Industrial Organization:
Behaviour and Control

Industrial Organization:

Behaviour and Control

Edited by JOAN WOODWARD

Professor of Industrial Sociology
Imperial College of Science & Technology

Oxford University Press

1970

Oxford University Press, Ely House, London, W.1

GLASGOW NEW YORK TORONTO MELBOURNE WELLINGTON
CAPE TOWN SALISBURY IBADAN NAIROBI DAR ES SALAAM LUSAKA ADDIS ABABA
BOMBAY CALCUTTA MADRIS KARACHI LAHORE
DACCA KUALA LUMPUR SINGAPORE HONG KONG TOKYO

Printed in Great Britain by
Alden & Mowbray Ltd at the Alden Press, Oxford

Acknowledgements

The research Unit responsible for the preparation of this book was set up at Imperial College in October 1962. Since then a large number of people and organizations have provided support for and co-operated with the research.

The initiative in bringing the research into Imperial College was taken by Dr Samuel Eilon, Professor of Management and Industrial Engineering, who, as many of the references given in Chapters 2 and 3 indicate, gave a lot of help and stimulation in linking production engineering and management science ideas about control with those of the research group. Roy Brewer, also of the Management Engineering Section, co-operated closely with the group until his death in 1965.

Three technical assistants, Angela Barnard, Felicity Rose and Angela Lloyd have worked with the Unit for various periods since its inception. Fran Hedley, the secretary to the Industrial Sociology Unit worked hard in preparing the manuscript for the printer. In doing this she was given help and advice by Ruth Pomeranz, the Nursing Research Officer at St George's Hospital, who has been working closely with the Unit.

The research workers are grateful to the Social Science Research Council which has supported projects financially and whose staff have given useful advice on a number of occasions during the course of the research.

Finally and perhaps most important of all we would like to express our sincere gratitude to the firms who have allowed us to investigate their organizational structure. As the chapters based on the case studies show, the contact with these firms has involved the collection of a great deal of detailed and in some cases confidential information. The firms concerned have not only been frank and friendly but also very patient in their dealings with the research workers. Some firms provided not only research facilities but also financial support. This has enabled the Industrial Sociology Unit to build up a research programme which is not only a mixture of theoretical and problem-centred research but which is jointly financed by the College, the Social Science Research Council and private industry.

Contents

JOAN WOODWARD

Introduction

A current generalization of Industrial Sociology is that the organizational structure and processes of a manufacturing firm are causally related to its technology. This is a comparatively new notion, for the ideas about management structure and behaviour developed in the first half of this century were based on a monolithic concept of organization and on the belief that there is one best and all-embracing way to run any manufacturing business. Although organization theory was applied to technical situations, traditionally it ignored technology as an element in its conceptual framework.

One of the pieces of research that contributed to the change of view was that described in *Industrial Organization: Theory and Practice* (1). This study of the organization structure of a hundred firms in South Essex showed that their organizational characteristics were not directly related to size, broad industrial classification, or to the degree of business success they enjoyed. An attempt was then made to relate their organizational characteristics to the technology of their manufacturing processes. In the first instance, firms were grouped together on the basis of the simpler features of their technology, the three main groups identified being, first, those producing units or small batches mainly to customer orders, secondly, large batch and mass production firms, and thirdly, process firms concerned with the continuous production of gases, liquids and crystalline substances. When the organizational characteristics of the firms studied were related to these three technical categories, it was found that specific organizational patterns were associated with each category.

The results of the research were sufficiently encouraging to suggest that the relationship between technology and organiza-

tional behaviour was worth further examination. They showed too
that this was an area which could be closed off for the purposes of
study. In 1962, therefore, a long-term research programme was
set up at the Imperial College of Science and Technology to
continue the work started in South Essex. It was hoped that this
programme would not only make a contribution to the development of organization theory, but also have a practical significance.
Questions of concern to industrial managements could not fail to
come under review. What actually happens to people in different
technological and control situations ? How can the appropriateness
of a firm's structure to achieve its objective be assessed ? What are
likely to be the organizational implications of any proposed technical changes ? What are the skills, abilities and knowledge required
to carry out the management task in the different technical
situations ?

Financial help in getting this programme under way and
supporting a research team was obtained, in the first instance,
from the Department of Scientific and Industrial Research, the
commitment being passed to the Social Science Research Council
when it was set up in 1965.

The South Essex studies had shown that in relating technology
to organizational behaviour there are two clear-cut extremes in the
technical scale—firms making units or small batches to customers'
individual requirements, and process or continuous flow industry
—and a large and difficult centre area in which are found medium
to large batch production firms and firms with the component
assembly type of production system. Structure and behaviour
appear to be more consistent and predictable at the extremes than
in the centre. It was on this centre, therefore, that the new research
group decided to focus its attention, seeking order and explanation.

One possible explanation of the apparent lack of consistency was
that the classification of technology used in the South Essex
research was inadequate. One of the tasks of the new research
team, therefore, was to try to find a more sophisticated way of
identifying technical differences between firms and then to relate
these to differences observed in organizational behaviour.

The earlier research had, however, identified another avenue
that might be explored. The analysis of the data on the basis of the
crude classification of technology appeared to indicate that the
physical flow of work through the system at the extremes of
the technical scale limited management's organizational choice. In

the centre area of the technical scale, the work flow did not appear to impose such rigid restrictions, with the result that technology did not determine organization but merely defined the limits within which organization could be determined.

Thus, the second task of the research team was to examine the kinds of choices available to management where the nature of the task and the tools, instruments, machines and technical formulae basic to its performance do not impose such rigid restrictions. This led to a detailed study of the way in which manufacturing tasks were controlled and of the relationship between technology and control.

Eilon (2) assumed that when the management of a firm makes a decision to manufacture a product, or series of products, a control system is automatically brought into existence. Objectives have to be determined in relation to the product, and a sequence of activities planned in order to achieve those objectives. Plans then have to be executed and information generated to enable the results to be assessed. If the activities are to be repeated, corrective action may have to be taken or the objectives modified in the light of the results obtained.

At the unit end of the scale, the nature of the work is such that the mechanisms of control are relatively simple and unsophisticated. Control is exercised mainly through the personal hierarchy of authority, work is largely unprogrammed, and end results are difficult to predict. In continuous flow production, on the other hand, a mechanical framework of discipline and control is built in with the erection of plant or installation of equipment. Decisions about how much is to be produced, what it will cost, and what its quality will be are an integral part of the design of plant and equipment. Relatively little discretion is left to the line supervisors responsible for the day-to-day operation of the plant.

In the centre area, however, the technology allows a much greater choice of control mechanisms. The ideas which express the goals of the work are less closely tied to the technology of manufacture. The separation of production administration from production operations, the rationalization and prescription of production methods, and the continuous attempts to push back the physical limitations of production, result in the emergence of control mechanisms that reflect top management's thinking. The degree of precision and sophistication with which standards are set, the system used to generate and evaluate control information, and even the explicitness with which objectives and plans are defined are related more to managerial policy than to technological limitations and constraints.

It is possible, therefore, that the variations in organizational structure and behaviour found among firms in the centre of technology are more dependent on the nature of the control system than on the technology itself. To test this idea it was necessary to try and find a satisfactory way of classifying systems of control and to relate the resultant categories to organizational variables.

The classification of control, even when the term control was used in a limited sense relating merely to the control of the manufacturing task, turned out to be as complex a matter as the classification of technical variables had been. As a first step, the research team tried to find out more about control processes. A number of case studies were made in which attention was focused on the setting of objectives in relation to the manufacturing task and on the consequent planning, execution and control stages of the cycle. This was done by using the tracer method, that is, studying the control system of a manufacturing firm by isolating a particular task or order and observing the way in which people become involved with it and decisions are made in relation to it during its progress through the firm concerned.

This book is a collection of papers arising from studies made by members of the research team between 1962 and 1967. It divides into two parts. The first three chapters are concerned with some of the ideas and concepts that have emerged during these five years. The first chapter discusses the place of technology in the determination of industrial behaviour. Among other things, an attempt is made here to define the team's position in relation to technological determinism in its wider sense. The second chapter deals with the various attempts made to identify technical parameters and to use them for comparing manufacturing firms. The third chapter covers the classification of control systems and the relationship between control and technology.

Part II contains a selection of the descriptive material obtained during the case studies carried out in the course of the research. Each member of the team was asked to select from his study, data illustrating at least one facet of the relationship between technology, the control system in operation and the behaviour observed. These chapters are self-contained in that they can be read without reference to each other or to Part I, and they have been written for practising managers as well as for students of organization theory. They cover a wide range of industry; Madingley, Hollington and Electra Ltd. operate in the electrical engineering and electronics industries, Division X is a general engineering organization, Mass-Bespoke is concerned with tailoring and 'Four' Works and Seagrass with chemical processes. The fact that these studies were all made within the same conceptual framework made it possible in conclusion to identify common threads and relate them back to the ideas presented in Part I.

Finally, it must be borne in mind that this book does not mark the end of a stage in the research in the way that the publication of *Industrial Organization: Theory and Practice* did. No general conclusions or middle range theories, even of a tentative kind, are drawn about the major questions towards which the work of the research team at Imperial College is currently directed. It is hoped, however, that discussion of the problems of organizational theory will be stimulated by the publication of these papers, and the results of such discussion fed back into the on-going research.

References

1. Woodward, J. (1965) *Industrial Organization: Theory and Practice.* Oxford University Press, London.
2. Eilon, S. (1965) Problems in Studying Management Control, *International Journal of Production Research*, Vol. 1, No. 4, 1962.

Part One

THE THEORETICAL FRAMEWORK

TOM KYNASTON REEVES,
BARRY A. TURNER,
JOAN WOODWARD

1 Technology and Organizational Behaviour

ORGANIZATIONS COMPARED AS SYSTEMS FOR GETTING WORK DONE

The research into organizational structure and behaviour at Imperial College takes as its unit of analysis the organization, rather than any of the discrete processes which are found within organizations; and it assumes that useful comparisons of behaviour at this organizational level may be made by taking as a starting point the task to which an organization is committed.

This 'task analysis approach' implies that organizations are studied, first of all by identifying the work undertaken within them together with the specific technology which enables this work to be carried out. After this initial step, it is possible to explore the structure of the organizations under investigation by the use of a variety of models.

Thus, cybernetic, decision-making or political models (or indeed many others) may be used to examine the diverse internal characteristics of the organizations studied; but comparisons between the organizations will be made, it is assumed, by relating these characteristics to the initial classification of the technology and the task of the organization. In many ways this approach is paralleled by the work of some social scientists in the U.S.A., particularly Bell (1) at North Carolina, Lawrence and Lorsch (2) at Harvard, Perrow (3) at Wisconsin, Thompson (4) at Indiana and Udy (5) at Yale.

There is no reason why this approach should be limited to manufacturing organizations. Bell, Perrow and Thompson have all carried out task analysis studies of schools and hospitals; retail

B

stores and other service organizations could be studied similarly. However, this book is primarily concerned with manufacturing organizations—that is to say with firms producing goods and offering them for sale, and with some of the organizational sub-systems found within such firms. We shall regard the precise specification of the goods which such an organization is to produce by means of its technology as the *production task* of the organization. To describe the production task fully, this specification would state the type, quantity and quality of the goods to be produced, and their rates of production. The specific *technology* of the organization is, then, the collection of plant, machines, tools and recipes available at a given time for the execution of the production task and the rationale underlying their utilization. Thus the *technology* and the *production task* of a firm are interdependent, since neither can be defined without reference to the other. For example, the term continuous process production may be used to describe either the physical plant and its operating procedures or the task carried out within this plant. This means that attempts to classify technology may make use of some of the characteristics of the production task.

TECHNOLOGY AND ORGANIZATION

It is evident that the adoption of the approach outlined above is based on the same assumption as the socio-technical system approach of the Tavistock Institute of Human Relations, namely that theories about industrial organizations will be incomplete and relatively unhelpful if they are limited solely to the technical aspects, or solely to the social aspects of organizations, without regard for interaction between the social and the technical. It is further assumed that the interaction which does occur between the technical and social spheres of an organization can be described at two levels (6).

Firstly, the overt behaviour of the individual operator will be limited or *constrained* in certain directions by that portion of the *technology* or of the production hardware with which he is most directly concerned. Of course, these limitations will not be the only ones, or even the most important ones which affect his behaviour, for he will also be limited by the requirements of the administration,* by the demands of his colleagues and by other

* The administrative system is here regarded as a major portion of the social system of the organization. It includes both the supervisory structure and other factors. Nor will the interplay between the individual operator and his immediate technical surroundings be necessarily one way, for often he may be able to bring out changes in his immediate technical situation, over and above those changes which he is expected to carry out as part of his job.

Similarly, we would expect to find a two-way relationship between social and technical aspects at a second level of analysis, when we consider the organization rather than the operator as the unit to be studied. In the long term, the technology of an organization is for the most part a result of a series of managerial decisions to serve specific markets, to acquire or build plant, to accept certain types of raw materials, and to address the organization to certain production tasks. But in the short term, as our definition of technology suggests, most of these considerations can be taken as given, and we may expect to see certain *salient* features of the technology of the organization limiting the administrative structures.

This does not mean that no immediate changes in the technology are possible; but rather that in most cases short- or medium-term technical changes occur against the backcloth of the relatively more enduring features of the technology and of the production task.

The relationship between technology and behaviour, therefore, can be studied at two levels, by examining the *constraints* placed upon the behaviour of those individuals who come into direct contact with the technology of the organization; and by looking at those *salient* features of the technology which limit the structure of the total organization to a greater or lesser degree. Although the research team at Imperial College is mainly concerned with technology at the second, organizational level, the need to take account from time to time of the behaviour of individual employees has led to a more rigorous delineation of the constraints at the individual level. This idea of constraints will therefore be examined in more detail.

CONSTRAINTS ON BEHAVIOUR IN ORGANIZATIONS

In any discussion of the effects of technical constraints on behaviour it is obviously necessary to specify clearly what aspects of behaviour are considered to be affected. Technical constraints can affect what

arrangements made to carry out and control the production of the organization. Thus the administrative system will include the allocation of authority and work roles, rules and procedures, management and supervisory style, systems of payment, etc.

people have to do in the course of their work; they can also provoke people to evade these constraints. A number of studies made by social scientists have suggested that technology, as this word is defined above, has implications for the behaviour of individuals (7). However the research workers concerned have not all been interested in the same areas of behaviour. Furthermore, the term behaviour has often been used, not in a general sense, but to refer to these selected aspects of behaviour. For example, Woodward (8) means by behaviour what people have to do in the course of their work including both conformity to constraints imposed on them and also the manner in which they exercise their discretion. By contrast, Walker and Guest (9), although they examine in some detail people's immediate jobs—their opportunities for social interaction at work; worker–supervisor relationships; union activity; attitudes to pay, working conditions and so on—they mean by behaviour merely what is revealed by labour turnover and absenteeism statistics. When they say that there is a 'correlation between mass production characteristics and overt human behaviour', they are merely stating that more people leave or are absent from their jobs in this kind of technical situation than in others. Sayles (10) also, despite the all-embracing title of his book, *The Behaviour of Industrial Work Groups*, is really concerned with the relationship between the nature of the work done and worker activity in relation to the acceptance or rejection of management procedures and job regulation.

The definition of behaviour adopted by the Imperial College researchers is the first one, with particular emphasis on the actions resulting from the various technical and administrative constraints to which workers are subject. In order to define this aspect of organizational behaviour and to link it with an analytical framework, a typology of behaviour was developed by Kynaston Reeves (11). The justification for trying to establish yet one more typology of behaviour lay in the fact that no existing typology systematically related behaviour to both technical and administrative features of organization.

This new typology is based on the assumption that every economic organization exposes its members at all levels of the hierarchy to a unique set of constraints and facilities. Technology and the system of administration restrict freedom of action; at the same time they also create facilities or opportunities for behaviour that is optional. A diagram will help clarify this and also show the relationship of constraints and facilities to other factors which influence organizational behaviour.

This diagram is specifically related to behaviour inside economic, goal-seeking organizations, and in discussing it the examples and illustrations are all taken from the manufacturing industry. There is nothing theoretically significant about this; it merely reflects the interests of the research team at Imperial College and the way that the typology was developed. There seems no reason why its concepts should not be applied, not only to non-manufacturing economic organizations, but also to other types of goal-seeking organizations. Indeed, in analysing industrial behaviour, there might be occasions when a trade union could usefully be made the subject of a similar diagram.

Since in social organizations there are few, if any, one way causal relationships, at least in the long term, the arrows in Fig. 1, representing causal relationships between variables, run, either directly or indirectly, in both directions. For example, the pecked arrows around the periphery of the figure indicate the possibility that an individual may change his environment as well as be influenced by it.

The production technology and the administrative system have been defined above. The behaviour of individuals in economic organizations can also be affected by the norms, values and informal rules operating within their particular work group, indicated by a separate circle. All organizational variables are subject to economic, political and social influences; this external environment is indicated around the periphery of the diagram.

The individual in Fig. 1 is portrayed at the focal point of a variety of environmental influences, both inside and outside the organization. However, the figure is not intended to suggest a simple deterministic view of his behaviour. What an individual does depends not only on the nature and force of environmental influences, but also on how he perceives and interprets them, on his attitudes to work, and on other personal factors.

The organizational constraints to which the individual is subject are defined in the broadest sense; the concept of 'job regulation' developed by Flanders (12) covers very much the same ground. They include the moral obligations of employment—the fair day's work for a fair day's pay ideology—the sanctions at the disposal of superiors, rules and regulations, the system of payment, tightness of control and degree of discretion, as well as exigencies

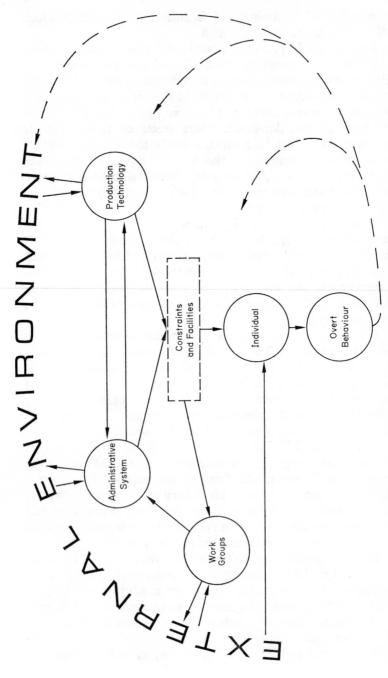

Fig. I. Derivation of behaviour in economic organizations

arising from the work situation itself, such as pace of work, job cycle, type and layout of production machinery, and the nature of the materials handled.

Constraints can be definite, that is to say they prescribe specific actions, or they can be indefinite, merely setting limits to action or specifying the end results of action. Constraints thus include the allocation of responsibilities which obliges a person to exercise his discretion and choose an appropriate course of action in order to discharge his responsibilities. In sum, constraints are all those elements or features of an organization which impinge on employees to decide or limit the behavioural content of their work.

Facilities provide an employee with the chance to engage in behaviour which is not directly concerned with the performance of his job. Facilities are the complement of constraints and include all opportunities for behaviour within an organization which is neither required nor precluded by constraints. A facility may be defined by the nature and extent of the constraints in the work situation. The most obvious example is the opportunity for social intercourse with other employees. For instance, on the automobile assembly line studied by Walker and Guest (13) any conversation between operators was restricted by the noise and also by the brevity of any spare time between job cycles. Furthermore, the range of people to whom an operator could talk was defined by his position on the line.

Constraints and facilities may not always promote the achievement of organizational goals. The identification of a set of constraints and facilities says nothing about their effectiveness from this point of view. Most constraints will of course have been deliberately designed to further organizational goals, and to the extent that they achieve this end they may be termed instrumental. But constraints may be inappropriate for their task; in these circumstances an evasion of the constraint might be instrumental while compliance would be non-instrumental. Moreover, not all the constraints will have been deliberately designed. Constraints—instrumental or non-instrumental—may have arisen as the fortuitous and unintended consequences of designing other constraints. For example, an incentive payment scheme for operators may result in supervisors having to devote an inordinate amount of their time to dealing with queries and complaints about wages. This in turn could conflict with other constraints on them that specify how they should spend their time.

Facilities may be only tenuously and indirectly connected with the achievement of organizational goals—if at all. There is of course a commonly held view that certain facilities help to promote morale and commitment to an organization, and that in this way they become instrumental. This case, however, is by no means proven.

The conceptualization of technology and the system of administration in terms of constraints and facilities provides a suitable basis for categorizing behaviour in organizations. The resulting typology consists of three categories of behaviour in relation to constraints, and three in relation to facilities. They are shown in Fig. 2 below. This figure is an expansion of the bottom circle of Fig. 1, that labelled 'overt behaviour'.

	TYPES OF OVERT BEHAVIOUR		
Behaviour in relation to:	Negative	Neutral	Positive
CONSTRAINTS	Constraint-Evasive Behaviour	Constrained Behaviour	Constraint-Exceeding Behaviour
FACILITIES	Facility-Detractive Behaviour	Facilitated Behaviour	Facility-Enhancing Behaviour

Fig. 2. A typology of organizational behaviour

The two central categories of this typology are constrained and facilitated behaviour. These are classified as neutral categories in that they do not imply any action other than simple compliance with constraints or response to facilities. Below are definitions and explanations of the six categories. The categories of behaviour in relation to facilities are only described briefly here; they have been elaborated more fully in Kynaston Reeves (14).

(a) BEHAVIOUR IN RELATION TO CONSTRAINTS

(i) *Constrained behaviour* is behaviour which has to be engaged in because of a person's obligations of employment and because of the administrative and technological constraints to which he is subject in his job. Constrained behaviour consequently covers everything a person has to do or chooses to do within the discretionary limitations of his job. Like constraints, constrained behaviour may be instrumental or non-instrumental for the achievement of organizational goals. It is sanctioned behaviour in the sense that its performance or non-performance is tied to the reward and punishment system of the organization.

It is not necessary for specific actions to have been prescribed for behaviour to be classified as constrained. Except in a sinecure, a person is under an obligation to choose some course of action even though the particular course may be unspecified, and therefore in carrying out this course of action, he is under a constraint. Were it not for the constraint of employment, the person would probably not be engaging in any of the alternatives. Constraints of course may be perceived as facilities by employees. It is possible that an employee enjoys his work and regards the opportunity to do it as a facility. However, for the purpose of this typology, which is based on the rules, norms and values of an organization, attitudes towards constraints are immaterial. It is possible to engage in constrained behaviour with enthusiasm or with reluctance.

(ii) *Constraint-exceeding behaviour*, or positive behaviour in relation to constraints, is behaviour that exceeds a person's normal obligations or call of duty and intended to further the organization's goals. Examples of such behaviour occurred during the initial enthusiasm for the 'Backing Britain' campaign of 1968.

(iii) *Constraint-evasive behaviour*, or negative behaviour in relation to constraints, is behaviour which constitutes non-compliance with, evasion of, or a reaction against the constraints imposed by an organization on its members. Constraint-evasive behaviour ranges from passive disobedience through various types of grievance activity, go-slows and strikes, to the total withdrawal of the employee from the organization. Constraint-evasive behaviour will usually be detrimental to the achievement of organizational goals, although this may not always be so; turning a blind eye to misguided constraints may be sometimes in the best interests of the organization.

(b) BEHAVIOUR IN RELATION TO FACILITIES

(i) *Facilitated behaviour* is behaviour engaged in in order to take advantage of the various amenities, facilities and opportunities that membership of an organization offers. It is permitted but not obligatory.

(ii) *Facility-enhancing* behaviour is behaviour intended to maintain, improve, or extend an existing facility.

(iii) *Facility-detractive* behaviour is either failure to use an existing facility, or behaviour aimed at getting an existing facility removed.

Of these six categories of behaviour, the one with which the Imperial College research team has mainly been concerned is constrained behaviour. As the various papers contained in the latter part of the book indicate, the researchers have typically been interested in identifying the implications for behaviour at different levels of the set of constraints that arise from a particular production technology or production control system. For the purpose of doing this, other influences on behaviour are taken as given. It is felt that the assumptions that are made in doing this are not too sweeping, and are justified, provided attention is focused solely on constrained behaviour. It is merely assumed that in so far as those employed by an organization accept the terms and conditions of their employment, it is possible to predict aspects of their constrained behaviour from the various technical and administrative constraints to which the organizational task gives rise. Nor is it assumed that all constrained behaviour can be accounted for in terms of organizational constraints. Indeed, it is taken for granted that the content of much discretionary constrained behaviour can only be accounted for by reference to factors which lie outside the organization.

However, approaches to organizational behaviour of this nature, which assume people's readiness to acquiesce in the demands made on them by their job, have led to misunderstandings. Some social scientists (15) have criticized what they see to be an implicit assumption that industrial workers respond like puppets to technical stimuli, or can be regarded as a passive mass. Although the major emphasis in the foregoing analytical framework has been on the influences in the work environment which affect an individual's behaviour, the researchers do not subscribe to a 'puppet on a string' hypothesis. It is accepted that behaviour in an industrial setting is voluntary. An individual may be more amenable or responsive to some influences in his environment than to others, but however compelling the pressures, he is, theoretically at least, able to choose whether or not he will comply with them, after weighing up the consequences of non-compliance. Causal relationships between technical or administrative constraints and the behaviour of employees depend on the willingness of those employees to allow their behaviour to be channelled by the norms and values pertaining to the social institutions of employment.

The research team's limited focus on constrained behaviour contrasts with that of many other social scientists who have written about the relationship between technology and behaviour. The category of behaviour on which attention has most often centred is constraint-evasive behaviour: the causes of strikes, voluntary absenteeism, excessive labour turnover, lack of response to incentive payment systems, disgruntlement and restrictive practices. Interest shown in constraints and constrained behaviour has usually been less for their own sake than to provide an explanation of why people evade constraints. For example, Walker and Guest (16) found an explanation of the constraint-evasive behaviour they encountered in an automobile plant in the arduous and uncongenial features of an assembly-line production in motor-car manufacture.

Goldthorpe and Lockwood (17), on the other hand, found an explanation of the fact that the motor-car workers they studied did accept the constraints of assembly-line production in the way in which their social and personal environment affected their perception of the work situation.

The findings of these two pieces of work are not contradictory, nor does one support the assumption that industrial behaviour is technologically determined while the other refutes it. All that can be said is that, because of their personal goals, the operators studied by Goldthorpe and Lockwood were more ready to tolerate the constraints of the work situation than those studied by Walker and Guest. It cannot, however, be assumed that the constraints were the same in both cases. Neither study tells us enough about them to make a comparison possible. It can be assumed that in both cases assembly lines were a feature of the technical environment but, as illustrated in Fig. 1, it is not only from the production hardware that constraints are derived. This apparent contradiction in the two studies does, however, emphasize the need for better methods of comparing technical situations and for relating technology to other variables as a basis for understanding industrial behaviour.

SALIENT TECHNOLOGICAL CHARACTERISTICS

In the preceding section, the emphasis has been on the direct influence that technology may have upon industrial behaviour as a result of the technical constraints of the production hardware: that is, the plant, machines, tools or equipment, the workshop layout, and the nature of the raw materials. We may now return to our second-level relationship to consider the effects which technology can have upon the administrative structure.

At any given time, the administrators and supervisors of a firm have, as one of their functions, to make the series of arrangements necessary for the achievement of the production task. It is evident that the nature of the arrangements which they make will be influenced by their current definition of the firm's production task; but in making these arrangements they will also have to take into account, among other things, the nature of the work force available at that time, and the state of the existing technology of the firm, which can be seen as a concrete, cumulative residue of previous decisions about the task of the firm. The resultant arrangements for the programming and control of work will form the basis for the administrative constraints which will be placed upon the individual employees.

It is not suggested that this relationship between the production task, the administrative structure and the constraints placed upon the individual production operator is necessarily direct.

Thus the extent to which the nature of the firm's overall production task influences the constraints at the operator level varies not only between organizations but also between different parts of organizations. While it might be expected that in many completely standardized production processes the operator would be required to carry out an extremely repetitive job, this repetitiveness is not inevitably eliminated in small batch or unit production systems. In the latter case the way in which the work is programmed and controlled is critical; Klein (18) found in Multiproducts Ltd. that variation in products had little impact on the shop floor because the system of breaking down and programming the work eliminated the variety as far as the shop floor operators were concerned. For the people concerned with the design of the production system, however, the variation in production range was of great significance.

As suggested above, the nature of arrangements made to carry out work may also mediate the influence of technology: when a number of motor-car firms were studied in connection with Brewer's work on the analysis of technical variables (19), it was found that although the hardware of production was similar in all the firms and the work was similarly repetitive, the body of ideas on which the programming and control of work were based varied considerably from one firm to another. This had a marked effect on the constraints in the work environments of the firms concerned. Further, it must be made clear once again that the separation between the two levels of technical influence is analytic rather than empirical, for as we have seen, there will be interaction between the administrative structure and the constraints placed upon the individual employee, as a result of decisions about the programming and control of production on the one hand, and as a result of individual or collective employee responses to the constraints on the other. Because of the complex nature of the relationships which connect the technology of a firm with its structure, it is likely that some, but not all, characteristics of technology will be reflected in organizational structure or in industrial behaviour. Turner (20) has referred to these as the salient technical characteristics, and has suggested that it may be possible to identify these at the organizational task level.

In terms of these characteristics it is possible to restate the findings of the South Essex studies, since the homogeneity of organizational structure shown by firms at the extremes of the technical scale would be expected if these firms had organizationally salient technical characteristics in common. That is to say, in process industry and in unit production there are similarities between the salient characteristics, regardless of the particular industry concerned. One characteristic that most process plants have in common is that the products are fluid during the production process and that most of the reactions that produce them occur in the fluid state. Only if we wish to differentiate between plants do the differences in chemical composition, density, viscosity, toxicity become marginally salient, that is to say they may account for smaller differences in the constraints of the work environment. It is obvious that there will be some characteristics of the nature of the materials, the refractive index, for example, which will rarely, if ever, be salient.

By comparison, in unit production or where small batches are made to order, whether the product is solid or liquid, acid or alkaline, is less important for the organization, and the salient characteristics of this system of production relate more to the design and sales aspects of the organizational task. In these terms, also, the heterogeneity in the central area of the scale may reflect the fact that the patterns of technical characteristics that influence the administrative structure vary between different mass production and large batch production firms. In these types of firms, the production task is usually broken down into a series of sub-tasks, and typically different technical characteristics will be salient for the performance of each sub-task. Thus the characteristics salient for the effective achievement of the total production task by the organization will include those characteristics salient to the parts of the organization concerned with each of the sub-tasks. It follows, therefore, that in this type of industry even relatively minor changes in the technology may be salient for at least one sub-task and this may lead to a different combination of salient characteristics for the whole firm.

This idea of salience also has implications for the possibility of measuring technical variables for the purposes of comparing organizational behaviour by limiting attention to the salient area. Counting or identifying the set of salient characteristics involved in a technical situation might be more useful and less time consuming than attempts to measure all observed variables on the assumption that they might have an important effect on structure and behaviour. The following chapter describes the attempts made to carry out such measurements and the difficulties encountered in doing this. However, the use of the intervening variable suggested by Turner opens up the second problem to which the Imperial College research has been directed—finding a way of measuring second-level technical variables to enable comparisons to be made of the constraints arising in different technical situations.

References

1. Bell, Gerald D. (1966) *Variety in Work*, Sociology and Social Research, 50(2).
   Bell, Gerald D. (1967) *Determinants of Span of Control*, American Journal of Sociology, 73(1).
2. Lawrence, P. and Lorsch, J. (1967) *Organization and Environment, Managing Differentiation and Integration*. Division of Research, Harvard University, Boston.
3. Perrow, C. (1965) Hospitals: Technology, Structure and Goals, in March, J. G. (ed.), *Handbook of Organizations*. Rand McNally & Co., Chicago.
   Perrow, C. (1967) A Framework for the Comparative Analysis of Organizations, *American Sociological Review*, 32(2).
4. Thompson, J. D. (1964) Decision-Making, the Firm and the Market, in Cooper, W. W., Leavitt, H. J. and Shelly, M. W. II

(eds.), *New Perspectives in Organization Research*. John Wiley & Sons, New York.

Thompson, J. D. (1967) *Organizations in Action*. McGraw Hill, New York.

5. Udy, S. H. Jr. (1959) *Organization of Work: A Comparative Analysis of Production among Non-Industrial Peoples*. Human Relations Area Files Press, New Haven.

Udy, S. H. Jr. (1961) Technical and Institutional Factors in Production Organization, *American Journal of Sociology*, **67**(3).

Udy, S. H. Jr. (1962) Administrative Rationality, Social Setting and Organizational Development, *American Journal of Sociology*, **68**(3). Or in Cooper, W. W., Leavitt, H. J. and Shelly, M. W. II (eds.) (1964) *New Perspectives in Organization Research*. John Wiley & Sons, New York.

Udy, S. H. Jr. (1965) The Comparative Analysis of Organizations. In March, J. G. (ed.), *Handbook of Organizations*. Rand McNally & Co., Chicago.

6. Recent developments in the socio-technical system approach involve the comparison of organizations in terms of their 'primary task'. See:

Miller, E. J. and Rice, A. K. (1967) *Systems of Organization: the Control of Task and Sentient Boundaries*. Tavistock Publications, London.

7. *See for example:*

Blauner, R. (1964) *Alienation and Freedom: the Factory Worker and his Industry*. University of Chicago Press, Chicago.

Dubin, R. (1965) Supervision and Productivity: Empirical Findings and Theoretical Considerations, in Dubin, R. *et al.*, *Leadership and Productivity*. Chandler, San Francisco.

Gouldner, A. W. (1954) *Patterns of Industrial Bureaucracy*. Free Press of Glencoe, Illinois.

Sayles, L. R. (1958) *The Behaviour of Industrial Work Groups: Prediction and Control*. John Wiley & Sons, New York.

Trist, E. *et al.* (1963) *Organizational Choice*. Tavistock Publications, London.

Turner, A. N. and Lawrence, P. (1965) *Industrial Jobs and the Worker: an Investigation of Response to Task Attributes*. Harvard University Press, Boston.

Walker, C. R. and Guest, R. (1965) *The Man on the Assembly Line*. Harvard University Press, London.

Woodward, Joan (1965) *Industrial Organization: Theory and Practice*. Oxford University Press, London.

8. Woodward, Joan. Op. cit. (See Ref. (7) above.)

9. Walker, C. R. and Guest, R. Op. cit. (See Ref. (7) above.)

10. Sayles, L. R. Op. cit. (See Ref. (7) above.)
11. Kynaston Reeves, T. (1967) Constrained and Facilitated Behaviour: A Typology of Behaviour in Economic Organizations, *British Journal of Industrial Relations*, 5(2).
12. Flanders, A. *Industrial Relations—What is Wrong with the System?* Institute of Personnel Management Broadsheet.
13. Walker, C. R. and Guest, R. Op. cit. (See Ref. (7) above.)
14. Kynaston Reeves, T. Op. cit. (See Ref. (11) above.)
15. *See for example*:
    Goldthorpe, J. H. and Lockwood, D. (1966) Attitudes and Behaviour of Car Assembly Workers: a Deviant Case and a Theoretical Critique, *British Journal of Sociology*, 17(3).
    Touraine, A. *et al.* (1965) *Workers' Attitudes to Technical Change.* Manpower and Social Affairs Committee (Introduction), O.E.C.D., Paris.
16. Walker, C. R. and Guest, R. Op. cit. (See Ref. (7) above.)
17. Goldthorpe, J. H. and Lockwood, D. Op. cit. (See Ref. (15) above.) Since this book was written their study has been described more fully in Goldthorpe, J. H., Lockwood, D., Bechhofer, F., and Platt, J. (1968) *The Affluent Worker: Industrial Attitudes and Behaviour.* Cambridge University Press, Cambridge.
18. Klein, L. (1964) *Multiproducts Ltd.: A Case Study on the Social Effects of Rationalized Production.* H.M.S.O., London.
19. Brewer, R. Appendix II in *Industrial Organization: Theory and Practice.* Op. cit. (See Ref. (7) above.)
20. Turner, B. A. (1967) Unpublished research paper on Technological Salience, Imperial College.

JEFFREY RACKHAM,
JOAN WOODWARD

2 The Measurement of Technical Variables

EARLY WORK ON MEASUREMENT

The underlying assumption of Chapter 1 was that different technologies impose different constraints on individual members of organizations and on the choice of organizational structure. To test such an assumption and to find out more about the causal relationships involved, techniques are needed to describe, measure, and compare both technical and structural characteristics of industrial organizations. Techniques of this kind are also a prerequisite to the formulation of guides to the appropriate design of new structures, to the assessment of existing structures and to the analysis of the management processes associated with them. This chapter is concerned with technical characteristics and the attempts made at Imperial College during the last five years to describe and measure them.

For comparing the firms studied in the South Essex research, from which the current research programme developed, Woodward (1) used a system of technical categories basically similar to the classification that a production engineer might use. That is to say, she grouped the firms into three main categories: unit and small batch production, large batch and mass production, and continuous flow or process production.

Woodward's conclusion was that the original system of classification, while adequate for the purpose of supporting a hypothesis on which further research could be based was too crude a measure to provide a basis for the comparative analysis of organizations (2). It became clear that a better instrument for classifying technical variables and relating one production system to another would have

C

to be found even before the South Essex hypothesis could itself be tested adequately.

Such an instrument had to satisfy two basic criteria. Firstly, the fact that its purpose was to relate technical variables to structural and behavioural differences meant that it had to be based on technical factors which could be isolated, at least conceptually, from structural and behavioural factors. This did not mean that it was necessary to avoid choosing technical factors likely to affect organizational behaviour. Indeed this would be the sensible basis of choice. But it was important to guard against the selection of any means of classifying technology that could only be expressed in terms which were themselves social.

For example, there have been research studies which have compared production tasks on the basis of whether they provide jobs which are more or less repetitive, more or less skilled, or more or less dependent upon the pacing of machines. But these variations are consequences, not basic characteristics, of the production task; they are concerned with the arrangements made for getting the work done and are therefore at least partly dependent on social factors. Thus to treat them as purely technical factors is misleading if one is trying to find out in what ways technical and social factors are related. It is only when the question, what is the nature of the production system has been answered that a second question can be asked: what are the consequences, for people, of working with a production system of this sort rather than another sort.

Secondly, the classification had to be related to the production task of the organization and take into account not only the specific technology, the production hardware and the features relating to it, but also the body of ideas that encompassed planning and control. As indicated in Chapter 1, the research workers assume that the production task of the organization is not merely an accumulated total of man/machine system components, but can be described and classified as an entity. The nature of the products, the nature of the market and the rationale of the manufacturing methods all contribute to the identification of the production task.

The questions on which Woodward's crude classification was based can be found in Appendix I to *Industrial Organization: Theory and Practice*. The relevant questions were:

(i) Is production predominantly,
    1. Single simple articles ?

  2. Prototypes?
  3. Large equipment, built in stages?
  4. Jobbing?
  5. Small batches?
  6. Large batches?
  7. Mass production?
  8. Continuous flow?
(ii) What types of products are they?
  1. Stable products firmly established with a minimum of variety and slow in development.
  2. Progressive products which are fairly new, subject to rapid development and considerable variety.
  3. Specification products 'made to measure'.
(iii) Have any major technical changes taken place in the last six months or are any such changes contemplated?
(iv) If so, is the nature of the production system affected in terms of questions (i) and (ii) above?

When the research programme was transferred to Imperial College in 1962, Brewer, a member of the Production Engineering staff, became interested in the problem of measuring technical variables. The details of his work are given in Appendix II of *Industrial Organization: Theory and Practice* (3). He started with Woodward's system of categories and tried to identify the parameters on which they were based. He saw them as representing bands on a scale of increasing rates of production. He developed this scale and it was interesting to find that the firms included in Woodward's batch production category covered a very large part of it. This meant that some of the firms in this category were closer to either continuous flow or unit production firms than they were to each other. Even where the production hardware was similar, as in motor-car or cathode ray tube manufacture, firms varied considerably in their rate of production.

For a variety of reasons, elaborated in Appendix II of this book, at this point the search for better ways of identifying and comparing the technical systems of different firms was given up for the time being, although some of Brewer's ideas, particularly about standardization, were followed up later. At this time, the research team was concentrating on the tracer studies discussed in the next chapter and on which many of the papers in Part II of this book are based. One of the general conclusions arising from these tracer studies was that they reaffirmed that any study of managerial control and its relationship with organizational behaviour was likely to be unsatisfactory unless the problem of the measurement of technical variables could be solved. It was almost impossible to tell whether the differences observed between the firms being studied depended on differences in control systems, differences in technology or a mixture of both.

VARIATION IN PRODUCT RANGE

On the conclusion of their first case studies, therefore, two members of the research team, Combey and Rackham, looked again at possible methods of comparing technologies. Like Brewer, they implicitly accepted Woodward's unit-batch-process 'scale' as their starting point. Eilon suggested that an important factor underlying both this scale and much of the Brewer work was the extent to which a firm's product range varied over time. Process production would normally involve the manufacture of a limited range of products that changed relatively little over a number of years. At the other extreme, unit production consisted, by definition, of the manufacture of single products, with continual change of design and specification from one product to the next. The category in which Woodward had found wide variations in organizational characteristics was the batch production category. It was thought that if this were an intermediate category between the two extremes of process production and unit production, then differences in batch size might be related to differences in variation in product range. It seemed to make sense to suppose that, other things being equal, those firms that made more changes in the specification of their products would probably make their products in smaller batches.

It was thought, therefore, that if a way could be found of measuring the variation in a firm's product range over time, this might help to provide what had previously been lacking, in the way of a method of differentiating between firms in the batch production category.

During 1965 attempts were made to measure the variation in product range in four firms covered by the research programme. The method adopted was to obtain figures for the number of different products made in 1963 and 1964. The number of different products common to the two years expressed as a proportion of the combined total of different products, was taken as an indicator of the degree of similarity in product range from year to year. The complement was taken as the indicator of the degree of variation. This procedure will be made clearer by describing the actual results.

The first firm, Madingley (see Chapter 7) made electrical and electronic equipment to the orders of six commercial Divisions of the parent Company, each concerned with the design and sale of products to a particular type of market. Madingley bought from outside suppliers such standard electronic components as resistors, capacitors, transistors and valves; but there were facilities at Madingley for making mechanical components, such as chassis, brackets, gears and spindles, as well as for certain electrical components, such as cableforms, coils and printed circuit boards. The firm therefore had a fairly elaborate production system, made up of feeder shops for the various types of component, together with sub-assembly and main assembly shops. This unit preferred to make products for which there was a firm order, although products which seemed to have a reasonably assured market were sometimes made for stock. But any continued assurance about markets was rare, owing to the continued development in electronic design. It was unusual for a batch of as many as 200 units to be made. It was also unusual to make as many as six batches of any product.

This situation—a complex production system, making a constantly changing range of complicated and advanced electronic equipment for six divisions catering for six types of market—had thrown up a fairly intricate production control system with the Production Control Department appearing to stand in a relatively powerful position. (As noted in Chapter 7, it sometimes seemed to the research workers that the production control system had developed to the point where it had an impetus that would carry it through the motions of its procedures even if the production departments somehow ceased to exist.) Luckily for the research workers, this production control system identified individual products at the point where an order was placed on the books by a Division, and all the subsequent procedures and paperwork and the activities arising out of them were connected with particular orders and, therefore, with particular products.

Thus the research workers had no difficulty in identifying, from production control records, the different products actually completed in the years 1963 and 1964.

Table I makes it easier to see that if all products were common to both years, so that the variation in product range were nil, then $1 - A/B$ would be equal to o. If no products were common, so that variation was at the maximum possible, $1 - A/B$ would be equal to 1. Thus the figure 0.7 suggests high variation in product range in this firm.

Table I. *Variation in product range in Madingley*

Product Division	Different products made in both 1963 and 1964 *A*	Different products made in 1963 and/ or 1964 *B*	$\dfrac{A}{B}$	$1 - \dfrac{A}{B}$
1	40	118	0.34	0.66
2	6	19	0.32	0.68
3	16	56	0.24	0.76
5	7	34	0.21	0.79
7	18	78	0.23	0.77
8	5	38	0.13	0.87
All	92	343	0.27	0.73

In the next firm where this was tried, the variation was less, that is, about 0.3. This was Pizzicato Ltd., a firm making musical instruments. Production was divided into two main sections, brass instruments and reed or woodwind instruments, and the following detailed figures were obtained:

Table II. *Variation in product range in Pizzicato Ltd.*

Product division	Different products made in both 1963 and 1964 *A*	Different products made in 1963 and/ or 1964 *B*	$\dfrac{A}{B}$	$1 - \dfrac{A}{B}$
Brass	86	128	0.67	0.33
Reed	24	33	0.73	0.27
Both	110	161	0.68	0.32

The number of people employed in the two firms was about the same. Both firms would be classified by the Department of Employment and Productivity or the Board of Trade as being in the engineering industry. Both would have been classified in Woodward's South Essex study as falling into the small batch production category. Pizzicato Ltd., like Madingley, had a number of feeder shops—for drawing and shaping brass tube, forming the bells of brass instruments from sheets, making keys and valves by forging and machining, turning and drilling the bells, joints and mouthpieces of woodwind instruments—producing the components that were soldered, lapped, screwed or otherwise fitted together in sub-assembly and assembly shops.

But, unlike Madingley, the design of the products in Pizzicato Ltd. had changed only imperceptibly in something like a century. The research workers were told two stories illustrating this. The first story was that the Company had developed a trumpet, made by non-traditional methods, which was said to have qualities of tone and ease of playing that were at least as good as those of a traditional trumpet. The method of manufacture allowed the trumpet to be produced at a significantly lower cost than traditional methods. But nobody would buy the new trumpet, and so Pizzicato Ltd. stopped making it. The second story was about a customer who wrote saying that he had a reed instrument that had been made by Pizzicato Ltd., and that he would like to have a second one, identical with the first. When the second was sent off, Pizzicato Ltd. were pleased to be able to include a letter saying that although the first one was then fifty years old, the second was made not only from the same drawings, but by four of the same people who had helped to make the first.

Compared with Madingley, the production methods in Pizzicato Ltd. had remained the same over a long period. Earlier in the century, a new method of bending tube accurately to required shapes had been devised. During the time when the research was in progress, experiments were being made with a new method of spinning brass sheet to make complex curves. Certain simple components were being made on automatic machines, which were markedly newer than most of the equipment. But much of the brass shaping was still being done by hammer and anvil methods; and the first stage in making a woodwind instrument still required a craftsman with a high degree of a rather esoteric skill, to chop up logs of wood with an axe in such a way as to make sure of getting the whole of the fifteen per cent of usable material out of a wood that was imported at high cost from East Africa.

In Madingley, the small batch, special-order character of the manufacturing system was dependent on the rapidly changing design of the products, which in turn arose out of the rapidly developing technology of the electronics industry. In Pizzicato Ltd., however, the batches were small because of the size of the market. The major problem was how to go on making and selling products for which there was a limited market and which could not be made more attractive by being offered for sale at a lower price, because the demand was not high enough to justify the introduction of low-cost methods of manufacture.

Variation in product range appears to be a salient feature of technology in batch production firms as it provides a basis for differentiation between them. Differences in structure and behaviour between the two firms could logically be related to this variation.

For example, Madingley employed a large number of graduates, while Pizzicato Ltd. had recently taken on a graduate for the first time. Madingley had large numbers of staff in design and development departments, while Pizzicato Ltd. had two employees who spent a small part of their time in such activities. The two biggest organizational problems in Madingley were, first, how to achieve some sort of compatibility or compromise between the needs of the sales and design staff on the one hand, and the production staff on the other; and, second, how to programme and control the manufacture of a wide and changing variety of products. These two problems had a considerable influence on the activities, attitudes, communication patterns and power structure within the firm.

In Pizzicato Ltd. the main organizational problem was how to improve the provisioning process so that the large number of materials and components, many of which were common to a number of different products, would be available in just the right quantities at just the times when they were needed.

These studies gave encouragement to the idea that it might be possible through further empirical research to link variation in product range with specific constraints in the work environment. The organizational problems of Pizzicato Ltd., however, also led Combey and Rackham to turn their attention to other factors on which variations in production systems could depend.

STANDARDIZATION OF COMPONENTS

The research in Pizzicato Ltd. suggested that it was not only variation in product range over time that had a bearing on standardization, the interchangeability of components between products being a critical characteristic of the manufacturing system. This raised the question of whether it might be possible to find a way of measuring the degree of standardization of components to draw comparisons between one firm and another.

Because standardization of components was recognized as a problem, records had been devised that readily yielded the kind of information required by the research workers. Using these 'applicability cards', they drew up a matrix showing what components were used on what products. The number of theoretically possible applications would be the product of the number of products and the number of components. The ratio of actual to theoretical applications was taken as a measure of component interchangeability. If all components were used on all products, this would give a figure of 1. If no components were used on more than one product, this would give a figure approaching 0, and the figure would be nearer to 0 the larger the numbers of both products and components.

This again seemed to bear some relation to Woodward's system for comparing production systems. Mass production and large batch production are more likely to use all components on all products, whereas this is least likely to be the case in unit production.

In *Industrial Organization: Theory and Practice*, reference was made to a group of firms which did not fit into any category satisfactorily. These were firms in which mass-produced components were subsequently assembled diversely. This situation was found within Electra Ltd. (see Chapter 9) in which another tracer study was carried out. This firm would have undoubtedly been placed by Woodward in the unit and small batch production category. Using figures for the two years 1963 and 1964, the variation in product range was measured. A figure of 0.8 was obtained; but the research workers had some doubts about the meaning that could be attached to this figure, for reasons that will be explained shortly. However, the high variation figure suggested, on the lines of the argument above, a unit-production type of manufacturing system, which might be expected to exhibit a low degree of interchangeability of components. And yet it was found that there was in fact a high content of standard components. This was largely achieved by means of designing and making a limited range of standard electronic modules, which were subsequently assembled into varying configurations to produce electronic equipment with a variety of specifications, forms and functions. When Combey tried to produce a figure for the degree of inter-changeability, he found that it was quite impracticable, because the complexity of the products was such that the numbers involved were very large and, at that time, unobtainable.

NUMBER OF PRODUCTION STAGES

This problem led Combey to suggest that another important variable to be considered in comparing production systems might be the complexity of the products being made; and it was suggested that a first rough indicator of this might be the number of separate assembly or conversion stages in a manufacturing process. The separation of assembly stages also directed attention to the points at which stock could be built up. From observations in some of the firms studied this too appeared to be a salient characteristic of technology in that it had implications for the constraints in the work environment. Where stock was held at a number of points, an effective system of inventory control was one in which there was a minimum of slack at each point in the manufacturing process. Combey used the phrase 'low comfort level' to describe such a situation.

THE DEFINITION OF THE PRODUCT

In Electra Ltd. the research workers encountered the main problem in their attempts at measurement. This arose because the measurement methods centred around the nature of the product and therefore depended on a definition of the product. In this firm, about half the different products made in 1963 and 1964 were regarded as 'special'. That is to say, they had some feature, component or configuration that made them different from the 'standard' products that comprised the other half. It was for this reason that the research workers were doubtful about the meaning that could be attached to the figure of 0·8 obtained for Electra's variation in product range. By the research workers' definition, each 'special' had a standard content that might in some cases be very small but which in others might amount to as much as eighty or ninety per cent, measured by the criteria of material or labour cost.

For this reason, the method of measuring variation in product range, which had been feasible in the first two firms, fell down as a generally applicable tool. This was confirmed by the experience of the research workers in the fourth firm in which the method was tried. 'Four' works (described in Chapter 5) made soap and synthetic detergents, and fell into Woodward's category VIII, batch production of chemicals in multi-purpose plant (4). This firm had made nine different products in 1963, and had introduced one additional product in 1964. The figure for variation in product range was therefore extremely low, at 0.1. However, this did not take account of the fact that while the names of the products did not change, it was possible for them to change in a number of ways—composition, packaging and the addition of bonuses to the packets in order to promote sales—several times a year. Had all these modifications been taken into account the figure would have been very much higher. Moreover, as far as the constraints in the work environment were concerned, in some parts of the organization they appeared to be related to low variation in the product range and in others to high variation.

The fact that this method of measuring the variation in product range could not be universally applied was depressing to the research workers who had spent so much time in developing it. They had started off with an hypothesis that the differences in structure and behaviour observed within the batch production area were explainable in terms of technical differences too detailed to emerge in the original crude classification. The work carried out on these various facets of technology had confirmed in an impressionistic way the assumption that detailed technical differences were important in providing explanations of differences in structure and behaviour in industrial firms, but a satisfactory and comprehensive measure of technical differences between one firm and another had not emerged.

One possible way of proceeding beyond this point might have been to abandon the idea of finding a general measure of technology on which a comparative framework could be built and concentrate instead on relating specific technical characteristics such as those described above, to differences in organizational structure and behaviour. An argument in favour of doing this was that the research had shown that crude classifications of the type used in the South Essex studies embrace a number of variables which may be independent of each other, and that the use of such a system of classification may mask the separate effects of the different variables.

But in spite of the negative results of this stage in the research, new ideas and new questions were being thrown up. The research workers saw a common thread emerging that brought together many of the ideas involved in Woodward's categories, Brewer's scales, and the subsequent attempts to measure technical characteristics. This was, simply, the idea of variety. All the work that had been done had in one way or another focused on the amount of variety in the system of production. The variety might depend upon the nature of the product, the nature of the market or the nature of the manufacturing processes themselves, but looking at it from the point of view of the constraints in the work environment, variety, whatever its cause, seemed to have similar effects on patterns of behaviour.

THE CONCEPT OF VARIETY

This concept of variety seems to underlie not only the various attempts made to measure technical variables at Imperial College, but also much of the work of other researchers interested in the relationship between technology and organization at either the descriptive or the measurement level. One researcher may have equated technology with mechanization, another with standardization, and so on, but all seem to have been concerned with variety of one kind or another.

The research group at the University of Aston (5) have produced and used a tool for measuring 'throughput continuity'. This is a measurement of differences observed between production systems and is concerned with variety in the same way as the Woodward classification from which it was derived. It is, however, still a crude measure and by becoming more specific, it is open to the criticism that it deals with complex phenomena in too limited a way.

The interest in variety shown by Easterfield (6) was stimulated in quite a different way. He was concerned because variety reduction and standardization have both been widely advocated as measures which would save British industry and equally widely attacked as threatening to ruin it. He therefore attempted to categorize those facets of organization that could be affected by the extent of the variety in the products made.

He lists eight factors on which the case for variety reduction can be made—simplification of classification systems for products and components, reduction of 'concealed set-up costs' such as those involved in holding extra sets of jigs and tools, reduction in sorting and packing problems arising from the probability that customers will order more items, the benefits of increased batch size, reduction in stock-holding, reducing the effects on people of disorganization, reduction of strain and worry, and higher levels of earnings. Against this, he lists five factors which suggest that variety reduction may be detrimental—less flexibility, restriction of opportunity for technical progress and for improvements in design, less opportunity to satisfy diverse customer requirements, and the boredom among staff employed.

This work encouraged the research workers in thinking that their interest in variety was not misplaced. In particular they were interested in the suggestion that a study of a firm's pattern of product variety was worth carrying out because of the insight it will give into the working of the firm. This seemed to imply that Easterfield had found a satisfactory way of doing this. Here, however, they were disappointed, for although he suggests possible ways of measuring variety, he does not appear to think that any of them provide reliable results. Moreover, he does not seem to have considered that there might be a problem in defining a product. He merely says, 'a logically classified list of the firm's products is necessary for a study of the degree of variety within the firm. As regards the final products for sale, such a list almost certainly exists in the form of a catalogue, and there is no difficulty'. The research workers knew to their cost that it was not so easy.

The difficulties of defining a product are also ignored in Smith-Gavine's (7) *percentage measure of standardization* which is referred to by Easterfield. Nevertheless this measure was interesting in view of its close relationship to what the research workers had tried to do.

This measure is designed in such a way that:

(i) a firm making one product only would rate as being 100 per cent standardized;

(ii) other things being equal, the more products a firm makes, the lower is its standardization measure;

(iii) other things being equal, the greater the proportion of its production concentrated in a few of its products, the higher its standardization measure; and

(iv) the more that common components enter a number of its products (more particularly if they appear in these in the same proportions), the higher its standardization measure.

Neither Easterfield nor Smith-Gavine seem to have taken account of the fact that variation in product range and standardization can be considered over a period of time as well as at a point in time or that the former may be as important as the latter in the insight it gives into the working of the firm.

The importance of variation in products over a period of time in terms of its effects on organizational structure and behaviour was demonstrated by Burns (8) in his study of firms in the electronics industry. He was concerned with a particular kind of variety. Unfortunately, however, Burns confined himself to discussing these effects at the descriptive and theoretical level and did not try to find an objective means of assessing degrees of innovation. It is interesting to note that two of the firms included in the Burns study were Madingley and Electra Ltd., where the research workers had tried to measure the variation in product range. Similar figures had been obtained for these two firms, although, as already pointed out, the variation was different in kind.

The implication that variety or uncertainty in the organizational task is a significant factor in relating technology to organizational structure can be found in the work of most of the social scientists adopting the task analysis approach to the study of organization. This comes out most clearly in the work of Perrow (9). It is typical of this approach that he starts his argument by disclaiming interest in technology at the man/machine level and concentrates on organizations at the overall task level. He says:

'there are a number of aspects of technology which are no doubt important to consider in some contexts, such as the environment of the work (noise, dirt, etc.). . . . For our purposes, however, we are concerned with two aspects of technology that seem to be directly relevant to organizational structure. The first is the number of exceptional cases encountered in the work; that is, the degree to which stimuli are perceived as familiar or unfamiliar. . . The second is the nature of the search process that is undertaken by the individual when exceptions occur.'

Perrow picks up one particular source of 'exceptional cases' for further consideration—the nature of the raw materials.

'Techniques are performed upon raw materials. The state of the art of analysing the characteristics of the raw materials is likely to determine what kind of technology will be used. . . . The other relevant characteristics of the raw material, besides the understandability of its nature, are its stability and variability; that is, whether the material can be treated in a standardized fashion or whether continual adjustment to it is necessary.'

Although, however, Perrow develops his ideas as a basis for comparison, his attempts at measurement are of an elementary kind. He merely states, for example, that 'the number of exceptional cases varies on a scale from low to high', giving very little indication of the exact techniques he would use to position a firm on this scale. In so far as he is concerned with the extent to which stimuli are perceived as familiar or unfamiliar and uses interviewing as his main research tool, his attention seems to be focused on the perception by organization members of the constraints in the work environment rather than on the constraints themselves. Indeed, he does what the Imperial College team had tried to avoid from the outset; he classifies technology in terms that are themselves social. This reduces the usefulness of his framework as an instrument for relating technical variables to structural and behavioural differences.

The affinity between the task analysis and the socio-technical system approaches is reflected in the similarity between Perrow's work and some of the work of the Tavistock Institute of Human Relations.

Emery (10) like Perrow sees the nature of the raw materials as an important source of variety in production systems; he refers to:

'the natural characteristics of the material being transformed or fabricated in so far as it sets limits on, assists or introduces the possibilities of uncontrolled variation into the labour requirements of the production processes.'

Emery also refers to seven other dimensions of technical systems adding that even this list may not be exhaustive. Included are the physical work setting, what he calls the 'spatio-temporal' dimension, the level of mechanization, the various unit operations of which the manufacturing process is composed, the degree of centrality of the different production operations, the maintenance operations and the supply operations. He draws no distinction between the two levels at which technology can have an impact on the social system. Although some of the dimensions refer to the total organization task, the emphasis is on the man/machine system. In introducing these dimensions, Emery indicates that they can be used not only to analyse a given technology, but also to enable comparisons of it with others. In practice, however, this conceptual framework has been mainly used to compare alternative work arrangements within firms. Moreover, relatively little attention has been paid to measurement.

VARIETY AND THE SOCIAL SYSTEM

Neither Emery nor the other research workers whose work has been referred to in this chapter have been interested in the classification of technology and the measurement of technical variables for their own sake. With the possible exception of Easterfield, their main objective, like that of the research group at Imperial College, has been the better understanding of the relationship between organizational behaviour and the manufacturing system. Technical factors are merely the starting point for the identification of the nature of the social system needed to cope with the problems these factors create.

This does not mean that the sole function of the social system is the furthering of the goals and purposes of the technical system; but merely that some aspects of organizational structure and behaviour can be explained by reference to the nature of the production task. It is this belief (based, for example, on the results of the South Essex study) that provides the justification for asking the questions: what, at any point in time, does the technical system require the social system to do, and how will changes in the technical system affect what is required of the social system.

The first question can be answered quite simply; to do what the technical system cannot or has not been designed to do. The general conclusion that emerges from all the research referred to in this chapter suggests that this is to cope with the uncertainty and unpredictability that arise from variety in the production task. The term production task, it will be remembered, has been used by the research team cover to both the specific technology—the production hardware and the features relating to it—and the body of ideas encompassing planning and control. Focusing attention on variety, highlights the relationship between these two facets of the technical system and also their link with the social system.

As the South Essex studies showed, in continuous flow process industry the technical factor which has the greatest influence on the choice of organization structure is the low degree of variety. There is relatively little uncertainty and unpredictability in the manufacturing task, and the control system is designed to cope with any there is. The social system has only exceptionally to deal with problems thrown up by the technical system, and its form was therefore more strongly influenced by social and psychological needs than by technical needs. In unit production firms, on the other hand, there was such a high degree of variety that it could not be controlled by mechanical devices or administrative regulations. Consequently, the nature of the social system was strongly influenced by the requirements placed upon it to function as a system through which the control of the production task could be effected. In mass production, variety was coped with in part by standardization of product and process, which allowed some mechanical control devices to be built in; and the relative influences of the control function needs and the social and psychological needs that the social system had to serve were much less clear than in either of the other two categories. In Chapter 4 an interesting situation is described where the control system itself introduced a higher degree of variety than the production task required.

If, as the work done so far suggests, the causal link between technology and organizational behaviour is the degree of uncertainty and unpredictability in the production task, it might be more profitable to find a way of classifying technical systems by identifying the types and degree of variety within them rather than by detailed measurement of particular technical characteristics.

Conceptually, Perrow's (11) approach of identifying the number of exceptional cases is an attractive one. It would lead to conceptualization at a higher level of abstraction, thus enabling organizations of different kinds, manufacturing firms, hospitals, shops, etc., to be brought within the same comparative framework. But in practice, as mentioned earlier, the problem would be to identify exceptional cases other than through the subjective perception of the people concerned.

Using 'variety' rather than 'exception' as a basis for comparison would not simplify the categorization process, and identification of the different sources of variety in the production task would not be easy. Variation in production range appears to be an important source, so does the nature of the raw materials, but these are probably only two of many. Variety, however, has the advantage that it can, in theory at least, be specified objectively.

References

1. Woodward, J. (1965) *Industrial Organization: Theory and Practice.* Oxford University Press, London.

D

2. Woodward, J. (1966) *Automation and Technical Change—The Implications for the Management Process.* Paper presented by Rackham, J. J. at the O.E.C.D. European Conference on Manpower Aspects of Automation and Technical Change, Zurich, 1st–4th February, 1966. Published by O.E.C.D.
3. Brewer, R. Appendix II, op. cit. (See Ref. (1) above.)
4. Woodward, J. Op. cit. (See Ref. (1) above.)
5. *See, for example:* D. J. Hickson, paper on The Measurement of Technology presented at the S.S.R.C. Seminar on Automation, 24th March 1966.
6. Easterfield, T. E. (1964) Optimum Variety, *Opl Res. Q.*, **15**(2).
7. Smith-Gavine, S. (1963) A Percentage Measure of Standardization, *Productivity Meas. Rev.*, Special Number.
8. Burns, T. and Stalker, G. M. (1961) *The Management of Innovation.* Tavistock Publications, London.
9. Perrow, C. (1967) A Framework for the Comparative Analysis of Organizations, *American Sociological Review*, **32**(2).
10. Emery, F. E. (1964) *Characteristics of Socio-Technical Systems.* Tavistock Institute of Human Relations, London. Document No. 527.
11. Perrow, C. Op. cit. (See Ref. (9) above.)

TOM KYNASTON REEVES,
JOAN WOODWARD

3 The Study of Managerial Control

In *Industrial Organization: Theory and Practice* two possible explanations were put forward for the fact that the link between technology and organizational structure was less obvious and clear cut in the group of batch production firms than it was in the groups of firms at each end of the technical scale.

The first, that the classification of technology was not sufficiently discriminating to cover adequately the technical differences between firms in the middle area of technology has been the reference point for the first two chapters. The second explanation, that organizational structure is not so much a function of technology as a function of the control system, will be dealt with in this chapter.

Every manufacturing business embodies a system for directing and controlling the production task. At its simplest this may be no more than the owner of the business or his representative having decided what he wants to achieve, issuing his orders and making sure that they are obeyed. With increasing size a more elaborate system is necessary and coordination becomes a more complex matter. But as Eilon (1) has pointed out, any system of managerial control, whether simple or complex, contains the four elements of objective setting, planning, execution and control, even though they may not be discrete or sequential stages in the process of management. Objectives have to be set in relation to the product; in particular, decisions have to be made about the nature of the product and the nature of the market. A sequence of activities must then be planned in order to achieve these objectives. Orders have to be given for the plans to be executed and for information to be generated through which results can be assessed. If the results are unsatisfactory, corrective action must be taken or objectives modified in the light of these results. The execution of the plans may depend upon persuasion and the influencing of employee motivation as well as actual direction.

In the literature relating to organizational behaviour there is ambiguity in the use of the word control. The confusion arises largely because to control can also mean to direct. Precisely defined, control refers solely to the task of ensuring that activities are producing the desired results. Control in this sense is limited to monitoring the outcome of activities, reviewing feedback information about this outcome, and if necessary taking corrective action.

But planning, setting standards and issuing prescriptions for action, are all prerequisites of control. Without some concept of what should be done, it is impossible to make any assessment of what has in fact been done. Thus the use of the term 'managerial control system' in connection with the research at Imperial College implies that the four elements identified by Eilon were all under review.

One of the assumptions underlying this research, therefore, is that the managerial control system of a manufacturing firm can, at a conceptual level at least, be regarded as an entity. This implies that a firm's control system can be studied independently of both the social system and the technical system and compared with the control systems of other firms in respect of various characteristics. Some of these defining characteristics would relate to systems as wholes, while others would relate to individual elements within the system and their relationship to each other. For example, it might be possible to compare firms in respect of the explicitness of the objective setting process or of the time lag between information generation and the taking of corrective action. It might also be possible to compare the amount of overlap between the different elements in the control system. In short, one of the aims of the research team was to develop a typology of control which would supplement the typology of technology on which work was concurrently being undertaken.

In the South Essex research, the homogeneity of the organizational structure and behavioural patterns found among firms at the ends of the technical scale appeared to be related to the consistency of the system of managerial control. In unit production firms, mechanisms of control were relatively simple and unsophisticated. Control was exercised almost entirely through the personal authority pyramid, work was largely unprogrammed, and end results were difficult to predict. In all continuous flow process firms, on the other hand, a framework of control was created when the plant was built or the automated equipment installed. The setting of objectives, in respect of time, quality and cost, the sequencing of the manufacturing activities and even in some cases the mechanisms for taking corrective action were specified and built into the plant design.

In the middle of the technical scale, however, there was much more variation in the kind of managerial control applied. This was in part due to the fact that the firms concerned differed technically from each other in a number of detailed ways. In part, however, the variations were linked with the fact that in batch production what has been referred to in a previous chapter as the body of ideas expressing the goals of the work was not so closely tied to the production hardware. Plant and machinery were more flexible than they were in continuous flow production and in most cases products could be modified with relatively minor plant modification. Decisions about what products had to be made and how plant and machinery could best be utilized had therefore to be made more frequently. Conflict between short- and long-term decisions occurred more often.

Management had therefore much more freedom of choice about when and how decisions should be made, how resources should be used and how simple or complex the system of control should be. Moreover, although in unit production it seemed that a larger number of decisions had to be taken, much less was involved in terms of risk.

The fact that structure and behaviour appear to be more consistent and predictable in situations where the hardware of the technology is the major determinant of the control system and less consistent and predictable where management is not so rigidly restricted by technology in deciding how the production operations are to be controlled, suggests that control may be an intervening variable between technology and industrial behaviour. The link revealed by the South Essex studies between technical and organizational characteristics may in fact be a link between technology and the nature of the control system, on the one hand, and between the control system and organizational behaviour on the other. In other words, the managers responsible for batch production firms can make deliberate decisions which may result in their firms being either more like continuous flow production firms from a structural and organizational point of view or more like unit production.

The first steps towards finding out if this was indeed the case were to test the assumption that control systems can be studied as entities and to try and reach a deeper and more sophisticated understanding of the way that organizational tasks are planned and controlled, particularly in the batch production area where management choice has the greatest impact.

CASE STUDIES OF CONTROL

A number of case studies were made, each the responsibility of one research worker, based on the 'tracer approach'. This implied the isolation of a particular order or batch of products, central to and representative of the firm's manufacturing activity, and following its progress through the planning, execution and feedback stages of the control system, observing the way in which people became involved in plans, decisions and tasks relating to it. Thus a very detailed study was made over a period of time of part of each firm's activities. The research methods used were those of social anthropology, involving direct and prolonged observation and open-ended interviewing, until patterns of interaction between events and between people emerged, which could be related to the comparative framework being built up jointly by the members of the research team.

Direct observation was not always possible. Where the tracer involved the simultaneous production of components, the research worker could obviously not be in two places at once and direct observation had then to be supplemented by diary keeping and work sampling techniques.

A brief account of the research method and of its main advantages and disadvantages has already been published (2). For reasons touched upon in the last chapter, the main advantage of the method over the more frequently used interviewing programme approach, was that the research team was operating in a real time context and was not limited to the perception of reality of the people involved. They could relate their own observations of what was happening to the way it was perceived. Its main disadvantage was that it was a time consuming and extravagant way of using research expertise. To some extent this was offset by its value as a training in field research.*

* For further discussion of this research method see Appendix I.

Although most of them have already been published in the article referred to (3), it may be useful to repeat here the questions that each member of the research team was trying to answer in the course of his field study. These questions fell into seven main groups.

1. *The setting of objectives in relation to the tracer*
   (i) How did the chief executive define the firm's objectives in relation to the tracer products?
   (ii) How had these objectives evolved in time?
   (iii) What had been the firm's achievement in the past in relation to the tracer or to similar products?

2. *The relationship between the four elements in the control cycle*
   (i) Were the elements in the control cycle separately organized?
   (ii) Were they sequential or overlapping. What discretion was allowed to those concerned with the execution of the plans?
   (iii) If discretion was allowed, what were the circumstances under which plans were modified?
   (iv) Were those responsible for execution able to take corrective action if things were obviously going wrong at the production stage?

3. *The setting of standards*
   (i) Who was responsible for the setting of standards relating to time, quality and cost?
   (ii) On what criteria were the standards based?
   (iii) Was there anything discernible in the way of a master plan that ensured that all the standards set could be met simultaneously?
   (iv) If conflict arose, which of these standards took precedence and whose responsibility was it to fix priorities?

4. *The awareness of standards*
   (i) To what extent were supervision and production operators at shop floor level explicitly aware of the standards being aimed at?
   (ii) How was this awareness transmitted to them?
   (iii) If aware of the standards, did the people concerned accept them and have faith in the accuracy and relevance of the tools used for measurement?
   (iv) If people were falling down in respect of any standard set and were conscious of this fact did it cause anxiety?

5. *The use made of control information*
   (i) What control information was generated and to where in the organization was it fed back?

(ii) If fed back, how was control information used ? In particular, was it used to develop or modify policy, or was it used as a basis for the performance appraisal of individual supervisors and managers ?

(iii) What was the time lag between the generation of the control information and the corrective action ?

6. *Informal controls*

(i) What informal control mechanisms did departments or individuals build up for themselves to supplement or circumvent the formal control system ?

(ii) Were subsidiary objectives built into the control processes at various points in the cycle ?

(iii) If so, were the subsidiary objectives compatible with the objectives set by top management ?

7. *The control system and the social system*

(i) What sections and departments inside the social structure of the firm had not been brought within the research boundaries ?

(ii) Were any such sections and departments concerned with any other of the firm's production activities ?

(iii) If not, what was their role and function ?

The collection of this information over a period resulted in a series of very interesting and detailed studies of organizational behaviour related to various aspects of managerial control. Most of the remaining chapters of this book are selections from this material. In some of the case studies, interest was centred on the objective setting or modification processes, and in others on the changes or the increases in prescription and formalization of the control system taking place while the research was under way. In one firm it was found that lack of realism in the original negotiations with customers in respect of delivery dates made planning or control almost impossible from the outset. The generation of control information deteriorated into a paper mill, remote from the reality of the production situation. The most interesting aspect of another firm's control system was its high degree of rationality and prescription and the implications this had for managerial and supervisory jobs. Other problems around which the case studies centred were the consequences of change in control procedures and the difficulties arising from the control of high variety production, where there were doubts about being able to reconcile the standards set for time, quality and cost. The combination of these circumstances appeared to be associated with particularly complicated problems of organization and management.

One general point about these case studies was that they reinforced the research team's belief that a more precise instrument for measuring technology was required before the complex relationship between technology, control and organizational behaviour could be properly understood. The studies had shown that relatively minor differences between the technology of batch production firms could have a marked effect both on the kinds of control mechanisms used and on modal patterns of behaviour.

CLASSIFYING CONTROL SYSTEMS

Simultaneously with the field studies, Eilon (4) was working on the development of a theoretically comprehensive scheme from an industrial engineering point of view, for the classification of control mechanisms identifying all the theoretically possible ways in which one control situation could differ from another.

The empirical work and the theoretical model building led to the same conclusion, that as had been found with technology there was little likelihood of being able to classify control systems along a simple scale in one dimension. Indeed, the Eilon approach identified eleven variables, his classification covering a very large number of possible combinations. These variables related to the way in which standards were set and results measured, the number and linkages of the controllers, the time span of control and the extent to which there was control of control in the system.

This classification, although it stimulated many ideas because it gave a very clear picture of the extent and nature of the possible variation in control systems, was obviously far too complex to provide a practical research basis for comparison between firms. The number of case studies that would be required before specific patterns of control could be linked with structure and behaviour would be far beyond the resources of a research team the size of that working at Imperial College.

It was necessary, therefore, either to select from this vast range of possible parameters those most relevant to the study of organizational behaviour or to try and find a way of combining characteristics to produce a cruder and simpler typology.

One characteristic of control that the data collected showed to be of considerable importance in its effect upon organizational behaviour was not directly covered by the Eilon typology, although many of the variables used in that typology were relevant. This was the general nature of the control processes.

As indicated at the beginning of this chapter the simplest form of managerial control is the owner-employer deciding what he wants done and seeing that it is done. Traditionally and historically, therefore, the successful achievement of the goals of a manufacturing firm depends upon the exercise of one man's influence or authority over others. The subordinate has his work allocated to him by his superior, is accountable to him for end results and refers back to him the problems which he cannot overcome himself. Spheres of influence and authority and the size or importance of the task over which he has discretion become greater as an individual moves up the hierarchical pyramid. This notion of a pyramidal structure of authority and influence is so deeply imbedded in our thinking and so much a part of both management ideology and sociological conceptualization that from Taylor and Weber onwards it has been almost impossible to consider control processes except in this context. Discussions among managers and sociologists alike, about such matters as division of labour, spans of control, leadership roles, line and staff relations, executive and advisory responsibility and centralization and decentralization, still centre on the relative authority and influence of people at different levels; that is, with the distribution and legitimization of power throughout an organizational pyramid.

Valid as the pyramid concept may still be where manufacturing firms are being compared as political or social systems, in terms of the task analysis approach it is inadequate. The more complex processes associated with the control of the task in modern industrial organizations cannot be explained adequately in terms of simple hierarchical lines running from the apex to the base of a pyramid. As Blau and Scott (5) have pointed out, a characteristic of such organizations is that their control processes are not necessarily part of the authority structure. They operate independently of the decisions of particular supervisors or managers.

With increases in size and technical complexity it becomes more difficult to exert direct hierarchical control. Line management can no longer have an intimate knowledge of the various specialized and complex processes that are intrinsic to the manufacturing task. To avoid the danger of losing control of the task, management builds into the organization impersonal processes of control to influence and regulate the work behaviour of those it employs. A feature of these impersonal controls is that they operate more or less impartially and more or less automatically. These processes may be administrative, covering such things as complex programmes for production planning, measurement mechanisms and cost control systems; or mechanical, as in the automatic control of machine tools or continuous flow production plant.

The fieldwork suggested that it might be possible to position a firm on a scale ranging from completely personal hierarchical control at one extreme, to completely mechanical control at the other. Between these two extremes come the administrative, but impersonal, control processes. Assuming that this idea of a scale on which firms can be placed in respect of the nature of their control processes is a valid one, what does movement along this scale imply as far as organizational behaviour is concerned?

The main implication has already been suggested: it seems that the assumption of managerial control being exercised through a pyramid of hierarchical authority becomes increasingly invalid as a firm moves towards the mechanical end of this scale. The introduction of increasingly complex and sophisticated control mechanisms ensures that more and more of the problems arising in the course of the firm's manufacturing activities are predicted and dealt with in advance as part of the planning process. A change in emphasis in line management's job inevitably results. Line managers and supervisors increasingly cease to concern themselves with the day-to-day problems of production operations and function primarily as adjusters and supplementers of the control processes. Ultimately, in theory at least, even the trouble-shooting role becomes superfluous as the control system becomes foolproof. At this stage, as Blau and Scott have suggested (6), the significance of management is no longer as the apex of a system of personal control but as the designer, in association with expert staff, of administrative controls of the impersonal kind and of the planning criteria on which mechanical controls will be based.

As far as the coordination and control of the production task are concerned, it may be more useful and more realistic to conceptualize an organization not as a pyramid but as two spheres, one embracing the design and programming of the production task and the other its execution. At the personal end of the control processes scale, there is almost total overlap between the two. This means that the planning and execution stages in the control cycle are often inseparable, and never discrete. At the other extreme of the scale, where control processes are completely mechanical, there is total separation. The designers and programmers of the production facilities not only have little to do with production operations, but do not even receive or act upon the control information generated, for the mechanisms through which corrective action is taken are also built in at the planning stage. An example of this is the way that viscosity and other quality controls are built into the instrumentation of the continuous flow plant producing liquid chemicals.

At different points on the control processes scale, there are different degrees of overlap; the progression being illustrated by Fig. 3.

At the mechanical extreme of the scale, the design and programming of the task is sometimes the concern of a second organization, independent of the one that is concerned with its execution. The planning and erection of a continuous flow automated chemical plant is often undertaken by a chemical engineering firm, and on completion the plant is handed over to the contracting organization. The erection firm will have its own control processes, probably of a much more personal kind.

An interesting question that arises from the increasing separation of a firm's design system from its execution system as it moves up the control processes scale, is what effect this movement has on the behaviour patterns established and on the type of managerial staff required. What, for example, are the problems that arise when organizations that are pyramidal in shape as political and social systems have to adjust to dichotomy between the design and execution systems?

The nature of the control processes also affects the role of the production operator. Where the control processes are personal the operators are more likely to be producers in the exact sense of the word; collectively, they make the products that go out of the factory gate. When the control processes become mechanical, however, the operators increasingly cease to be responsible for making the product. They may monitor its manufacture or their role may be that of controllers of control. Where control is administrative but impersonal there are elements of both roles in the production operator's task.

The nature of the production operator's task has implications for personnel administration. It is obviously important for a realistic assessment of this role to be made before any system of rewards and punishments can be evaluated.

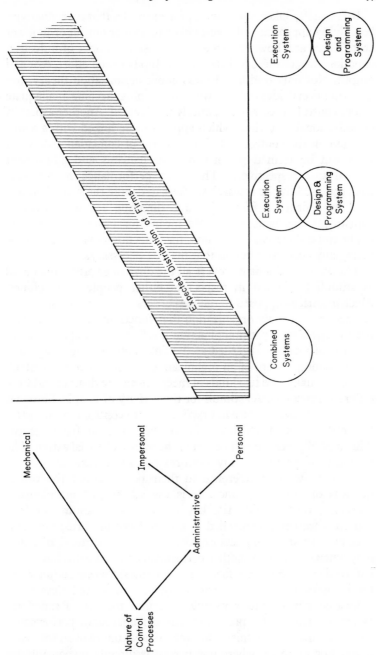

Fig. 3. Relationship between nature of control process and degree of separation between design and execution systems

It is usually taken for granted, for example, that a productivity bargaining approach will result either in greater output or in lower cost. There are, however, an ever increasing number of industrial situations where there is little relationship between effort, cost and output. Not only traditional ideas about organization theory, but also traditional ideas about wage bargaining become inadequate where control processes are entirely mechanical. Another aspect of organizational behaviour which appears to be linked with a firm's position on the control scale is the degree of coincidence between what can be termed performance mechanisms and adjustment mechanisms respectively. The term performance mechanisms has been used by the research workers to denote the various means used by a firm for motivating and directing activities, whereas adjustment mechanisms are the means for ensuring that what ought to be done has been done, for detecting deviations and for taking any corrective action that may be necessary.

The word mechanisms covers all the devices or procedures used as stimuli for action in respect of either people or machines. Mechanisms, as opposed to random orders or *ad hoc* prescriptions, are necessary in any organization that functions as a system and has to cope with repetition of action. Performance and adjustment mechanisms can be regarded as the links between the design and programming system of an organization and its execution system.

Conceptually, the two kinds of mechanisms are distinct and have different functions. As stimuli for the activity of people, however, this is not always the case in practice. Where control is administrative rather than mechanical, the distinction is far from precise. This lack of precision is inherent in the nature of social action. The response of people to any performance mechanism cannot be understood without reference to their beliefs about the consequences of non compliance. It is the adjustment mechanisms, therefore, that provide the key to the understanding of how activities are being controlled in a manufacturing firm; performance mechanisms being less important, as they assume significance only when enforced. Whether performance mechanisms have been enforced or not cannot in fact be known unless there are adjustment mechanisms for detecting and correcting undesired deviations. Adjustment mechanisms include of course the use of sanctions. Where control is of a predominantly personal kind, performance and adjustment mechanisms are inextricably interwoven with each other. For example, where one person is directly responsible for seeing that work of others is successfully completed, he is likely to use his personal authority both to direct and to check that work.

Even where control is impersonal, it is sometimes difficult to decide whether particular mechanisms are mechanisms of performance or of adjustment. For example, the ostensible purpose of a system of payment by results may be to stimulate higher performance, but in so far as it identifies and penalizes the low performer, it is also an adjustment mechanism. Its value both as a performance mechanism and an adjustment mechanism depends, however, on how far the people concerned are motivated by money.

But in general, the more impersonal the control processes, the greater the likelihood of being able to distinguish between the two kinds of mechanisms. In the garment factory described later in this book, one of the performance mechanisms was the exhibition of notice boards in the workshops indicating the categories of work that currently had priority. There were, however, no built-in consequences of non-compliance, with the result that the effectiveness of the notice boards as performance mechanisms was impossible to measure.

There are, of course, adjustment mechanisms which have no corrective action content. For example, a quality control procedure that operates only to reject substandard products contains no features to directly influence future performance. In the garment factory referred to above, the quality control system incorporated two adjustment mechanisms. Faulty garments were either returned to be put right by the operator who made the mistake or corrected by an alteration hand or supervisor. From the point of view of the control of the task, by getting faulty garments put right, both courses of action were equally effective adjustment mechanisms. But only the first mechanism, the returning of garments to the operators concerned, incorporated a specific device for influencing the standard of their performance. The operators worked on a payment by results system, thus they could lose earnings when reworking substandard garments. This in itself was likely to make them more careful in the future. If the second procedure was followed the likelihood of the operators learning to avoid similar mistakes depended entirely on the extent to which there was feedback about their errors, and on the effectiveness of the reprimands they were given.

Although this idea of performance and adjustment mechanisms seems to be a useful one in analysing and comparing organizational behaviour related to control processes—particularly as the degree of coincidence between the two kinds of mechanisms appears to get progressively less as controls become increasingly mechanical—it is important to stress that management is unlikely to be able to devise enough mechanisms of performance and adjustment to ensure that every aspect of the organization's activities is adequately covered. Inevitably, in some areas of activity, management has to rely on more or less spontaneous co-operation from its employees. Moreover, mechanisms devised by management as part of the administrative control process always depend to some extent on reinforcing influences in the environment and on the willingness of the people involved to allow their behaviour to be influenced by the constraints imposed by management.

FRAGMENTATION OF CONTROL

The field studies undertaken by the research team in the last few years have certainly supported the view that an understanding of the nature of the control processes is helpful in the analysis and prediction of industrial behaviour. There was, however, another characteristic of managerial control which seemed to be very important in its behavioural effects; this had been identified both in the South Essex studies and in the Eilon categorization. This was the extent to which the various control processes were linked with each other. Was there single-system (unitary) or multi-system (fragmented) control?

Some firms—that studied by Klein (7), to which Chapter 5 refers, is a case in point—made considerable and continuous efforts to relate the standards set for various departments by the different functional specialists, and the performance and adjustment mechanisms associated with them, into a single integrated system of managerial control.

In others, either because different departments made different products by different methods and for different markets, or because departmental standards and standards related to such factors as cost, quality and time, were set independently and never related to each other, control was fragmented. For example, it might be taken for granted that an operator could reach the desired level of quality and earn an acceptable bonus simultaneously, without any systematic appraisal being made of how far this really was the case.

Here again it seemed possible to envisage control systems on a scale, ranging from a single integrated system of control at one extreme, to multi-system fragmented control at the other.

As with the scale identifying the nature of the control processes, movement along this second scale had behavioural implications too. One result of extreme fragmentation seemed to be that the performance and adjustment mechanisms relating the design and programming system to the execution system tended to break down. Production could become completely dissociated from the planning and control elements in the system and an independent set of informal mechanisms of performance and adjustment generated. The design of procedures for setting standards and measuring actual against anticipated results then became a separate activity, carried on for its own sake; it was a paper work system bearing little relationship to production reality.

Multi-system control implies that there are a number of control criteria which people in an organization are trying to satisfy at one and the same time. A particular task has to be completed by a predetermined date to satisfy the production controller; it may involve using certain methods to satisfy the work study man; and a limited number of people to satisfy the personnel manager; it has to comply with certain quality standards to satisfy the inspector; it should not involve more than certain costs, to satisfy the cost accountant; and so on. With these control mechanisms operating in parallel, and the different goals not always being compatible with each other, the supervisor's main task is to violate each of the standards as infrequently as possible. Furthermore, he will presumably rank his goals in a diminishing order of nuisance value, depending on the expected outcome of failure, frequency of past failures, the latitude that each goal provides and the relative power positions of the people he is trying to satisfy. Lesser goals may be sacrificed at times to ensure that other critical ones are attained, and in any one field there is little incentive to do better than the goal specified.

In a situation of this kind it becomes extremely important to meet the actual standards even if in doing so hidden costs are generated or the primary objectives of the firm overlooked. Several examples of this kind of behaviour reported by Jasinski (8) were observed; of foremen rushing all work in progress through the measuring point, of procrastination in making decisions about operating repairs and protective maintenance and of 'batching down' or switching components to an order being chased.

Even where the links between the design and programming

E

system and the execution system did not break down, there was a tendency to set up informal controls to supplement them. This was due in part to the confusion created by a multi-system of control which often led to blockages in the communication channels. In others, the lack of acceptance of the standards set, because of their incompatibility, led to various forms of evasive action. For a shop floor worker, the logic of fragmented controls which enable him to get work through a quality control inspector because of its urgency, although it might be of a quality which would normally be rejected, is difficult to perceive.

In some cases, therefore, the function of the informal controls was to enable those involved in the system to retain the initiative and thereby increase their own discretionary powers.

To sum up, a multi-control system is associated with conflict and irreconcilability between the standards set and with the domination of one control process by another, either through circumstances, as in newspaper production where every goal is subservient to that of reaching the time targets, or through internal factory politics where one functional specialist is more powerful than another.

Referring back to what was said about the nature of the control processes, it now becomes clear that control systems, like technology, are not measurable along a simple scale in one dimension. Where the control processes are of a fragmentary kind the controls may not all be of the same nature. Personal and impersonal, administrative and mechanical control processes could all be found within the same organization.

CATEGORIES OF CONTROL

It is not claimed that the two aspects of control processes that have been described in this paper are the only ones with implications for the study of organizational behaviour. More work is envisaged on the development of scales relating to other characteristics of control suggested in the Eilon (9) typology.

In the meantime, however, the two scales described, when used together, do provide a simple system for dividing manufacturing firms into four groups and relating organizational characteristics to these control process groups in much the same way as organization was linked with technological categories in the South Essex studies.

These categories are:

A1 Firms with unitary and mainly personal controls.

A2 Firms with unitary and mainly impersonal administrative or mechanical controls.

B1 Firms with fragmented and mainly personal controls.

B2 Firms with fragmented and mainly impersonal administrative or mechanical controls.

Moreover, although there are the usual problems of what Brewer (10) called the 'borderline complex', that is, of fitting marginal firms into the categorization, it is possible to allocate any manufacturing firm to one of the four categories by taking a fairly superficial look at its control processes. Consideration is now being given to the kind and amount of information needed to delineate more precisely the position of any firm being studied on the personal/mechanical and single/multi-system scales of control. A balance has to be found between undertaking a prolonged and detailed investigation of the tracer study kind, and relying entirely on the subjective and impressionistic judgement of the individual research worker.

The four categories have been listed in what can be called chronological order. The normal processes of industrial and technical development would move a firm in the direction indicated by the arrows in Fig. 4.

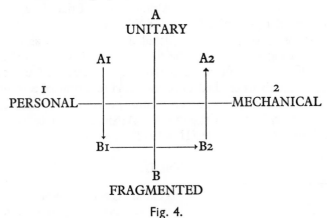

Fig. 4.

An entrepreneurial organization would be likely to fall into the A1 category: the single system control processes being the master plan developed by the entrepreneur himself, he would, for example, almost automatically relate time and quality to cost. The authority to direct and check the work would be directly delegated down the line of command. Growth and specialization normally lead to fragmentation in the control processes unless positive steps are taken to prevent this happening and the firm would probably move into the B1 category. The interest of the study of Electra Ltd. lies in the fact that the firm was moving through the early stages of the control process. At a subsequent stage, production engineering and operations research techniques, administrative rules and procedures, and the growth of computerization, result in the emergence of impersonal control mechanisms of both an administrative and a mechanical kind. These developments would initially be unlikely to result in a reduction of fragmentation and the firm would probably move in the first instance into the B2 category. Finally, as a result of integrated data processing or the use of computers for programming and controlling the total manufacturing process, a master plan would again emerge and the control processes would then become single system again, but of an impersonal kind.

CONTROL AND TECHNOLOGY

To try and identify the way in which control and technology are linked, a re-examination was undertaken of the data collected during the South Essex study. Although out of date in a general sense, this data contained a lot of facts and figures relating to organization structure, and detailed information about the manufacturing processes of the firms involved, which had been collected at the same time. The data was comprehensive enough to enable the firms studied to be allocated to a control category.

Clear links emerged between control processes, as classified in the way described, and the original classification of technology. These are shown in Table III below:

Table III

	Control system A1 %	Control system B1 %	Control system B2 %	Control system A2 %
Unit and small batch production	75	25	—	—
Large batch and mass production	15	35	40	10
Process production	—	—	5	95
Total firms	28	21	18	33

The links between control and technology revealed in this diagram throw interesting new light on the South Essex study results. It will be remembered that the research (11) showed that in respect of some organizational characteristics, unit production firms resembled process firms, while in respect of others, these two types of firm were at the extremes of the scales used. Table III suggests that the similarities between the two groups depend upon the fact that in both groups single system control processes predominate, and the differences, on the fact that in one group it is personal control processes that predominate, while in the other it is mechanical control processes.

Moreover, the heterogeneity in structure and organizational behaviour associated in the South Essex study with the batch and mass production group, may be linked with the fact that they spread across the whole of the control processes spectrum. Although the control systems of seventy-five per cent of these firms came into the lower half of Fig. 4, there are batch production firms in every category.

The final point brought out by the re-examination of the earlier data is that the organizational structure of the large batch and mass production firms with predominantly personal controls approximated to the organizational structure of unit production, while the organizational structure of the firms with predominantly impersonal controls was more like that of process industry.

As suggested at the beginning of this chapter, there appears to be more freedom of choice for the management of batch production firms than for other categories, in deciding what kind of control processes to use. Why and how the decisions are made is an interesting question in itself, and more light may be thrown on this in future research. It does appear, however, that once the choice is made, constraints in organizational planning then develop in predictable ways. This suggests that the control system may be the underlying variable linking organizational behaviour with technology. If so, an alternative solution to those put forward in Chapter 2 to the problems of measuring technical variables suggests itself. If control processes proved to be easier to measure and classify than technology, there would be little to be gained in persevering with what is, as has already been shown, a complex exercise. The classification of control processes outlined in this chapter, crude as it is, might provide a better instrument for predicting certain facets of organizational behaviour than the classification of technology.

References

1. Eilon, S. (1962) Problems in Studying Management Control, *International Journal of Production Research*, **1**(4).
2. Woodward, J. and Eilon, S. (1966) A Field Study of Managerial Control in Manufacturing Industry, in Lawrence, J. R. (ed.), *Operational Research and the Social Sciences*, Tavistock Publications, London.
3. Woodward, J. and Eilon, S. Op. cit. (See Ref. (2) above.)
4. Eilon, S. (1965) A Classification of Administrative Control Systems. *British Journal of Management Studies*, **3**(1).
5. Blau, P. M. and Scott, R. W. (1963) *Formal Organizations: A Comparative Approach*. Routledge & Kegan Paul, London.
6. Blau, P. M. and Scott, R. W. Op. cit. (See Ref. (5) above.)
7. Klein, L. (1965) Rationality in Management Control, *British Journal of Management Studies*, **3**(1).
8. Jasinski, J. (1956) Use and Misuse of Efficiency Controls, *Harvard Business Review*, **34**(4).
9. Eilon, S. Op. cit. (See Ref. (4) above.)
10. Brewer, R. (1965) Appendix II, in Woodward, J., *Industrial Organization: Theory and Practice*. Oxford University Press, London.
11. Woodward, J. (1965) *Industrial Organization: Theory and Practice*. Oxford University Press, London.

Part Two
THE CASE STUDIES

BARRY A. TURNER

4 Control Systems: Development and Interaction

The *Hollington* factory (this name was selected at random from a telephone directory), where the study on which this paper is based was carried out, is a manufacturing unit of a large electronics company. About 500 people are employed. The outward appearance of the factory is totally unremarkable. Most of the offices are housed in a single storey building which presents an inoffensive façade to the road on which it is situated, while the manufacturing shops are at the rear and to one side of this office building.

Some components, such as transistors and printed board circuits, are brought in from outside, but with these exceptions the factory has the production facilities to carry out the whole of the process of manufacturing, assembling, finishing and testing electronic equipment. The factory is also fairly self-contained as far as other functions are concerned, so that once the design for the equipment has been received, the Hollington factory has a high degree of autonomy in its handling of the production process, in spite of the inevitable restrictions which arise from the links with the wider Company.

This study was one of the tracer studies referred to in Chapter 3. The research consisted, therefore, of following an order, that is a batch of products, through the production and control processes.

The course of the production process, however, is similar in broad outline for most of the range of products made. During the early stages of manufacture, components and small sub-assemblies are produced in several departments. Mechanical components are manufactured in two departments: the machine shop, which is able to handle a variety of turning, milling, jig boring and gear cutting; and the associated metal fabrication shop which deals with sheet metal work and small mechanical assemblies.

On the electrical side, the large number of coils needed for electronic equipment are made by women in the coil winding section. Most of these coils are small and fragile, and for this reason they are encased in a protective plastic capsule whenever possible. Women in an adjacent section assemble the completed coils, together with transistors or resistors, on to a prepared printed board circuit, and solder them into position. In the same area, another group of women employees make up the 'cable forms' or bundles of wires needed to connect up the components in the equipment. They tie the wires neatly together, bare the ends and fit any necessary connectors, in order to facilitate the wiring up of the equipment.

All of the production areas mentioned can be thought of as 'feeding' sub-assemblies and components into the large assembly section where the equipment is fitted together into its final state. From the assembly section, completed equipment passes into the test department, where it is subjected to a lengthy series of performance checks, and adjusted if necessary, before being despatched to the customer.

This outline of the production process is of course grossly oversimplified. While the broad product flow tends to follow the lines indicated, an individual sub-assembly may be fabricated in, say, a dozen steps, moving backwards and forwards between all of the departments mentioned. Such movement means that the work flow is complex and for this reason a number of stores exist, both to hold work between operations, and to accumulate and 'collate' the sets of parts needed before an assembly operation can begin.

The control of this sequence of production tasks involves the monitoring of cost, quality and delivery times; and in this factory distinct and separate systems have been set up to deal with each of these aspects of control. As each system has a separate set of goals, the overall control picture is an example of what in Chapter 3 was called 'multi-system' control.

The study examined the control systems and evaluated their appropriateness for the technological task. Explanations of the interrelationships between them were sought and an attempt was made to link them with the problems encountered by management.

THE HISTORICAL BACKGROUND

A brief account of the history of the Hollington factory is an essential preliminary to the understanding of the present situation.

It was set up originally after the Second World War by a large electrical manufacturer and subsequently taken over by the present Company in 1961, with the consequence that the existing control systems represent an amalgam of influences from the old parent Company, the new parent Company, and the people employed by the Hollington factory itself.

The factory came into existence at a time when the original parent Company was laying a number of people off as part of a major re-organization, and Hollington was started with a nucleus of people coming from the parent Company as an alternative to being made redundant. Looking back, it appeared from what was said that the three outstanding characteristics of the factory at that time were: a friendly atmosphere, a high standard of work which could not be reached elsewhere in the parent Company, and an ability to draw red herrings across the tracks of any investigation from Head Office. Whatever their cause, these characteristics seem to have persisted, and may to some extent apply to the present situation.

Before the takeover, the factory was leading a protected existence by manufacturing on a cost-plus basis. In the view of the new owners the factory was overtooled in anticipation of long runs; it had high indirect costs and a high proportion of staff to production workers. Some of the staff were aware of the problems: 'We knew the takeover would have to come, or the factory would have to close down.'

Among hourly paid employees there seems to have been much resentment of the takeover, 'because a lot of people were attached to the old Company' and a lot of them left (although many of these subsequently returned). As it happened, the people who had more cause for alarm were the management and supervision, for staff numbers were allowed to waste considerably, and there were a number of changes at the top. 'We wondered where the axe would fall next', one supervisor put it. Another member of the senior staff commented:

> 'We got through four Personnel Officers, three Heads of Production Engineering, two Production Controllers, and two Works Superintendents. Only the Buyer and Works Accountant have survived from those days'.

These staff changes were made by the manager appointed to run the factory shortly after the takeover. He is spoken of as having a very forceful personality, and a blunt, aggressive way of dealing with situations. This forthrightness, however, together with his considerable technical background knowledge, seemed to win the respect of most of the staff who survived and who joined with him in his efforts to ensure the factory's continued existence. In the words of one member of staff, 'within eighteen months he made Hollington a place that you were proud to work in'.

Thus the new manager 'shook things up in the factory' and 'got things moving'. And in the process he managed to reinforce to a considerable extent the feeling of unity which seemed to have existed among the staff, although some of the effect must be attributed to a fear that the factory might close down altogether. However, at the same time he took a number of strategic decisions which affected the factory's future. He recognized that although the factory was now working on more commercial contracts and less cost-plus work, the existing inspection system was a powerful and effective means of controlling quality, and he left it largely unchanged.

His first concern was to set up a production control system that would highlight delays and shortcomings in the flow of components, and thus satisfy the primary requirement of getting the equipment 'out of the door' on time. This concern led him to institute a new production planning system modelled on that of the new parent Company, where standards were set and plans made in respect of individual orders for a product or batch of products on a sequential basis.

Secondly he set up a progress system which presented highly detailed progress information on a weekly basis to the Works Manager (and for orders at an earlier stage, to the Production Controller). Thus, he was said to have 'got the factory out of trouble by becoming a glorified progress chaser'.

Having instituted this system, and after several attempts having recruited a Production Controller with the combination of temperament and ability necessary to keep such a detailed system in operation, he turned his attention to the question of cost control. Here again the existing procedures were inadequate and he directed some of his accounting staff who were familiar with the factory to devise a means of presenting feedback on the cost performance of the factory with respect to each contract, month by month. Given this brief, the accounting department produced the ingenious procedure for cost reporting described below. As the system was based on 'guestimates' of the state of production and the state of the 'spend' on each contract, using the detailed knowledge of the factory possessed by the Production Controller and the 'cost investigator', it was not expensive to operate.

This new arrangement appears to have been effective in the sense that a considerable reduction both in manufacturing costs and in the amount of capital tied up in work in progress followed its introduction. It seems a good point, therefore, at which to begin the review of the control system as it operates at present.

THE CONTROL SYSTEM

(a) *The control of costs*

In beginning this examination of the way that manufacturing at the Hollington factory was controlled, it is important to stress again that the factory was one of the production units of a larger organization, and that control has therefore to be considered at two levels. Firstly, there is the control system connecting the factory with the Head Office; there are a number of links that form part of the Company-wide control system. Secondly, there are the internal mechanisms of control operating within the Hollington factory itself.

At the first level of analysis, we find that Head Office issues directives to Hollington on such matters as general policy, accounting, specification of materials and supplies, and guidance on certain aspects of pay. Head Office also exercises a more specific control over the factory, by setting the framework for the allocation of contracts to the various manufacturing centres.

The placing of orders seems to be governed by two factors:

(i) The policies laid down by the Head Office Production Scheduler. These policies determine the type of work that factories will normally handle, the associations between certain design teams and certain factories, and the balancing of available work.

(ii) The estimates submitted to the Product Divisions of the company by the factories in response to estimate requests. These estimates are supposed to be estimates at cost, and, other things being equal, the order goes to the factory with the lowest estimate.

Thus, in the Company-wide cost control system, one function of the Hollington estimating department is to act as a source of information about how cheaply (or expensively) Hollington can produce orders which Head Office may be considering sending them. As we shall see when we look at the cost control system operating *within* the factory, these estimates fulfil a different function in that context.

The operation of these internal cost control systems can best be approached by a consideration of the two formal cost-monitoring occasions; the *Management Meeting*, and the *Manufacturing Cost Meeting*, both of which are held once a month. The Management Meeting is attended by the senior managers in charge of each of the functional areas of the factory: production, production engineering, production planning, inspection and testing, purchasing, accounting and personnel. The Manufacturing Cost Meeting is attended by only some of these functional heads, together with some junior managers, but both meetings are chaired by the Works Manager.

The Management Meeting provides the occasion for a monthly review of the state of the factory, as reflected in a report from the accounts department. This report presents senior management with a picture of the factory level of production and output, of stocks and work in progress, of personnel, wages, hours worked and factory overheads. All of the figures in this report are 'live', and the senior staff have become accustomed to using them to gauge their position. Their interest is heightened since factory overheads in particular are broken down among the various functions and compared with monthly budget figures submitted by the senior managers. These budget figures are themselves the result of complex bargaining processes which take into consideration the Works Manager's policy directives, the Works Accountant's specialized knowledge and the senior staff's knowledge of their own departments.

Thus, the monthly review and budget comparison carried out by the Management Meeting is concerned with the overall position, the balance of contracts, and the likely ultimate profit or loss on all the contracts currently being processed. The other dimension of cost control which is monitored relates to individual contracts; an assessment is made of how money and time is being spent in relation to standards set by the estimate. This dimension is the concern of the Manufacturing Cost Meeting which takes the figures given by the estimate as a goal, and provides up-to-date assessments of performance relative to this goal. The goal is not completely taken for granted, however, for the estimating process itself is being reviewed at the same time. Since the estimates are supposed to be estimates at cost, a profit on a contract may mean *either* slack estimates *or* particularly effective production. A loss may mean *either* too tight an estimate *or* ineffective production. It is clear that there is a conflict built into this situation; a running dispute between the estimating department and the production departments. While at times this conflict may become severe, it seems for the most part to be accepted as part of the system. This is recognized by the ritual references to it, usually of a joking nature.

It is of interest to note that in the setting of this not very large factory, the formal system for monitoring manufacturing costs recognizes the nature of the informal knowledge which certain people have of the factory, and incorporates this knowledge.

This means that the operation of the manufacturing costs system depends upon a series of 'guestimates'. The Production Controller assesses the percentage of work which has been done on a contract, based on his 'feel' of the contract from the weekly progress meetings. In a similar fashion he assesses the number of hours' work that remain. The Cost Investigator makes an estimate of the eventual profit or loss on each contract.

Both of these assessors have considerable knowledge of the factory: they walk round the factory and are able to assimilate information from a large number of sources. The Cost Investigator 'knows accounting and engineering, and the men on the shop floor, and he knows the system here from A to Z'.

The Production Controller augments his information by leaving his door open, and encouraging anyone to drop in and chat, so that he can listen to people telling him 'things they think he knows already'.

The subjective element in the system is reflected in the many references made at the Manufacturing Cost Meetings to the 'feel' of the order, the 'feel' of production costs, the 'feel' of materials and so on.

In looking at the relation between the two formal cost-monitoring occasions which have been described, it is not possible to say that one is the meeting at which major cost decisions are taken, while at the other only minor matters are considered. In one sense, the Management Meeting *is* presented with a condensed version of some of the information generated as a result of the monitoring activities of the Manufacturing Cost Meeting. Thus the latter appears to be pursuing sub-goals set by the Management Meeting. But the Manufacturing Cost Meeting also has a certain degree of independence and, particularly since it is chaired by the Works Manager, it can pursue goals which have not been set at the other meeting. Therefore, these two sections of the cost control system are operating simultaneously on slightly differing aspects of the factory's cost situation. They are operating partly as a two-step or two-level control, but at times they also operate in parallel. They do not, however, appear to be in conflict with each other.

There is one further aspect of cost control which must be mentioned, although the term 'control' is hardly appropriate. The factory inherited a decaying piecework system, which has a number of drift-inducing mechanisms built into it. This means that the management is not in control of the cost of labour. It would be impossible to regain control without changing the wage system in a number of ways, and the unions are challenging management's authority to do this. Meanwhile, management can only try to regulate, through the rate-fixing department, the extent of the increase. Even this is difficult however, as the daily bargains that rate fixers make with individual employees on the shop floor are inevitably affected by the common expectations within the factory that rates must continue to rise. Attempts to control through the rate-fixing department, therefore, are ineffective.

The Factory Manager was probably not overstating the case when he told the unions that failure to control wage drift could lead to Hollington being priced out of the market by other Company factories, particularly as there are other uncertainties about the future of the factory. Thus the lack of any effective control system in respect of labour costs could have very serious results for the factory.

(b) *The control of quality*

The procedures for controlling quality are more independent of overall Company policy than those for controlling costs. This does not mean that the Company quality control system has no links with Hollington, but that these links are not so extensive and ramifying. As indicated above, to understand the system it is necessary to go back to the days when under the previous ownership the factory was producing only government work on a cost-plus basis.

A common belief at Hollington is that the system operating at that time led to a 'money-is-no-object' approach to manufacture; this meant that great stress was placed on high-quality work.

The idea that maintaining very high standards was important was continuously reinforced by the presence of a team of six or eight government inspectors permanently stationed in the factory to monitor the work of the factory's own inspection department.

'They were respected. The chief was very fair, but they were very powerful. They could stop a whole line of equipment going out if one small fault was found. And they could withdraw an inspector's stamp, which would mean that he couldn't get a job on A.I.D. work anywhere else in the country.'

The operation of this system meant that detailed records were kept of who inspected each piece of work, so that in the event of a faulty part being discovered, the inspector responsible could be identified and, if necessary, have his stamp withdrawn. Consequently, if any job diverged from the standards laid down, it would be rejected without debate. The internal inspectors were gradually trained to recognize the standard of work which was required, by a process of being shown the specification of jobs, and then being shown examples of work which met this specification. After passing through a stage where he referred doubtful cases to an experienced inspector, the new inspector gradually built up a standard of his own. Thus the new Company took over, with the factory, a team of inspectors with high prestige in the factory and with a set of internalized standards about what was acceptable work.

The products which the new Company intended to manufacture at Hollington were similar to those made before the takeover, both Companies being concerned with the manufacture of electronic equipment. The changes in the production technology following the takeover were less fundamental than the changes that took place subsequently as a result of the introduction of transistors, printed board circuits, and modular constructions.

A significant change in attitude towards quality was, however, associated with the takeover. The new owners were not producing government work on a 'cost-plus' basis—they were manufacturing equipment to be sold commercially, either to government departments or to private industry. As a consequence, although operating in a market where the quality of the equipment was important,

F

they had to produce high-quality equipment at a competitive price. The inspection department had to revise its standards accordingly and probably felt that this reduced its prestige.

'What was thrown out one week under the old Company, was accepted by the new Company and you had to train people up in a similar way to a new standard. The older men still feel that they are passing rubbish, even though the standard is still high by commercial standards.'

In practice, commercial standards seem to mean: 'Work to the specification whenever possible, but before scrapping border-line cases, consider the cost of rejection, consider the function which this particular part fulfils, and consider whether the equipment can be modified so that the part can be used.'

This was impossible to do on government contracts because the government agencies stated as a condition of the contract that any modifications *must* be authorized, and that all parts with a given part number *must* be made accurately enough to be completely interchangeable.

It is worth pursuing a little further the idea of 'internalized standards of acceptable work', particularly in order to compare this type of standard with the hardly articulate and highly subjective 'craft' standards of inspection in the tailoring factory described in Chapter 6. Although electronics manufacture is a very precise procedure relying on an advanced technology, in which properties can be specified to a high degree of accuracy, the very complexities of the technology make for difficulties in inspection. There are so many characteristics laid down in the component and material specifications, and in the handbooks of workshop practice, that it is impossible to check all of them without stopping production completely, which means that subjective judgements are still important.

The inspectors rely on their memory, or on files directing their attention to points which are particularly important, or to points which have been found to be faulty in the past: 'We don't check all of the characteristics—we couldn't do; but we check the important ones, and any which seem suspicious. For example, if a material *feels* wrong we may send away for a lab analysis of it.'

The difficulty of inspecting the product increases through the production process, as the assemblies become progressively more complex, and it is at its most extreme when the final equipment is to be inspected.

In the course of the study, the research worker accompanied an inspector from a government department on his examination of some finished equipment which his department was purchasing. Since he had perhaps three hours to inspect a complete equipment which had taken two-to-three weeks to be checked by the test department, it is clear that he could not carry out a detailed inspection, and he admitted this. He relied first on a visual inspection, checking for any obvious faults; secondly, on an examination of the details of the performance of the equipment recorded on test sheets by the Test Engineer; and thirdly, on asking to see a repeat measurement of one or two of these figures carried out. He conceded that this was inadequate as a quality control device on its own, and for this reason he thought that it was also necessary to get to know the firm and to establish a personal relationship with the Test Engineers, in order to satisfy himself of their competence, reliability, and integrity. Overall, the picture of the inspection system at Hollington, then, is one of a system with a tradition of power and high standards which still exerts a considerable effect on the quality of the work passed.

But although the system has *power*, and works to high standards of accuracy, its effectiveness is limited by the large number of standards set, and the impossibility of monitoring all the characteristics involved. This means that the real goals aimed at are not the standards of the drawings, handbooks, and inspection standards, but some personal amalgam of these which each inspector builds up. Moreover, although the inspection system had reasonably rapid feedback, the nature of the product is such that some components cannot be finally checked until they are installed in the completed equipment, so that there is inevitably a time lag of several months in inspection feedback for such components.

(c) *The control of time*

Having considered the ways in which cost and quality are controlled and bearing these in mind, there remains what is perhaps the predominant control system at Hollington: the system for controlling delivery dates, and for controlling the timing of production in order to achieve these delivery dates.

All production at Hollington is initiated by the placing of an order by a Product Division, sometimes acting directly for a customer and sometimes, although less often, placing a stock order which may subsequently be allocated to a customer. The responsibility for allocating the work available among the different factories rests, as we have already seen, with the Head Office Production Scheduler. While the state of the order book is of concern to all the senior staff at Hollington, the Production Controller is the person most directly linked with the Head Office Production Scheduler's work. He is responsible for ensuring that the factory is as fully loaded as possible and that there is capacity available to meet the requirements set.

The current work load on the factory is assessed in terms of the money value of the orders placed, and it is claimed that this is as effective as more sophisticated methods. This assumes that the ratio of work content to contract value is approximately constant. Although this ratio varies from two to five hours to the £1 for individual contracts, it is said that the ratio for the combination of contracts in the factory is effectively constant. A consequence of this method of loading is that the formal shop load is not planned out in detail in advance, but worked out on a week-to-week basis by the progress section and the shop floor loaders.

The planning process as such revolves around the preparation of a production control schedule for each contract. The Planning Officer combines his information about the contract with any information which he has about similar work which has been done before. Using this information, he works back from the promised delivery date, by rule-of-thumb methods, a network that indicates the dates when drawings should be received, when parts lists should be issued, and when each stage of the contract should be started.

The main function of the production control schedule is to provide, at minimum cost, an arbitrary reference scale which can be used to generate all the paper-work necessary to see the contract through the factory and to indicate, other things being equal, the order in which the different parts and assemblies should be issued and made. Once the schedule for an order has been worked out it is seldom altered; all modifications are made by adjusting the subsidiary paper-work.

The production control schedule is then passed to a planner, who compiles from the drawings of the equipment a detailed breakdown of the assemblies and sub-assemblies of the contract, and a list of all the parts which are needed for the order. These parts lists, together with the production control schedule and a set of production layouts, can then be combined in a routine fashion to produce all the job tickets, accounts slips, wage slips, warrants and progress cards necessary to get the required components produced or made, and to get the contract manufactured.

This sounds an extensive amount of paper-work to generate in a rule-of-thumb manner from a very small input of information, but in fact for each contract the amount of paper-work required is not very great. The arbitrary nature of much of the paper-work generated seems to be accepted by people in the factory, for the forms are treated as aids, not as controllers. This attitude seems to be summarized in this comment by one of the production control staff: 'Systems are all very well, but they're only as good as the people who operate them. That's why we try to operate with a minimum of systems, and bring people in who think in a certain kind of way.'

To understand where the adjustments that enable this arbitrary rule-of-thumb planning to operate successfully in the real world are made, it is necessary to look at the progress system. The effects of this system are so pervasive and far reaching that any attempt to alter it radically would mean fundamental changes in the entire organization and control of work. There are two mechanisms, one major and one minor, through which the progress system makes its impact. The major one is the Production Meeting, normally chaired by the Works Manager and attended by all the senior staff with the exception of the Accountant and Personnel Manager. This takes place weekly and is known throughout the factory as 'the Monday Morning Meeting' or simply 'the Meeting'.

The framework of this Meeting is provided by the production minutes. These list the different products that have to be manufactured and tested in the monthly period and the numbers of each required. The monthly target-setting takes place at a meeting of the Production Controller and his assistant with the Works Superintendent, the Head of Test, and the foreman of the Final Assembly section.

The Meeting revises the minutes, thus indicating the weekly progress made towards the completion of the monthly target. In control terms, therefore, the Meeting is a monitoring of the progress towards a series of sub-goals which are reset each month, and an examination of the obstacles that lie in the way of such progress. The target-setting exercise is to some extent a bargaining process, but as the people involved in it know both the factory and each other very well, room for manœuvre is limited. The Production Controller is in the strongest position, for in addition to his knowledge of the state of production he also has information about outside pressures on the factory for delivery of equipment. There is, moreover, beneath the bargaining a basic acceptance of the fact that the demands must be met, and the Production Controller's comment: 'I tell them what I want, and they say why I can't have it; in practice I usually get my way' seems to be a very accurate description of the bargaining process, although it perhaps suggests a formality which does not in fact exist.

The fact that most of the senior staff and the Works Manager are involved in the 'Monday Meeting' makes it a powerful mechanism of control. The power is transmitted by means of the revised Production Minutes, thirty-nine copies of which are distributed on Tuesday morning. These Minutes are in effect a series of orders or directives, for unless all the items mentioned on the Minutes have made progress by the end of the week, at the next Meeting the Works Manager wants to know why.

Six copies of the Minutes go to the senior staff at the Meeting, two go to Test (one each to the Chief Test Supervisor and the Chief Test Planning Engineer), one goes to the Assistant Buyer, one to the Materials Controller, and one to the Chief Foreman; four to the Senior Inspectors and the Quality Control Investigator, twelve to the Progress Department, two to the Cost Investigator, and ten to all Foremen and Senior Chargehands.

Not only are these lists ubiquitous within the firm, they are even distributed by the Purchasing Department to regular sub-contracting firms, to enable them continually to readjust *their* production priorities.

The wide distribution throughout the factory of this list of production targets and holding items (with the initials of those responsible for each item marked alongside) means that there is an explicit and common awareness of the weekly task. This is reflected in the selection of quotations given below:

Foreman A: 'The Monday Meeting Minutes are the most important single bit of paper for me. . . .I work with Progress: they have to make sure that the work keeps coming through—I keep my men happy and push work that is highlighted.'

Foreman B: 'I work to the Monday Meeting list.'

Inspection Supervisor: 'I work to the Production Minutes.'

Test Engineer: 'We know that some items are under pressure.

This unit I'm working on now had three asterisks put against it
at the Meeting on Monday with the big boss.'
Progress Chaser: 'The fact of an item being on this list gives me
more strength to push.'

The second and minor programming mechanism is the Pre-
production Meeting held on Friday mornings. This is a meeting
of the functional staff concerned with progressing the work. It is
chaired by the Production Controller, and attended by his assistant
and several of the key progress chasers. This is a much more
routine occasion than the Production Meeting, partly because the
contracts are at an earlier state of manufacture, so that crises are
rarer and less urgent, and partly because so many small items are
involved that considerable application is needed to get through
them at all. The form of this meeting is rather curious: the Production Controller has his copy of the Pre-production Minutes, which
is a list of about two thousand items. He reads out the number of
each part, and the progress chaser concerned reports, as briefly as
possible, on the movement of that part since the previous meeting,
indicating whether it is 'off' (finished), 'issued to shop', 'on op. three
of five' (that is, on the third operation out of five operations required
to complete the part), 'waiting for other parts', and so on. The Production Controller records this information in a shorthand on his
Minutes, and calls out the next number. This boring, almost ritual
process, occupies this member of the senior staff and most of the
staff of the Progress Department for at least three hours each week.
It should be evident from the foregoing that the Production
Controller exercises considerable influence over the flow of work
through all departments of the factory, and this gives him considerable power to influence happenings in areas outside his own
department. It would be possible to describe Hollington as a
factory which, although it has a strong quality control system and
a system of cost control, is dominated by the production control
system operated by the Production Controller. One comment made
was: 'I find that this factory has got more progress chasers (although
not necessarily designated as such) than anywhere I know, even in
the electronics industry, where making sure that the right parts are
in the right place at the right time is a major job.' Other people
echoed this: 'Supervision here have never had to supervise since
the War.' 'The foremen here are only glorified progress chasers.'
'Their concerns are those Progress Meeting Minutes.'

Several devices are used by the Production Controller to balance the conflicting demands of the orders on the factory. Work can be sent out to sub-contractors or to other Company factories, and work can be brought in from other factories. One internal device which is used, however, is the procedure known as 'batching down'. Although orders may be placed on the factory for quantities of 50, 100, or 200 units of equipment, these units are rarely required all at the same time. Therefore, the contract specifies that say, 60 units will be delivered as an initial batch of 20, and four subsequent monthly batches of 10 units. If each unit requires, for example, two of a certain type of coil, or printed board, or bracket, the planning process will provide for the manufacture of one lot of 120 coils, boards, or brackets. But if some of the components necessary for the coils, etc., have not been bought or made or if pressure on production facilities is too great for the 120 coils to be made in one batch, then it is possible for the progress chaser to 'batch down', so that they are made in two lots of 60: or in an extreme case, he could break the job down into five batches, one batch of 40 and four subsequent batches of 20 each. This procedure is obviously useful in meeting the conflicting demands of a batch production situation, since it gives considerable flexibility, and at the same time provides the components needed to meet the delivery dates. But it has serious disadvantages that are apparent even in a superficial examination of the factory.

Foreman: 'I dislike batching down; for example, if 1 000 off are ordered this may be batched down to 10 for a production meeting schedule. One job we did involved eighty hours' setting-up time on it alone. I've been continually on to the office to change this.'

Foreman: 'There is far too much batching down going on. On small quantities you don't get a run, you have to pay extra setting time, and the operators go on section average for batches under 25 so you pay more in the end. I'd rather hold a job up for two days. They are on your back, but it's more economic.'

Operator: 'I often have to set up a batch (on the machine) and then have to do another batch the same week, sometimes. I don't lose by it, but it bothers me to think that they are so stupid.'

Operator: 'You can get one job, then the same job the following week, but that's the designers' fault, and the fact that they're planning by contracts. It means that someone in planning has slipped up.'

Thus the issue of batching down is a controversial one, on which opinions are divided. On the one hand it provides the flexibility necessary to ensure that delivery dates are met, but on the other hand 'if you are going to assemble equipment in batches of five, you aren't going to make a profit. If you ignore the internal arrangements and make them in batches of 100, you make a profit'. More will be said about this dilemma later in this paper.

Overall, then, the production control system at Hollington can be described as one which has its broad goals set by some sort of negotiating process with Head Office and with the Head Office Production Scheduler. The ultimate responsibility for production is taken by the Works Manager, who monitors the performance of the Hollington Production Controller. Much of the initiative and control of production lies with the Production Controller himself, who sets the goals of the internal system and uses the authority of the Works Manager to provide the ultimate power that makes his control system work. A number of goals have to be reconciled within the system. Each contract must be made on time, in order to satisfy the customer's requirements; to achieve this, a multitude of steps must be taken at an early stage, and these steps must be combined in the correct order, and the facilities must be available to take these steps. At the same time that this is being achieved for one contract it has to be achieved for all others. Moreover, there is another goal, that of ensuring that the facilities available are fully utilized—that the factory is not working either over or under capacity.

Thus the task of the production control system is a highly complex one, and it is interesting to consider how appropriate the system is to the nature of the manufacturing process which it monitors, and to the other controls which are operating in the factory.

THE INTERRELATIONSHIP OF THE CONTROLS

This description of the control system in the Hollington factory has shown that it is of the multi-system fragmented type. A major problem of this kind of control is the necessity of reconciling the various sub-goals in the system if production is to take place at all.

Although in many firms this reconciliation is a painful process, with the responsibility for it falling on the shoulders of lower-level line supervision, it does not appear to be a major source of distress for the foremen at Hollington. It is true that, in addition to their responsibility for the supervision of the people in their section, the foremen are expected, as one of them put it, 'to get good quality jobs out at the right time, at low cost', but there was little indication that they found the task impossible or even difficult. The question arises, therefore, of why this was so.

One feature of the controls which probably has a bearing on this is their explicitness. In terms of both quality and delivery dates, the line supervision were left in little doubt of what was required of them. The words 'good quality' and 'right time' in the quotation above had specific meanings; they were not left to the foremen to interpret subjectively.

Another important factor is the friendly, or at least co-operative, atmosphere in this small factory. The foremen as a group share a number of common characteristics: all but one of the foremen have been promoted by the new Company since the takeover; with one exception, they have been promoted from within the factory; and most of them also eat together at mid-day. Against this background, it is easy to deal with conflicting production demands by adjusting work loads between sections, or to provide some commiseration and social support to make unavoidable conflicts easier to survive.

The preceding paragraph overemphasizes, perhaps, the separateness of the foremen as a group, for the factory as a whole is characterized by a complex network of informal relationships which tend to cut across department and hierarchical divisions. Within the factory, it is rarely necessary to make an appointment to see anyone, and the informal atmosphere is constantly being contrasted with the formality of Head Office. Several people were aware that the informality and the small size of the factory were major factors in ensuring that the factory control systems operated at all, and were prepared to admit that if the factory size were doubled, they would have to adopt different control systems.

The importance of small size and informal co-operation can be seen most clearly at the senior staff level. The senior staff within Hollington 'live in each other's pockets'. They eat together daily in a separate dining-room, they spend much of their time in contact with each other, and their jobs are highly interdependent. Although they are acutely aware of each other's qualities and faults, they are conscious of the need to present a united front to the factory, and at times to the Works Manager. As a group, they are extremely aware of the demands placed upon the Hollington factory, and of their separate and collective responsibilities to meet those demands. And since, in spite of individual differences, they are frequently able to operate as a team, some of the reconciliation of the disparate control systems takes place at this senior staff level.

But although the informal co-operation which occurs at a number of levels enables the three managerial control mechanisms to exist side by side, there are some contradictions in the system which cannot be resolved by informal co-operation. Two problem areas are of particular interest.

(a) *Batching down and product variety*

We have already mentioned briefly the process of 'batching down', which occurs to enable conflicting production requirements to be met, but which at the same time increases the degree of variety with which the control systems have to cope. What is the significance of this procedure in the context of the links between the control system and the task of the factory?

From the shop floor, batching down is seen as an uneconomic activity, caused by a failure of planning. What is not so generally recognized is that this criticism can be levelled at the planning process itself, in particular at the separate planning of each order. It is possible for several batches of identical components to be required for several different contracts, and since there is no formal mechanism for linking up the batches, components are manufactured in smaller numbers and therefore more expensively than is necessary. Informally, it sometimes happens that a member of the production control department or line supervision exceeds his normal duties and browses through the work waiting to be issued, picking out batches that could with advantage be combined.

A parallel situation exists in the buying department, to which the planning system sends purchase requisitions. Because of the way in which the planning department breaks down each equipment into assemblies and sub-assemblies, the purchasing department receives a separate requisition for each component in each sub-assembly. Moreover, if the component is also required for other contracts, further bundles of requisitions will be generated by these contracts.

The considerable price reductions which are available when large quantities of most components are purchased means that the purchasing department have to make some attempt to collate purchase requisitions in order to buy components or materials in more economic quantities.

The planning of each product separately not only has cost implications, but also makes it more difficult to load the factory in advance in a detailed manner. The forward loading has therefore to be assessed in terms of the money value of the contracts to be handled. While this loading is adequate in overall terms, it inevitably leads to frequent local pressures upon production resources, or to unused production capacity.

In the process of operating the very detailed progress system, the Production Controller has to identify the areas of overload or underload, and to cope with overloads by arranging with the foremen for work to be subcontracted, or to be sent to other Company factories, or to be batched down. Underloads are dealt with by requesting or attracting work *from* other Company factories, or by paying for waiting time.

These devices for handling overload or underload are also needed to cope with adjustments to the production programme. It is assumed within the Company that equipment going out will be of a certain quality, and the autonomy of the quality control system, as we have seen, ensures that this is so at Hollington. Thus urgent priority requirements for a given contract must be met, not by pushing work through at a lower standard, but by off-loading or sub-contracting work, by pushing back the delivery dates of low priority contracts, and by batching down.

Observation of the problems associated with the planning of each contract separately led to the question of whether there was any alternative. It can be argued that this is the most appropriate, or even the only possible procedure where there is a high variation in product range and where products are subject to rapid development, as in the electronics industry. Was this the type of production with which the Hollington factory was primarily concerned? Certainly, the range of products made varied from year to year, certainly a technical advance by a competitor rendered one equipment obsolete before the first five had been made, and certainly many of the employees at Hollington felt that they were operating in a constantly changing situation.

But against this we may set the consensus among the senior management of the factory, that the product range could be separated into two categories: 'bread and butter' equipments which had changed little in the past five or ten years, and a proportion of equipments made in batches of five-off or ten-off which were subject to much more frequent modification or change. Since the 'bread and butter' equipments are ordered in batches of 200-off, and since a new order for a further 200-off almost automatically follows the completion of the preceding one, it seems that at least a proportion of the work passing through the factory is large batch or standardized production, rather than small batch production.

This is, of course, an oversimplification, because as would be expected, the long-running equipments are the most 'old-fashioned' ones. With time, these equipments are being redesigned, and the new designs tend to be of a modular form. The inherent nature of modular equipment is such that a number of permutations are possible, and there is certainly more variety in the modular equipments being made. Thus, the long-term trend to modular production could be seen as a tendency for the factory to move from the large batch production area to the small batch production area. However, modular production also opens up the possibility of producing commonly used modules in large batches, and subsequently assembling small batches of special combinations of these modules, and this process is also under way at Hollington.

The possibility, therefore, that the control system at the Hollington factory is designed to cope with more variety than the nature of the task requires cannot be overlooked. Two pieces of circumstantial evidence can be offered in support of this view.

First, it was stated by Head Office that the amount of variety at the Hollington factory was much lower than that in the Company as a whole. That is to say, the Hollington factory tends to deal with the most standardized end of the Company's product range, although the total amount of standardization of products over the whole range is low.

Second, an indication of the degree of product variability can be worked out by the use of the formula suggested in Chapter 2, that is, the calculation of the number of different products manufactured in two successive years as a proportion of the total number of products manufactured in those two years. Accepting that this measure is very crude, and can be invalidated by a number of factors, it seems nevertheless to support the Head Office assertion. The ratio was calculated for Hollington and for another of the manufacturing units of the same Company. The value obtained for Hollington was 0.24 while the value obtained for the other factory was 0.7. This is such a wide difference in results that it is unlikely to be explainable in terms of the crudity of the measure and is consonant with the idea that the Hollington factory is subject to rather lower rates of product change than are common in the rest of this electronics Company.

Hollington appears, therefore, to be a manufacturing unit in which the system of production control is less appropriate to its own task than to the overall task of the wider organization to which it belongs. Looking at Hollington from the Head Office point of view, there are certain advantages in a system which enables the factory to cope with more variety than it needs to do. It is, for example, well able to cope with unexpected demands, and the flexibility versus maximum economy dilemma is expressed in the Head Office assessment of it as 'not our most efficient factory but our most effective'.

This means that because of the flexibility offered by the various devices which have been adopted to make up for the crudities in the planning process, and because of the ability of the factory senior staff to operate informally as a team, Hollington is able to offer the Company as a whole two facilities.

These are, first, the facility to fit in small prototype or one-off fabrications or sub-assemblies, on an informal foreman-to-foreman basis, so that the jobs are carried out rapidly, without excessive paper-work and without disturbing the factory's routine. This facility is developed because an ability to attract work within the Company is needed to cope with local underloads, which the foremen are anxious to avoid. The second facility is to be able to rush any given high-priority contract through, at high speed, with a minimum amount of time spent on planning. This facility normally means, of course, that other contracts suffer to a certain extent, but at least Head Office knows that no effort will be spared on the urgent contract.

(b) *Design standardization*

The second problem that puts a strain upon the informal, friendly co-operation, both within the Hollington factory and between it and other parts of the Company, is that of the relationship between production and design. Here again, a difficulty arises from the fact that the Hollington manufacturing task is to some extent atypical of that of the Company as a whole. At Company level, the design element in the task is most critical to success. It is, therefore, a Company in which those concerned with design have high prestige and considerable power. There is a tradition in the Company that

the future rests with the designers and that it is therefore impera-
tive that their demands should be met.

The Company is divided below board level into a number of
Divisions specializing in different forms of electronic equipment,
and each Division has its own design office and chief designer.
However, manufacturing centres are not broken up in this way, so
that each factory is working on contracts from several Divisions.
There is little standardization of components across the Company.
Any standardization that has taken place has been within the
province of each Chief Designer. The sets of electronic equipment
manufactured at Hollington may serve different purposes but the
growing use of transistorized modular sub-assemblies means that
the equipment is becoming increasingly similar in construction.
Unfortunately the production process is unable to take advantage
of these similarities because the separate design units meet similar
constructional problems in different ways.

There does exist an elaborate mechanism for informing the
production centre of modifications to equipment, which makes
provision for those concerned with production to request modifications in designs, but these requests are only seen as legitimate if the
design is difficult or impossible to manufacture. Any requests from
the factory for designers in one unit to conform to the practices of
designers in another unit seem to be interpreted as attempts to
reduce the designers' autonomy and thus, in the context of the
Company as a whole, they have little chance of success.

THE COIL WINDING EXAMPLE

The main problems of the control system and its appropriateness
to the factory's technical task have now been described. There is
one section of the Hollington factory where a number of these
problems manifest themselves and are interrelated. It is interesting
to look specifically at this section, particularly as it was also
recognized by management as a problem area at the time of the
research.

This area was the coil-winding section where a large number of
women were employed in winding a variety of small coils. Difficulties arose at first because a very high proportion of some types
of coils were found to be unsatisfactory when the final equipment
was tested.

This high wastage seemed to result from two factors: first, the
long time lag already referred to between manufacturing the coil

and testing the final equipment meant that the operators did not have a rapid feedback pointing out their failures and reinforcing their success. Secondly, the specifications for the coils were written on the basis of one-off coils installed in the prototype by the designer who measured the characteristics of these one-off coils, and estimated tolerances. If his estimates were too wide, coils which had been passed by inspection failed to function in the equipment. By the same token, if his tolerances were too narrow, coils which would have been adequate were rejected by inspection.

The pressure upon coil production resources to remake these coils then showed itself in bottlenecks both in coil inspection and in coil production. The inspection difficulties arose because efforts were being made to step up inspection of coils at the point of manufacture, by means of more detailed and more accurate inspection. The production difficulties arose because the situation was exacerbating the inherent problems of coil manufacture. Most of these coils are very small, and are manufactured of fine gauge wire. This means that their final properties are very sensitive to small changes in the varnish coating of the wire, the length of time for which the wire has been exposed to the atmosphere, the individual operator's style of winding and 'tying-off', and so on. These difficulties are met by repeatedly inspecting the first coils of a batch until a satisfactory coil is produced, then holding all conditions constant while the remainder of the batch is wound.

This system seems to operate satisfactorily under light load conditions, but the presssure on inspection was slowing up the necessary feedback on the quality of the coils, and the very existence of a bottleneck demanded that coil production should be batched down in order to provide coils for as many contracts as possible. But since small batches reduce the length of run which can be made when satisfactory conditions have been achieved, batching down increased the pressure on inspection but did nothing to improve the standard of the coils being produced. It should be pointed out that there is effectively an upper limit to batch size, since 'first-off' inspection must be repeated whenever a new reel of wire is used, but with small coils this limit does not seriously restrict batch size.

The immediate problems of coil production were solved by keeping up the rate at which the coil winders were working and by bringing in new equipment and extra personnel to inspect coils. However, the episode also indicates that coil production is likely to be a recurring problem. As one manager said: 'Coils are the only live component which we manufacture here, and we can't expect to deal with them in the same way that we deal with assembly work.'

This remark implies that coils should be manufactured on a stock basis, to reap the maximum benefit from long 'steady state' runs, and the close quality control which such runs make possible. However, the two features of the analysis discussed earlier make such a course of action very difficult to follow.

In the first place, since the tradition of designer autonomy embodies few pressures towards the use of standardized components, there is a great variety of coils. This means that a large amount of capital and space would be required if stocks of the whole range were to be kept. And in the second place, the contract planning system is, as we have seen, so pervasive that any attempt to manufacture on a stock basis in one production area would have far-reaching consequences for the flexibility and effectiveness of the planning/production control system.

CONCLUSIONS

This study has attempted to describe the control systems devised in a small factory to cope with its tasks. The problems identified can be explained only by reference both to the peculiar local circumstances of the Hollington factory and to the beliefs of central management, subscribed to by local management, about the form of organization which is most appropriate to the electronics industry. Looking at these problems from the Hollington point of view, it seems that some reappraisal of the factory's position on the small/large batch continuum is needed. The present contract-by-contract planning process, designed to cope with maximum variation between contracts, may not be wholly appropriate for a situation where much of the factory's task is concerned with the manufacture of large batches.

If a system of planning were adopted which recognized the elements of stability in the situation, instead of injecting increased amounts of variety into the system, it seems likely that improvements in planning of factory load and in detailed advance costing would become possible, and it might then prove unnecessary for senior management to be so closely linked with the progress system. Moreover, it might be slightly easier to cope with wage drift, although the main causes of this are probably outside the system being examined.

G

At the Company level, however, it might be felt that such gains in 'efficiency' could only be won at the expense of 'effectiveness', since the changes would be likely to reduce the factory's flexibility to cope with non-routine situations. It would certainly be important to make a deliberate policy decision based on the acceptance of the fact that 'effectiveness' and 'efficiency' may be alternative goals.

The second problem, from the Company point of view, that might arise from a change in the control system at Hollington would be the challenge that this change would present to the beliefs that underlie the present structure.

Two components of these beliefs have been seen as significant in this study. The high regard placed upon designers within the Company manifests itself in an elaboration of the task which the Hollington production centre is expected to perform, while the examination of the interrelationship of this task with the local control systems suggests that a belief in the appropriateness of Company-wide modes of control may lead to difficulties where the local task deviates from the Company norm.

LISL KLEIN

5 Prescription in Management Control*

The study on which this chapter is based differed from the other
tracer studies in that it was the only one carried out in a chemical
process firm. The tracer was a brand of soap which was made and
packed in one Department. The 'making end' had the characteristics of process technology although the process was not continuous; the technology was what Brewer (1) described as batch
production of dimensionless products. The machinery and operations of the 'packing end' made it more akin to engineering
production.

THE RESEARCH CONTEXT

The factory in which the study was made is a manufacturing
unit of a large international Company making soaps, detergents and
related products. While this is an industry which has shown consistent growth, based as it is on rising standards of living and expand-
ing populations throughout the world, in this country the market
for its products is probably almost saturated. Any increase in
sales, therefore, is likely to come from an increased share of the
existing market, and there is fierce competition.

The competition rages on several fronts: technologically there is
the race to be first in the field with new or improved products;
this involves heavy expenditure on research, including research in
packaging. Secondly, there is the competitive wooing of the
consumer, with its comprehensive apparatus of market research,
advertising and advanced selling techniques. Reference has already

* A briefer version of this chapter was published in the *British Journal of
Management Studies*, 3(1) 1965, entitled 'Rationality in Management Control'
by Lisl Klein.

been made in Chapter 2 to the way in which the special packaging and free gifts offered to attract the customers to this firm's products made measurement of the variety in product range in the firm extremely difficult. Finally, and probably of greatest significance in relation to this study, competition shows itself in the need to keep down or reduce unit costs, involving technological improvements and advanced management techniques.

The factory went into production in 1940 and at the time of the study employed about 600 people, roughly one-fifth of whom were managerial and clerical staff. The chief executive on the site was the Works Manager, to whom were responsible a General Production Manager with five Group Managers under him, and the heads of four functional departments—the Chief Chemist, responsible for quality, the Personnel Manager, the Chief Engineer and the Industrial Engineer.

The tracer product, called here product 'Four', was a batch of a particular brand of soap tablets representing one month's production of a small Department. Liquid soap was pumped from a storage tank into this Department. There it went through a number of chemical and physical processes at the end of which it was extruded as a bar. It was then cut into tablets which could be of two sizes, stored on racks, dried, stamped, packed and despatched to a warehouse. The entire process took place in one room and involved about fifteen operators and one Manager. The Manager was in turn responsible to one of the Group Managers referred to above.

The choice of 'Four' as the tracer turned out to be a fortunate one. The Department in which it was made was small enough to be studied in depth and the manufacturing process simple enough to be understood. Nevertheless, all the policies of this very large international Company impinged upon it. Scheduling and production control, budgeting and cost control, the determining and implementing of working methods were all applied to the manufacture of 'Four' in the same way as to any of the Company's products. The procedures caused the occasional flurry but on a small enough scale for one research worker to be able to see how they operated and talk to all the people involved. The Department also formed a unit for most of the firm's accounting procedures—in the words of the Works Manager: 'It's a microcosm.'

METHODS OF RESEARCH

The fieldwork was carried out in two phases. During the first phase interviews were held with everyone involved with the making and packing of 'Four'. This included the line management hierarchy: the Works Manager, the Group Manager and two Department Managers, as the post changed hands during the course of the research, as well as the Manager of Manufacturing in the Company's Head Office; five men and eleven women operators; and all personnel of service and functional departments who had contact with or were in any way responsible for what happened in the Department.

These interviews were unstructured, but as with those carried out in the other tracer studies, they started off by asking the people concerned what they actually did in relation to 'Four'. This always produced responses on which further questions could then be based, and it also provided information on how people perceived and structured their jobs.

The second phase of field work consisted of four weeks spent observing what happened in the 'Four' Department. Production was scheduled in four-week periods and one whole schedule was traced from the decision to make it at Head Office through the various incidents that took place during its production to the collection and assessment of all the control information relating to it. During the four weeks the same people (operators, mechanics, Department Manager, Group Manager, Works Manager and inspectors) were visited each day and asked what had happened since the previous visit. For the Department Manager, a questionnaire was filled in every day, and for the process operators there was also a questionnaire. All the operators were asked what had been happening in relation to (a) the product, (b) the equipment, and (c) the people. The Group Manager and Works Manager were asked whether 'Four' had come to their attention since the last visit, again under the heading of product, equipment, or people. Where incidents had occurred involving people not on the regular visiting list these were followed up as well. All the relevant management meetings held during the month were also attended.

Finally, two hours a day were spent in detailed observation in the Department. These were timed so as to cover the whole working day once, i.e. to observe everything that happened from 6.00 – 8.00 a.m. one day, 8.00 – 10.00 a.m. another day and so on.

The month's observation served to put flesh on the bones of the formal description of how the system worked as given in the interviews. During this period the barriers came down and feelings, relationships and problems emerged. It was here, too, that the interaction between the social, technological and policy aspects of the organization showed most clearly.

The interviews with people at management level had taken a course that was curious and unprecedented in the experience of either the research worker or her colleagues, but which provided the first clue to understanding the situation.

The introductory question 'what do you actually do?' led in most cases to the production of one or more manuals and there would follow a session averaging two hours, in which the Manager behaved as though he were training the research worker to do his own job. He would describe policies and procedures, read from instruction manuals and sometimes hand over copies of extracts from these manuals for retention. The information was certainly useful but it was difficult to assess to what extent people were describing what they were expected to do and to what extent describing what they actually did. This process happened too many times for it to be attributable to personality characteristics.

The explanation lay in the fact that managers moved around frequently from job to job and, as will be seen later, the training of others to do their job was in itself part of the system of managerial control. Everyone was always ready to train either his successor or a new trainee being sent round the firm and therefore had official job descriptions ready to mind. Unlike the operators therefore, the managers tended to pass on what a trainee would need to know about the job, rather than the feel of the job with its satisfactions and problems.

Shortly after the observation phase had been completed, a meeting was held, attended by all the Managers employed in the factory, in which the analyses and impressions of how the factory operated were discussed. Although the meeting was not originally planned as part of the information gathering process, what happened in it was useful in assessing the significance of the data, and the meeting itself provided more information.

THE NATURE OF THE CONTROL PROCESSES

A clue having been provided by the manuals and instructions produced during the interviewing, it became clear on analysis that within the frame of reference provided by Chapter 3, there was in this Company an exceptionally clear cut and explicit distinction between the process of designing the system and that of operating it.

Here was a Company that had consciously and deliberately based its management practices on the concept of control systems. System design was the responsibility of a Management Systems Department which in reporting on its own activities in June 1962 had identified its functions as follows:

(i) designing, installing, improving and maintaining control systems for business activities, resources or objectives;
(ii) developing and improving organizations;
(iii) developing and improving the work place;
(iv) developing and installing improved working methods and procedures;
(v) developing and promoting the widest possible use of tools and techniques, the application of which help to maximize performance and effectiveness;
(vi) developing and maintaining the means for measuring the effectiveness of the use of resources and for appraising performance.

The thinking and the procedures did not all originate from the Management Systems Department, but somewhere in the Company there seemed to be a central intelligence, a 'mind', which had taken the trouble to think through 'what do we want?', 'how are we going to get it?', 'how are we going to know whether we have got it?' and 'when we know, what are we going to do about it?'.

In some instances this 'mind' seemed to be located at the international Headquarters of the Company and in others at the Head Office of the British factories. Sometimes it was difficult to identify its location. This corresponded with reality in that the responsibility for actual decision-making lay at different levels of the organization according to the size and importance of the decision that had to be made. What was striking, however, was that whatever the size and scope of the decisions and whatever the level at which they were made, the method of approach was consistent. It was this consistency of approach that differentiated the firm from any of the others studied and that created the impression of central direction.

As regards the actual control of operations, the explicitness of the systems approach meant that, for all the parameters of quantity, quality and the different types of cost, targets were set; methods for arriving at targets were laid down, and ways of auditing the methods of arriving at targets were also laid down. Similarly, actual performance was measured; methods for measuring the actuals were laid down; and ways of auditing the methods for measuring the actuals were also laid down.

The control of *design and quality* was a detailed and highly logical process. There was a basic design card for each product: one half contained the required characteristics and qualities for production; the other half the required characteristics and qualities for the product going out. The limits specified were of two kinds, 'expected' and 'rejection'. 'Expected' limits meant that on a sampling basis ninety per cent of production must come within the standard specified. 'Rejection' limits meant that there was an absolute injunction to scrap. Between the two sets of limits there was an area of discretion allowed to the Works Manager, which was in practice delegated to the Chief Chemist, who made the decisions whether a product should be despatched.

The maintaining of design and quality standards called for a complex organization of controls and controls of controls. It came functionally under the Chief Chemist to whom was responsible a Laboratory Manager and, under him, laboratory analysts and inspectors. Only the Chief Chemist was professionally qualified, since all the work in the laboratory was routine analysis and testing, with no research or development work going on. In turn, laboratory equipment and procedures were regularly audited in detail and compared with those of the other factories in the Group.

The principle on which quality control operated was that if closely controlled, that is adequately sampled and tested, raw materials were processed in a controlled manner, then analysis of the finished product should be superfluous and merely for record purposes. There were therefore two sets of standards and instructions for raw materials and for processing.

By the time soap was in 'Four' department, the word 'quality' did not therefore denote anything to do with its chemical composition. It referred, by then, to the physical characteristics of the soap—weight and appearance of the tablet, colour, odour, tendency to smear or crack, clarity of the imprint, etc., as well as to such things as the strength of the seal on cartons and cases. The operators in the Department, as well as inspectors, had a responsibility to watch for the various physical flaws.

Instructions for making each product were contained in a series of Manufacturing Standards. The form of these was again standardized, each set consisting of an index, a product flow chart, and lists of material standards, operating standards and operating instructions.

Standards were also laid down for packing, covering dimensions and weights of cartons and cases, code markings, etc. Finally there was a series of rules associated with the storage arrangements. For example, the product studied was not allowed to be shipped from the factory to a depot if it was more than thirteen weeks old or to a customer if it was more than six months old.

The setting of *quantity or scheduling targets* was not quite so detailed or so precise. It was difficult to devise measures to test the accuracy of scheduling and some research was currently being done on this.

The explicit objective of scheduling was to achieve the greatest possible control of inventory, i.e. of finished stock. Company-wide inventory control was based on a scheduling equation comparing the stocks available with those needed. If a period of two months was taken so that P_1 and P_2 represented production in the two months (the controllable variables), E_1 and E_2 the expected demand in the two months (the uncontrollable variables), I the existing stock at the beginning and T the target stock at the end, then

$$P_2 = E_1 + E_2 - I_1 - P_1 + T$$

T being computed from a number of fixed and contingency components.

The resulting Company production requirements were then broken down into factory schedules. These reached the factories half-way through the period before the one to which they applied, together with estimates for the three following schedules. They were the only direct instruction to the factories, signed on behalf of the Director of Manufacturing. The 'King Pin' in the process was said to be the Sales Scheduling Department, who applied the scheduling equation and made the crucial decisions about the level of T. A good deal of clinical judgement had still to be used at this point and it was also necessary to allow for occasional 'crash action'.

Any possible uncertainty about this was not felt at the level of the product 'Four' Department, however. It might express itself in manufacturing amendments originating from the Sales Division. These could be accepted up to the first day of the manufacturing period in question, but were not supposed to be made after that.

Late amendments were occasionally requested and it was in the factory's interest to be as accommodating as possible about them, as it was to some extent in competition with the Company's other manufacturing units in this country. These occasional late amendments were welcomed as a break from routine: 'There's nothing quite as boring as you get a schedule and it goes like a bomb.'

The comparative lack of disruption was in marked contrast to the situation in most firms studied of the batch production engineering type, where changes in production plans were probably the biggest single factor in creating a sense of urgency, crisis and pressure. In this case any changes required were limited to quantity—there could only be a request to make more or less, not to make something different—and they did not interrupt production but merely increased or decreased the machine utilization and hours worked. It was interesting to find that in these circumstances changes were regarded as a challenge which was not only bearable but stimulating. ('Packing' was different in this respect from 'making'. It had a higher labour content so that changes in schedule involved some 'juggling' with labour.)

The main reason for this situation lay in the nature of the market. When detergents were first introduced around 1949 the demand for household soap declined sharply. This decline had by 1961 levelled off but was still slight and, above all, predictable. The Department had changed from a double day shift to daywork and production capacity was not now fully used.

When the schedule was received, the Department Manager had to make a rough plan of when and how he was going to make it, requisition soap from the previous manufacturing stage and other raw materials from stock and advise the Despatch Department. The schedule was broken down into both a weekly plan of production and a daily production target, agreed with Despatch. The requirements of the schedule then had to be translated into work loads for operators. This was done through a system of work assignment. Key lists were maintained containing details of every operation necessary, the time each one should take and the frequency at which it should be repeated. On the basis of these key lists the Department Manager would assign to each operator his detailed work load for the day. The purpose of this mechanism was to control the work load in such a way that it would be known in advance what people should be doing and when, with minimal reliance on reporting.

Detailed rules for actually coordinating production within the Department were not laid down in Manufacturing Standards. It was the Manager's job to get the schedule made (a) with safety, (b) with quality, (c) with good housekeeping and (d) with economy. That was officially the order of priorities, although the operation of performance indices tended to push economy rather higher up the list. Failure to meet the schedule was almost unthinkable, and had not happened within living memory. The problem, rather, was to make it at minimum cost, i.e. with optimum use of labour, minimum loss of materials, etc.

Soap had to be made, dried and packed. There were two sizes of tablet, Large (L) and Small (S). They were scheduled separately, made on the same production line (with a change of die at the cutter), but packed on different lines. L took about eight hours to dry in the drying oven, S took about four hours in the drying oven, and about eight hours if left to dry in the atmosphere. The weekend was too long for S, leaving it too dry and brittle. Therefore, none was made on Fridays which could not be packed on the same day.

Thus after start-up in the mornings, as soon as 'O.K. soap' was coming through, the day's S schedule, which was smaller than the L schedule, would be made first. The S packing girls would be given other jobs to do, or lent to another department, while it dried, and S packing would begin in the afternoon. Meanwhile the L packers would be packing the previous day's production.

Various things could go wrong with this plan, for instance the feeding in of clean scrap (misshapen tablets, etc.) could slow down the machinery at the process end. Or there might be re-packing to do, if cartons or cases were found to be faulty. Or particular atmospheric conditions could affect the drying process.

If the day's schedule was completed before the official shut-down time, the girls cleaned their own machines. If not, the men cleaned the packing machines on overtime. Other cleaning jobs were scheduled to be done weekly, usually on Friday afternoons. In addition, there were some cleaning jobs like rack-washing or cleaning the dry-houses which were used as fill-in jobs.

Thus the Manager's scheduling task within the Department involved the coordination of two products, for which there were separate schedules, which were made on the same production line, took different amounts of time to dry, were packed on separate lines, and made necessary a number of auxiliary cleaning tasks. Drying time was not precise, but within a range, and so acted as a slightly flexible storage link.

Cost control was the responsibility of the Industrial Engineer and it was his Department that operated the Company's Cost Control Plan. For control purposes costs were divided into wage costs, repairs and maintenance, losses and depreciation (in respect of materials used in making and packing the products), and fuel, water and power costs. The methods used for setting standards under these various headings were perhaps the most complex, analysing every possible source of costs into the degree to which it was knowable and controllable; for each source of costs, at each degree of controllability, there was then a number of ways of computing targets, to be used in order of preference. In every facet of costs the Department Manager was thus presented with a target in the same way that he was given targets for quantity and quality. Similarly, there were mechanisms for measuring or calculating the actual as opposed to the target costs under each heading.

The comparison between the target and the actual figure for each item and in each department resulted in what were referred to as Performance Factors, or P.Fs. All these Performance Factors were brought together at the end of each month in a matrix type cost control summary. There was a weighting system which related the different standards to each other, thus ensuring that the more important were given the most attention and that they were reconcilable with each other. Read horizontally, this summary then gave the overall performance of each production department. Read vertically it showed the results obtained throughout the factory in respect of quantity, quality and each type of cost.

This Performance Factor scheme was not only a mechanism for controlling the task, it also had implications for managerial behaviour, for it was used as a basis for a management incentive scheme. Line managers responsible for departments could earn up to twenty-five per cent of their monthly salaries as a direct bonus. The functional managers responsible for the setting and control of the various standards were indirect participants and could earn bonus up to a 'restriction level'; that is to the average bonus paid to direct participants.

Referring back to the categorization of control systems attempted in Chapter 3, this Company provided the nearest example not only of the separation of system design from system operation, but also of what was referred to in that chapter as a single integrated system of control. The mechanisms were impersonal, but at the same time, the technology and high management ratio made possible a good deal of personal contact. For instance, managers whose P.Fs. fell below a certain standard would expect to be interviewed about this by the Works Manager. Moreover, the results and the systems were, at regular intervals, audited by people.

Of course, in detail the system was sometimes difficult and often complex in operation, and not all the procedures were completely foolproof. For example, it was not possible to take personal judgement out of every phase of the quality control process, in spite of the detail with which standards and procedures were laid down.

Laboratory inspection was organized in teams, one for each shift. On each shift one member of the team was a girl inspector who toured the production departments. The route had been worked out by Job Study methods and carefully timed and the girls were paid on a bonus scheme. They did seven or eight tours per shift. The job was to check and record at various quality points and if anything was found below standard to point this out to production supervision. In the Department under review four recording sheets had to be filled in at different points on the production line. If in doubt about any quality criteria the inspector could freeze stock in the warehouse until a more thorough investigation could be made.

This freezing had, however, to be agreed to by the Department Manager and it was clear that the personal relationship between the inspector and the Department Manager introduced an element of uncertainty into the process. This relationship was for the inspector the most difficult part of the job. If the inspection girl thought something was below standard and the Manager said: 'Oh that's all right', she was in a difficult position, being of considerably lower status than the Manager. Slanging matches were not unknown, and if sure of the point the girl might refer to the Chief Chemist. The status difference was then reversed as he could if necessary override the Department Manager. An incident of this kind would however modify the relationship between the inspector and the Department Manager.

From interviews with the girls involved, a number of other personal factors also emerged as contributing to their standards.

One was the fact that these were household products in common use, which they were testing from the customer's point of view rather than the scientist's—'you think to yourself I'm a housewife —would I like to buy this or not?'

Another was a growing familiarity with the Chief Chemist's standards: 'I don't think he would let anything go if it was wrong, even if they were screaming for it. You get to know what his standards are, what he'll let go.' Another was a familiarity with a particular problem and identification with the production department—'the marbling and scuffing, we've always had that' (note the 'we'). There were standard samples in the laboratory with which to compare when in doubt, but the comparisons did not always seem to resolve the doubts.

But the fact that there remained parts of the Company's operations which had not yet been brought under detailed control was well recognized. This in itself ensured that the uncertain area was circumscribed and limited and therefore in one sense also controlled.

It is not easy to assess to what extent the single (i.e. integrated) system of impersonal control described was due to the nature of the technology. Although soap manufacturing is a process industry, the production system in the Department described was batch production and the body of ideas underlying the system of control was a product of top management policy. There were alternative ways in which the manufacture could have been controlled.

On the other hand it is very unlikely that such a prescribed system of control would be feasible, say, in the batch production of engineering products, with its implication of variety rather than intermittence.

IMPLICATIONS FOR OPERATORS

The description of the control systems may have already pointed to the main comment that can be made about their impact: it is that this was primarily and most directly on management. By the time they were mediated through management to the operators in 'Four' Department the impact of the systems was less strong and less direct, and other factors, like the way the packing machinery behaved or why the soap seemed so much harder or stickier at times became more salient.

In its details, the everyday life of the operators was much as it would have been anywhere else, or at least as it might have been under a different systems philosophy. The period or observation in the Department yielded a number of stories or incidents: there was the young man who was very bored with 'racking' (a repetitive manual job), who started coming late, took time off for unlikely reasons because he was looking for a job and finally got sacked. There were arguments about when to 'bodge up' a fault and when to stop production and do a basic repair. (Clearly cost control influenced these, but not in a way which would be very different under a different cost control system.) There was the new girl who was slow to learn how to feed tablets into the stamping machine, thus affecting the packers' bonus. For two days they were protective and tolerant, then they got more and more angry until there was an explosion. There was the saga of a faulty die box and its diagnosis and modification, which had all the drama and incident of a serial story. There were part-time lady packers who confounded everyone's ideas of good management by enjoying being taken on and laid off at short notice to meet fluctuations in the schedule. They were all married, did not need the money for essentials and liked the unpredictability with which they were presented either with some extra money or with a chance to catch up on housework. What was regarded by management as a flaw in the system, and what operators in other circumstances might regard as intolerable uncertainty had become a source of pleasure—a constraint was perceived as a facility.

The operators were most directly affected, of course, by wages cost control via the bonus systems. An operator's take-home pay depended on three factors: his basic rate, the operation of one of several incentive schemes, and the way his working day was arranged by the system of work assignment into daywork hours, incentive hours, and overtime. Basic rates of craftsmen were governed by Trade Union agreements, and all jobs were allocated into one of five grades by a process of job evaluation. Bonus schemes were of two kinds: one provided an incentive for the operator to complete a work cycle or task in less than standard time; the other was applied to those operations in which the worker was thought to have control over quality as well as quantity of output. The incentive was divided into quantity and quality components with some combinations of these components producing a higher bonus than others.

The operators' responses to these payment systems were not very different from those found in many other situations: they were, on the whole, satisfied with the general level of wages; they did not understand how the systems worked, but knew how much they were making; they resented the occasions when the amount of bonus was not within their own control; and where they did have control they used it in ways which were not always those intended by management.

IMPLICATIONS FOR MANAGEMENT

The systems described yielded a mixture of aesthetic satisfaction and frustration both for the observer and for the managers who operated the systems. By and large, however, management satisfaction was a much more powerful force than management frustration. This was to some extent due to the safety valve devices built into the system. It is also possible that because of the nature of the system it was difficult for managers out of tune with it to remain within the organization. At one stage in the research, the possibility of trying to trace and interview managers who had left the firm was discussed. In the event, however, the idea had to be abandoned as impractical.

To the manager who approached his job as an intellectual exercise and challenge, the rationality in the system was attractive. Very occasionally the rationality behind the aim to know what was happening in order to control it could yield to an irrational and obsessive desire for detailed knowledge for its own sake: the system of work assignment already described may have begun to cross this border-line. In some departments it may have been useful for the Department Manager to have to plan and assign his operators' work in detail at the beginning of each day. But in the 'Four' Department, where the operators knew the work, which was more or less the same each day, and where the small variations due to machine stoppages could not in any case be predicted, there seemed little point in work assignment, except perhaps as an exercise for a trainee manager. The expressed objective, 'that any senior manager walking through the Department at a quarter to eleven, should know exactly which bit of the floor the clean-up man is supposed to be cleaning' seems to show anxiety or obsessive tendencies rather than rationality.

One of the two department managers responsible for the 'Four' Department during the period of the research did not apply the work assignment system. As will be discussed later, he was not typical of the Company management and there was ambivalence in other people's attitudes towards him.

On the whole, however, the systems were to a high degree rational and effective. Moreover, and this is an important factor in the situation, they were explicit and documented. Every manager and senior manager had a bookshelf full of manuals, describing and prescribing the different aspects of his job. One of them, the Job Control Book, was one that he would have compiled himself as a part of his own training. Between them these various manuals provided instructions or guidance on how to proceed in every imaginable circumstance, sometimes down to the most minute detail. For instance, the Managers' Manual included instruction to managers on what to say to an employee who asked whether he should join the Trade Union. The answer he was to be given was a sensible one, and would ensure that an inexperienced manager could not harm the industrial relations of the Company. On the other hand, only an inexperienced manager was likely to welcome, or indeed to tolerate, being told exactly what to say on an issue of this kind.

Some of the consequences of managing in this particular way begin to be apparent. One was that the Company could employ surprisingly young and inexperienced men as managers. It did not have to rely on the personal experience of individuals, since the accumulated experience of past and present Company management existed on paper in the form of detailed explanations and instructions for everything. Moreover, because it was operating in a process technology in a relatively stable market, very few contingencies could arise that had not been foreseen and allowed for.

The second consequence was that, for similar reasons, it would not take the young manager very long to learn to run a department. Thus the third consequence was that managers could be moved easily from job to job.

The Company's practice was to recruit good quality graduates straight from university, in fairly large numbers; approximately nine a year came into the factory in which this study was done. The trainee was then placed with an existing manager—line or service—for a training period of about six months. He would then take over that particular department or service job, and run it for about eighteen months. By that time he would in turn be teaching the job to his successor and would then himself be moved on to another management post. Moving around could also include moving between factories, but this was more usual at senior management level. It was reckoned that, by the time a man was twenty-six or twenty-seven, he would have held two or three

H

management posts, probably one in a line department, one service post such as Job Study, and one in the Personnel function such as Safety or Training Manager.

At about that stage the young manager was considered for promotion to the senior grade of Group Manager. If such promotion was not forthcoming, and the young man was ambitious, the chances were that he would leave the Company and many managers did in fact leave at this stage. They were then in a very good position in the labour market, since they had had an undoubtedly excellent training, and it was known that some firms would automatically short-list a man with experience in this particular firm.

This frequent moving of managers from job to job was perhaps a unique feature of this Company. It probably explains to a large extent the remarkable consistency of approach mentioned earlier. It led the manager to identify himself with a way of tackling a new task or a way of approaching a problem, rather than with the problems of a particular department or function.

This job rotation was also the major safety valve referred to earlier. Moving around prevented the frustration and boredom that could develop around a job that was well known and of limited discretion.

Several of the managers interviewed commented on the fact that the main disadvantages of job rotation lay in relation to projects. This implied that although the design of the production system had moved functionally away from its operation, production management was not cut off from the design aspects. During his tenure of a post a manager was encouraged not merely to run the Department but also to initiate one or more projects to tackle any outstanding problem or defects in its operation. The objective here would be to generate information and produce ideas which might lead to modifications in the system itself; to rewrite the manual rather than to modify the current practice on an *ad hoc* basis.

If a manager was moved from his department before a project of this kind was completed, it was unlikely that his successor would identify himself with it to the same extent. Projects, especially difficult ones, were therefore sometimes left incomplete. The operators in the 'Four' Department, for instance, complained that a difficult cleaning job had had no time set for it, since over the years successive job study engineers had begun to study it but had never actually got to the point of setting a time.

Although this state of affairs could have some long term practical disadvantages, it ensured that managers did not get too involved or develop the limited perspective which can be associated with long tenure of a particular post. They were more likely to develop a Company-wide perspective.

Moreover, the consequences of the disruption were to some extent mitigated by the methods programme under which every manager was allocated to one of a number of methods teams. The teams worked to financial targets on cost reduction projects, their success in reaching the targets influencing the P.Fs. of the members. Thus managers were rewarded for their part in systems design, too. A methods team cut across departments, and thus provided a little more continuity in the pursuing of projects (although the criteria for deciding on projects were different ones and therefore the type of project tackled may have been different). Again, however, being involved in an inter-departmental methods team was at least as likely to impress the Methods Approach on the young manager as the details of any particular project he worked on.

Generally speaking, however, continuity is less vital in a system of this kind than it is where control is less formalized and more fragmented. Continuity and any undocumented know-how in a department were provided by the operators and not by the manager. Operators saw managers come and go, and appeared not to mind this. An operator on 'Four' explained that 'a manager in this firm is a chap who asks you how to do the job', but he said it in a tolerant and good-humoured way. This acceptance was helped by the fact that the managers were generally very young and, provided their behaviour was not clumsy or arrogant, the operators could feel protective towards them. It was, however, a slightly uneasy relationship.

The fact that managers were moved around had important implications for control. A fairly short tenure of a job meant that one did not have time to learn to deviate from the job as laid down. There was a lot to learn, the procedures were often complicated, and one cannot normally develop short cuts or by-pass procedures until one is very familiar with them. In this way, therefore, moving people from job to job provided a mechanism for controlling the controllers. How far this was a deliberate part of the policy was of course impossible to tell—one could only observe that this was its effect.

There were other, perhaps more deliberate, ways of controlling the behaviour of managers. After a preliminary period in a department and before he got down to a detailed learning of all the jobs, a trainee would have had a full discussion about his findings and views on the department with the Group Manager. At this discussion the manager to whom he was immediately responsible was not present, 'in case the manager isn't operating according to the Group Manager's policy'. Moreover, when the trainee had been with the same manager for about six months and they both felt he was ready to take over the job, he had to 'qualify'—that is, he was tested on his knowledge of the different aspects of the job and on his ideas for running it. This testing was carried out by various functional staff and the Works Manager. The manager from whom the trainee had learnt the job again took no part in it.

There can hardly be a more effective way of keeping control of what a manager is doing than by finding out what a trainee has learnt from him. If he is not 'operating according to policy', but the results he produces are satisfactory, he may well be allowed to continue operating in his own way. But at least his successor can be deterred from operating in this way and encouraged to revert to the proper and official way, so that the deviation will not be continued. And at least the extent of the manager's deviation is known; and he knows that it is known.

The 'Four' Department highlighted some of these points. One of the two managers concerned and the Section Engineer were the only two exceptions in the factory to the pattern of management training and development described. Both were older men who had held their jobs for a considerable time, and they had entered the firm before the training scheme became formalized. They had their jobs at their fingertips and planned their activities in their heads, with as little use of the formal systems as they were allowed to get away with. They were the only two people of manager grade who when interviewed described their jobs without reference to a manual.

The 'Four' Manager had been running the Department, on and off, for about twenty years. Every now and again he would be moved out of the Department to allow a new, young manager to run it for a time, and would then come back to pick up the threads again. During the periods he was running the Department there were greater differences between the formal and the informal systems than at other times, or than elsewhere in the factory. He flatly refused to do work assignment, and there were various other procedures which, through experience and familiarity with the job, he by-passed or used flexibly.

There had been rows about this with senior management, but his informal handling of his job was tolerated because he was an old servant of the Company, for whom there was considerable affection, and because his P.Fs. were good.

It was interesting to see the way in which the social system accommodated this 'deviant'. In general the problem of what attitude to take towards him was resolved by treating his behaviour as a joke—'Oh well, everybody knows Peter!' There was, however, considerable ambivalence in the attitude of senior management towards him. Mostly the attitude was one of exasperation, tempered by affection and made bearable by amusement. This had been the picture presented during the field work of the research. But at the meeting held to present the findings of the study to management the picture changed dramatically. Peter, who had been rather a thorn in the flesh, suddenly became a hero, an example of individuality and initiative of whom the whole body of management was proud.

One well-known difficulty in presenting a descriptive account of a situation studied is that feelings of praise or blame may be projected on to it by the audience or readers. When the material collected in this study has been used in talks on managerial control to audiences of managers from outside this particular Company, the common reaction has been 'you are holding this up for us as a perfect system. You think this is good'.

But when the material was first presented to the Company's own managers, the response was exactly the reverse: 'you think we are all organization men. You think this is bad'. There was a general resistance to the implication that managers were conformists and that they had a very limited area of discretion. The immediate reaction was that 'if this were true we also would think it bad, but then it is not true, look at Peter'. Peter's behaviour was suddenly seen in a completely different light as demonstrating that the system could and did accommodate itself to individualists.

THE PROBLEM OF INITIATIVE

Underlying this reaction was one of the dilemmas of industrial management. Although the system of managerial control in this Company cannot be described as perfect—perfection is of course too absolute and philosophical a term—it does seem to be effective. It must be true that the nearer a system gets to meeting the requirements it is set up to serve and the less a reasonable man can find in it to criticize and improve, the more it must call forth acceptance and therefore 'organization man' behaviour. This fact in itself then becomes a source of criticism to those who, like Whyte (2) and possibly many industrialists in this country, are still committed to the protestant ethic, with its emphasis on the virtues of individualism and independence.

The dilemma is becoming greater as management education increases in both quality and quantity. There is a growing emphasis on the design of effective systems and on quantitative management methods. But as far as management philosophy and values are concerned there is still a strong assumption that control 'ought' to be personal and hierarchical, and that 'man-management' is what counts. Whyte concerned himself only with the behaviour of the organization man and avoided taking into account the nature of the organization itself. A manager must either quarrel with the objectives or *raison d'être* of the organization; or with the systems set up to achieve these objectives; or he must accept and conform. If none of these postures is tolerable, then one is in an insoluble dilemma.

There remains the question of where and how initiative occurred within the organization. On this subject the control system described presents some apparent contradictions.

The managers in this firm genuinely did not know whether their jobs were challenging and exciting, or merely routine. At different times they claimed both, and the movement from job to job helped to confuse the issue and prevent them from finding out. As one senior manager put it:

> 'It takes six months to learn the job, it's exciting then. Then for about three months you develop it and have ideas. Then it would begin to get boring, but if you are moved around you don't get bored and you don't discover that it's essentially routine.'

But even with the moving around the contradiction exists. Two examples will serve to illustrate it. In line management, it is a valid question to ask in what sense the 'Four' Department Manager was 'managing' at all. If he had suddenly disappeared, the Department would have continued to function. The operators knew what to do, the product would continue to be produced and packed, and it might be two or three months before anything started going seriously wrong. On the other hand the system of control was not entirely mechanical, it required monitoring and adjustment devices and it is likely that after a time the P.Fs. would begin to deteriorate, costs would go up, quality problems become more frequent, and coordination with other departments begin to creak. Senior management would eventually have to intervene, or the operators be given some additional training.

An example from a service management post was that of the engineer responsible for Losses and Depreciations Cost Control. This meant losses in material being processed, through inefficient processing, leaks, evaporation, etc. The post was held by a young philosophy graduate, in his first job, with no vocational training except a two-week course in statistics organized within the Company. Loss of material was the biggest potential cost item in the factory, one per cent loss involving a cost of £6000 per month. On the one hand it was tremendously exciting and challenging to think that only his own intelligence stood between him and savings of this order to the factory. On the other hand, if he merely read the meters, filled in the forms, applied the formulae and did the routine calculations, he would still be fulfilling his job adequately, and the result at the end of the month might be no different.

In these conditions it became very much a matter of the perceptions of the individual how he interpreted the job. If he had some initiative but saw his role merely as the monitor of the system he was likely within a fairly short space of time to feel constrained by the comprehensiveness of the system.

For the manager to regard himself as more than a monitor he had to become involved in improving the performance of the system and in improving the system itself. Reference has already been made to the fact that managers were expected to involve themselves in projects. At the feedback meeting, the majority of the managers showed they felt that the very comprehensiveness of the system set them free in a more general way to think creatively about the job. Whether these feelings of freedom were real or illusory would depend upon how much objective possibility there was of making improvements.

CONCLUSIONS

As indicated already the main interest of this particular tracer project was that it provided an extreme case as far as the clear distinction between the planning and control of a system and its operation was concerned. Although this firm is probably exceptional in its approach, the tendency will be for more of industry to move in this direction as modern management techniques develop and become more widespread.

This tendency will therefore mean a shift in the relative importance of different management activities. Industrial management involves three distinct types of activity:

  (i) the setting up of a workable system for production or service;

 (ii) the maintaining of the system by planning the work, co-ordinating the materials and services needed, keeping quality and cost within acceptable limits, and so on;

(iii) improving the performance of the system and improving the system itself.

Firms in different technical and market conditions use the energies and skills of their managers to different degrees in different parts of this schema. In the situation of small batch production engineering in the firm of 'Multiproducts Ltd.' (3), and in the firms in which the other tracer studies described in this book were carried out, the problems of (i) and (ii), and especially of (ii) were so great that they took up all the energy and initiative of the managers on the spot. For product 'Four', and for the service systems surrounding it, the problems of (i) had been largely resolved. The challenge to management ability no longer lay in working out how to make soap. Activity (ii) still required attention and ability, and a little initiative in spotting problems, but the solving of problems could be handled in a routine manner since those which arose were hardly ever new ones. It is also certain that the intelligence and sophistication which had gone into devising the control system meant that it was not difficult to keep it running.

The real challenge lay in improving the system itself. The important difference between (i) and (iii) on the one hand and (ii) on the other is that (i) and (iii) are never as urgent as (ii), or rather, even if economic circumstances make them urgent, their urgency is not as immediately apparent as that of (ii). If one does not feel like working on the new formula for inventory control today, one can work on it tomorrow without any apparent harm coming to the Company. Indeed, if one does nothing at all to improve the system, it may be a long time before anything very terrible happens.

This is without doubt one reason for the atmosphere of calm which was a marked feature of the factory. The observer, especially with experience of batch production engineering, is very impressed by a general atmosphere of security and confidence, an absence of panic and pressure. Since there are always processes of adaptation going on between a firm and its environment and between sub-systems within the firm, this absence of pressure is never likely to characterize a whole organization. But in large and advanced organizations there may be quite substantial units which are sheltered from external pressure and which have few internal problems. For them the greatest long-term problem may be how to cope with calm.

References

1. Brewer, R. (1965) Appendix II, in Woodward, J., *Industrial Organization: Theory and Practice*. Oxford University Press, London.
2. Whyte, William H. (1957) *The Organization Man*. Doubleday, New York.
3. Klein, Lisl (1954) *Multiproducts Ltd. A Case Study on the Social Effects of Rationalized Production*. H.M.S.O., London.

TOM KYNASTON REEVES

6 The Control of Manufacture in a Garment Factory

INTRODUCTION

This chapter presents a case study of the system of production planning and control in a garment factory and discusses its implications for those employed, particularly at supervisory level.

The Factory to be described is one of several production units belonging to a firm of multiple tailors, called here Mass-Bespoke. Mass-Bespoke is engaged in the manufacture and retailing in its own shops of men's bespoke suits, and to a lesser extent, men's ready-made outer wear. The 'Q' Factory, where the research was carried out was several hours' travelling time from the firm's administrative Headquarters. Although some of the management services most closely tied to production—work study for example —were based on the Factory site, there were very few non-production staff.

The authority hierarchy on the production side consisted of a Factory Manager and an Assistant Factory Manager under whom were foremen (and forewomen) in charge of the different departments and sections. Each foreman was assisted by one or more supervisors and by chargehands.

Over a thousand people—mainly women—were employed in the Factory. The only men were management, foremen, cutters and maintenance staff. The largest number of operators worked in the Sewing Room—the shop floor there gave the impression of being jammed with sewing machines and operators.

The main method of data collection was interviewing. The firm had asked the researchers to do an attitude survey and a one in six random sample of operators was interviewed using a set questionnaire. This chapter, however, is based mainly on semi-structured interviews of supervision carried out by four research workers in January and February in 1967. These interviews were tape-recorded and covered a wide field, centring around three basic questions; of what did the various supervisory jobs consist, how did supervision achieve what was expected of them and what happened when they failed to do so.

The interviewing programme was supplemented by a consider-able amount of casual observation. The Factory was not large and the initial contacts with both supervision and operators were made at their work locations. Thus it was possible to check to some extent what was said about how the system worked by direct observation.

ORGANIZATION OF PRODUCTION

Production organization was relatively simple; orders for suits received by the retail shops were all processed at the Headquarters site by a central Production Control Department who then planned weekly production schedules for each factory. This planning was done on the basis of a notional production capacity for each factory—about 5 000 suits per week for the 'Q' Factory. Depending on seasonal fluctuations in the tailoring trade, these suits would nearly all be bespoke, or if there had been a fall-off in the number of customers coming into the shops to be measured for suits, production capacity was utilized by making ready-to-wear suits for stock. However, it was not always possible in slack periods to keep the factories working at full capacity.

The period of the field work was a slack period for production. There had been a rush before Christmas to get suits away to the shops. After the Christmas rush a higher proportion of stock suits was made. Production of 'measured' suits was expected to build up again shortly after the completion of the research, when people started ordering new suits for Easter.

Switching from stock to measured suits had few implications for the production system and *vice versa*, since stock suits went through most of the production processes in exactly the same way as measured suits. The simplest way of describing the production system, therefore, is to deal with the manufacture of measured suits first and then to indicate briefly how the manu-facture of stock suits differed.

There were three main groups of production operations: the

cutting of the cloth and linings, the making and assembly of the suit in the Sewing Room, and the finishing operations, principally pressing and final inspection.

The production process started at a central warehouse on the firm's Headquarters site where lengths of cloth selected by the customers were cut off from the bale. The production process at the Factory began with the receipt of the suit lengths. These passed first into the Cutting Room. Cutting of the cloth was done by hand using standard patterns. The cutter chose a pattern which was nearest to the customer's measurements and then in marking out his 'lay' made any necessary allowances to achieve the customer's precise measurements. The cloth was then bundled separately into its component parts: jacket, trousers, and vest if there was one, and taken to the Trimming and Fitting Sections.

Trimming, as its name implies, was the process of adding the trimmings (linings and canvas interlinings) to the cloth. Different sizes of canvas interlining were cut in bulk and all the trimmer had to do was to select a piece of canvas of the appropriate size. Linings on the other hand were cut individually using the cloth as a pattern. Cloth and trimmings were then bundled together and taken by a service girl to the next process—jackets and vests to the Fitting Section and trousers direct to the Sewing Room for making up. The fitters added the finishing touches to the cutting process. Fitting is perhaps a misleading term to describe what they did, which was mainly marking out and cutting pocket flaps and welts and marking their position on the jacket or vest body. After fitting, jackets and vests also proceeded to the Sewing Room for making up.

The Sewing Room was divided into three departments: Jackets, the largest, employed about 450 operators; Trousers, about 300 operators; and Vests only fifty operators. In each Sewing Room Department the manufacturing process had been sub-divided into small operations with a cycle time ranging from a few seconds up to three or four minutes, but there were significant differences in the system of work organization.

The assembly of trousers was carried out on conveyor belts. There were five of these, each handling about 1000 pairs of trousers per week. Complete pairs of trousers were made on each belt. The process of making trousers had been sub-divided into about forty separate operations. Balancing the production line presented the usual problems associated with the pacing of work.

Not all the operations on the belt took the same time and therefore some had one operator allocated to them and some had two. The speed of the conveyors was governed by the time of the longest operations or the speed of the slower operators. This meant that some operators were engaged in a continual struggle to keep up, or as they put it, they were always 'getting in a drag'. Others were nearly always in hand with their work. Operators were paid on a group bonus system depending upon the number of pairs of trousers produced by their conveyor during a week.

In the Jacket Department, on the other hand, work was organized on what was known as a 'divisional' or 'bundle' system. All operators performing the same operation were grouped together in small units. There were nearly sixty of these jacket units. Operators could work at their own pace. Each operator worked from a skip by her side which was kept topped up with work by a service girl. On completion of the operation the garment was placed on a transporter belt which conveyed it to a skip at the end of the unit. The work was then collected by the service girl and taken to the next unit.

Work in the Vest Department was organized in much the same way as in the Jacket Department. But instead of a service girl bringing work to a box at the operator's side, trays of work were distributed and collected by means of a semi-automatic transporter belt operated from a control console. Consequently it was possible for supervision to see at a glance how the work was progressing and whether any bottlenecks were developing.

The work arrangements in the Jacket and Vest Departments were relatively new. In the Jacket Department the divisional system had replaced conveyors about two years prior to the research and the Vest Department transporter had been installed even more recently. The Work Study Department had played a major role in the modifications; in particular it had worked out the time-studied individual incentive scheme for the Jacket and Vest Departments.

On completion of the Sewing Room operations garments were pressed. Jackets were pressed in a series of operations in the Press Room after which their buttons were attached. Pressing of trousers and vests was carried out by Press Room operators stationed at the foot of each trouser conveyor and at the end of the vest transporter.

After pressing, jackets were taken to the Final Passing

Department. Final passing of trousers and vests, like pressing, was carried out at the foot of the conveyors and transporters. The Final Passing Department incorporated a small alterations section where minor faults were put right. More serious alterations were sent back to the production departments concerned.

It was in the Despatch Department that the two or three separate parts of a suit—jacket, trousers and vest—were collected together and received final inspection. Suits were then despatched by van to the Company's central warehouse from where they were distributed to the shops.

The manufacture of suits for stock differed only at the cutting and trimming stages. Cloth and lining material for stock suits were cut in bulk. Once stock garments passed out of the Trimming Section they followed the same route and were treated in the same way as measured garments.

Occasionally, the specification for a measured garment could not be accommodated within the production system. This would typically be a suit for someone with a very distorted figure, for example a hunchback. When this happend the suit would be 'made through' in a small tailoring shop which was attached to the Factory. The main function of the half-dozen tailors who worked in this shop was to carry out complicated alterations to completed garments that could not be handled on the shop floor.

Variations in style in men's tailoring are rarely radical although they may make a difference to the appearance of the finished suit. For example, whether a jacket is single or double breasted affects only a limited part of a jacket body. A style variation of this nature could readily be incorporated into the repertoire of the relevant operators.

At the time of the research, however, a system change had occurred which did have major implications for the organization of production. This was the renewed popularity of three-piece suits. While the Factory could produce upwards of 5000 jackets and trousers per week, it had capacity for only about 1500 vests. Therefore the question had arisen of whether to increase production capacity for vests. This was of course something which could not be decided lightly—fashion trends provide a hazardous basis for planning. The problem had been temporarily resolved by having vests in excess of capacity made at another of the firm's factories. At the time of the research, however, more vests were being scheduled to the 'Q' Factory than could be comfortably handled, and between 300 and 400 jackets and trousers belonging to three-piece suits were stored in the Despatch Department awaiting their vests.

Apart from the imbalance of capacity between the three Sewing Room Departments, there was also an imbalance of capacity between the Sewing Room and the Cutting Room. Cutting, fitting and trimming operations occupy a relatively large amount of floor space compared with sewing operations. Limitations of space on the 'Q' Factory site prevented the enlargement of the Cutting Room so a proportion of the suits were cut at other units of Mass-Bespoke. One consequence of this imbalance of Sewing Room and Cutting Room capacities was that the figure used as indicating the production capacity of the Factory was based on the capacity of the Jacket and Trouser Departments. It was here that the main production pressures were felt.

THE CLASSIFICATION OF THE TECHNOLOGY

The work system of Mass-Bespoke, although simple in itself, was extremely difficult to classify in terms of any of the measures of technology developed by the Imperial College Research Unit. Classification based on the nature of the products would have placed the firm in the unit production category, for in one sense every measured suit made was unique in certain respects.

Variation in size, cloth and style had implications for individual operations. Size and shape were determined at the cutting stage. Differences in style would be noted on the job ticket filled in by the salesman in the shop and it would be up to the operators working on that garment to note instructions regarding trouser turn-ups, width and shape of lapels, numbers and style of pockets, length of jacket vents if requested, number of jacket buttons and so on.

But these details would have to be dealt with whether the garments were for individual customers or for stock. Thus the variation in product range measure, that is the ratio between the measured and the stock garments made in each of two successive years, would have been quite meaningless for research purposes.

Moreover, the uniqueness had little significance for the production system as a whole. If the nature of the production methods rather than the nature of the products was made the basis of the classification, the Mass-Bespoke system of production would fall into the mass production category.

The problem of classification was even more complex, however, for as the description that follows of the organization and control of work will show, production really proceeded in a sequence of batches, and while some of the constraints on those employed were those normally associated with unit and continuous flow production, it was the pattern of constraints linked with batch production, particularly where managerial control is fragmented, that predominated.

THE TIME FACTOR IN PRODUCTION CONTROL

Getting suits made by the time they had been promised to the customer was the main preoccupation of management and supervision in the Mass-Bespoke 'Q' Factory. As long as the Company had a full order book there was an incessant pressure on the Factory personnel to meet production schedules.

Control of the time factor comprised two elements: rate of production and sequence of production. As far as rate of production was concerned reference was made above to the fact that production capacity was related to the facilities in the Jacket and Trouser Departments. The figure of about 5000 two-piece suits per week had been arrived at by agreement between the central Production Control Department, the Production Director, and the Factory Manager, and was probably rather less than the Factory's maximum capacity. Once agreed upon, this capacity figure remained constant until some change in production facilities necessitated its revision.

With few exceptions no adjustments were made to weekly production schedules to allow for such factors as excessive absenteeism of operators, backlogs of work from previous weeks, or any other contingencies. Most of the management and supervision interviewed felt, however, that 5000 suits per week was not an unreasonable target. Difficulties in meeting it were attributed to deficiencies in the organization of work within the Factory or to absenteeism. Both these factors could produce delays and bottlenecks and could result in a foreman having to produce, say, 800 garments one day and 1200 the next.

It was important for the Factory not only to produce the total number of suits scheduled for each week, but also to make sure that the suits completed in each week were, in fact, those required for delivery. Production of garments in the correct sequence was obviously a more complicated task than simply producing garments indiscriminately at the required rate.

Most suits were scheduled for delivery to the customer within four or five weeks of the time of ordering. Customers were warned, however, that this was only an approximate time for delivery and that they would be notified by the shop when their suit was ready for collection. Although Mass-Bespoke did not guarantee specific dates for delivery, every effort was made to get suits to the customer on time. If deliveries became overdue, customers became impatient and good will could be lost. In addition to the normal four-week delivery, shop managers were permitted to accept a small proportion of their orders for delivery in three or even two weeks. This was in order not to lose the trade of customers who wanted suits made in a hurry and these shorter delivery periods were usually guaranteed. The fact that shop managers were subject to direct pressures from customers made delivery dates particularly significant.

In order to simplify the task of making suits in the correct order, all measured suits scheduled for completion in the same week were batched together and tagged with the same coloured job tickets. Suits for delivery in the following week were marked with a different colour and so on. In theory this colour system meant that for a week each operator would work on garments with that week's colour and then at the end of the week change to garments marked with a different colour. About eight different colours were used so that in normal circumstances there was no risk of confusion resulting from having different delivery weeks marked by the same colour in the Factory at one time.

Regarded simply as a performance mechanism (see Chapter 3)—that is, a means for directing activities—the colour system was admirable. It was simple to understand and easy to communicate. Large notice boards were hung prominently over each section indicating the colour that operators should currently be working on, together with the last and the next week's colours, and the day on which all work on the current colour had to be complete.

But there were complications. To begin with, the monitoring of production operations by the foremen was complicated by the existence of orders for shorter delivery periods than the normal four weeks. These 'short order' suits, which were tagged with another kind of job ticket, had gradually to overtake the four-week delivery suits in the production process. This involved each foreman in keeping track of short orders and making sure they were given priority. Possibly because foremen had to pay special attention to these suits and also because the numbers involved were relatively small, the short order system seemed to work well.

In the case of the four-week delivery suits, however, the situation was unsatisfactory. Although suits of the same colour ticket were batched together when they entered the Factory, for various reasons they failed to stay together as they progressed through the Factory. Colours could begin to override each other as soon as the suits left the Cutting Room. Because it was impossible to synchronize the times at which cutters finished work on the old colours, the new week's colours would begin to trickle out of the Cutting Room before the old colours were finished. If the fitters and trimmers were waiting for work, they would get on with these new colours. Consequently, there might be up to 100 garments of an old colour overlapping with a new colour. On top of this lack of synchronization in the changeover of colours, old colours might be held back in the Cutting Room—sometimes for several days—because mistakes had been made in the cutting and new cloth had to be obtained. This overlapping increased as the work progressed through the various sections of the Factory, with the consequence that the foremen were always uncertain about how many garments of the old colour remained to come through once the new colour had started. As far as possible foremen tried to speed the old colours through so that they caught up, but obviously with many other demands on their attention, some inevitably lagged behind. The problem of keeping colours batched together was further complicated by the fact that colours from previous weeks would continually be coming back to the production sections for alterations.

Keeping colours batched together was far less of a problem in the Trouser and Vest Departments than in the Jacket Department. This was because of the technical difference; in the Trouser and Vest Departments the sequence of garments worked on by operators was governed by the order in which they were loaded on to the conveyors or transporter. The only problem for the Trouser and Vest foremen was to make sure that they had obtained all the old colours from the Cutting, Fitting and Trimming Sections. Once they had checked this, the colours proceeded through the production processes in the right sequence without much need for supervision. In the Jacket Department, on the other hand, the 'bundle' system made it more difficult for foremen to regulate the sequence of garments.

Management and supervision had hoped that the distinctive labelling of weekly batches with colour tabs would make operators aware of what garments they ought to be working on. But their hopes did not seem to have been fully realized. As one Jacket Department foreman commented:

'I don't see anybody taking any notice of them. I think it's a waste of time. I mean there's a bloody great big notice stuck up in front of them. You can go up and say "Well, what colour's urgent?" They don't know. . . . If only I could get the girls to work the colours without being told—get them colour conscious . . . . I'm not blaming the girls. The girl on the machine just does the job at her side. It's my own fault if I don't get the colours out. Actually, I've just started trying to put a squeeze on them just lately to see if it will have any effect—the signs weren't just put up there for the foremen.'

These difficulties in operating the colour system were undoubtedly increased by the fact that there was a dearth of control information about how batches of colours were progressing in different parts of the Factory. In fact virtually no quantitative information was available about progress of colours until the garments became overdue in the Despatch Department. By that time it was usually too late to identify the original source of delay, and consequently it was rarely possible to attribute responsibility for late colours to any particular foreman. From time to time foremen were brought together by the Factory Manager and told that they must improve their performance in progressing colours. But because of the lack of information about when or where colours were being held back, they had no idea of the corrective action necessary, nor were they able to judge the adequacy of their performance.

In fact the only available systematic feedback information about progress of work through the factory was related to the total volume of garments produced. Daily summaries of the total number of garments produced by each section were compiled from records kept by booking girls employed by each production foreman. Although it was generally accepted that the booking girls were unreliable in their recording—they sometimes missed garments and booked work through a section that had not in fact gone through—the daily production summaries provided the Factory Manager with a reasonably reliable guide as to whether or not the various sections were meeting their production targets. The result was that the production foremen were in no doubt that 'totals' were the only thing for which they could indisputably be held to account. It is not surprising, therefore, that they tended to concentrate their energies on achieving the required volume of production. This emphasis on volume was reinforced by the payment systems in operation in the Factory. Most direct operators were working on a payment by results basis, which as a performance mechanism for rate of production made achievement of 'totals' a prime consideration for them too. In nearly all our interviews with both supervision and direct operators the strongest emphasis was placed on 'getting one's totals out'.

There was yet one more mechanism concerned with the delivery of suits to customers on time: a longstop device. This was a small Order Seeking Department responsible for expediting the progress of overdue garments. The activities of this department may be regarded as a means for effecting adjustments to the sequence of production. The Order Seeking Department made no attempt to monitor all the garments passing through the production system, for although a record of the serial number of each garment was kept by the booking girls in each production section, their recording, as we have already noted, was not always accurate. Instead the staff of this department obtained information about late garments independently by having three order-seeking girls stationed in the Despatch Department picking up the serial numbers of garments that were overdue. They notified these numbers to other order-seeking girls stationed around the production sections who then chased up the late garments by searching through the bottom of skips, under benches, and so on. Most garments, it was claimed, could be found in less than half an hour. In fact the search process was not entirely random; there were a variety of clues which the order-seekers could pick up in order to find out where they should start looking for a particular garment. For example, it was often possible to find out how far a jacket had progressed by checking the serial numbers of linings waiting to be attached to jacket bodies.

The records kept by the booking girls in the production sections were only consulted as a last resort. Once an overdue garment had been found, the order-seeking girls would personally push it through the production process until it arrived in the Despatch Department.

The jurisdiction of the Order Seeking Department extended to the whole Factory except for the Press Room. The foreman of this section had been in his post ever since Mass-Bespoke began production in the Factory. He had designed the lay-out of the Press Room, and his system of work organization included a booking and order seeking system. When garments reached the Press Room it was almost time for them to be despatched. Also, garments which were sent back from Final Passing to the production sections for alteration had subsequently to be pressed again. The Press Room foreman was convinced that if he was to get these garments out on time he had to keep track of them himself. Consequently the Press Room was by tradition taboo territory for the Order Seeking Department. The order-seekers monitored the progress of late work into the Press Room and picked it up again when it came out. But for information about its progress within the Press Room, they had to rely on the Press Room foreman.

This description of the way that the control of time was applied to the Mass-Bespoke Factory makes it abundantly clear that in terms of the framework suggested in Chapter 3, control was fragmented; there was a multi-system of control even within the time parameter.

Moreover, the control mechanisms governing the rate of production were working against those governing the sequence of production. Although meeting delivery dates was critical for Mass-Bespoke, there was a tendency for the programme of weekly colour batches to take second place to the achievement of gross output.

The main reason for this was the fact that the monitoring of the sequence was far less effective than the monitoring of the gross output. The situation was aggravated by the fact that the only control mechanisms which had sanctions of any substance attached to them were those regulating the rate of production, that is to say the system of payment by results for operators and the system of booking work through each section which led to regular and unambiguous identification of the performance of foremen with respect to output. On the other hand, the colour system since it contained no built-in consequences for non-compliance, operated solely as a guide to performance.

The fact that the control mechanisms had proved inadequate as a means of ensuring the timely delivery of suits was reflected in the existence of the order-seeking system which undoubtedly played a large part in ensuring that suits left the Factory on time. But here again, since the order-seeking system did not generate any feedback information that could affect the performance of supervision or operators in adhering to the priorities indicated by the colour system, no corrective action could be taken to ensure better results in future.

The inadequacies of the time control mechanisms had been recognized by management and at the time of the research they were introducing a change into the control system in an attempt to overcome the problem. The bookers of the work on the various sections were being provided with push button counters, one for each colour, so that the daily summaries of production could be readily broken down by colour. The results of this change are not yet known but it is likely that the fact that their performance in progressing colours through their sections can now be monitored will lead foremen to attach more importance to this aspect of their job.

THE QUALITY FACTOR

As stated above, the main concern of management and supervision at Mass-Bespoke was getting suits out on time. At a slightly less pragmatic level, however, poor quality workmanship was considered to be the Factory's most serious problem.

Between twenty and thirty per cent of all garments entering the Final Passing Department were rejected for one reason or another. About a quarter of these faults were minor and could be dealt with by the alterations section in the Final Passing Department. The remainder were sent back to the appropriate production section for alteration. In almost all cases mistakes were discovered and put right before the suit left the Factory, and only about a dozen complaints per week were received from the shops, representing a mere 0·25 per cent of all suits despatched. But delays incurred through having to make alterations to faulty garments were said to be one of the major sources of difficulty in meeting delivery deadlines and making the Factory efficient.

The responsibility for controlling quality in the 'Q' Factory was divided between production management and a Quality Control Department, centred at the Headquarters of Mass-Bespoke. All inspectors in the Factory were responsible to the Factory Manager. The foreman of the Final Passing Department was, from an organizational point of view, regarded as a production foreman, and the final inspectors in his Department were classified as direct production operators. Intermediate inspection was the responsibility of the various production foremen. The Quality Control Department had only a small staff: a Group Quality Control Manager based on the Headquarters site and, within the Factory, a Quality Control Manager and two foremen. Garment manufacture is not the kind of production that lends itself to the setting of precise and measurable quality standards and, as it had no authority over either intermediate or final inspectors, the function of the Quality Control Department was a very limited one in the application as well as the setting of standards. In fact it did little more than try to plug some of the leaks in the system of quality control operated by production supervision.

The basic quality objective was to make a suit which would satisfy the customer who had ordered it. The suit had to be made in the style and cloth ordered by the customer, it had to fit, and it had to look smart. Errors in cloth could only occur at the central warehouse before the suit length was sent to the 'Q' Factory for making up. Fit of a jacket or vest could only be tested on the wearer, so only measurements of trousers had to be checked. This left customer fastidiousness as the most important consideration in making decisions about whether or not to pass a suit.

Gross mistakes in style had to be put right even if it meant remaking a complete garment. For example, if a customer had ordered slanting jacket side pockets, tulip-shaped lapels, or trouser turn-ups, he would obviously be unlikely to accept something different. On the other hand, a customer might never notice that an inside ticket pocket was missing, or that there were two instead of three cuff buttons. Decisions about whether a suit looked good enough could be even more difficult. For example, checks might not quite match, or the stitching of a seam might be slack at one point. If it was conspicuous, the garment would have to be altered. But what was conspicuous to the tailor might pass unnoticed by the vast majority of customers. Assessment of the general appearance of a suit was inevitably a matter of subjective impression. This was summed up: 'We're not asking for a perfect job, but a presentable job. What the customer's eye doesn't see in the mirror. . . .'

The need to satisfy the requirements of the individual customer in this direct way is characteristic of the constraints of unit production. But there were also problems in quality control reminiscent of large batch production. Where the work was broken down into small operations, certain mistakes in one operation not only spoiled the look or fit of the finished suit but also made subsequent operations more difficult or even impossible. This was particularly so in the manufacture of jackets, where a variety of components—linings, sleeves, collars, body forepart and back—were made separately and subsequently assembled. But if the various parts fitted together despite any mistakes, in many cases the customer would be none the wiser. Provided it fitted him, no customer was likely to be concerned whether the side seams on his jacket were half an inch instead of the specified three-eighths. The production foremen, in making their judgements about what was or was not an acceptable standard of workmanship, had to consider not only the end result but also the problems that were likely to arise in subsequent operations in the production process. This led to ambiguity in their expectations of the operators. On the one hand, they relied for the achievement of good quality work on the operators' adhering scrupulously to the methods laid down for each production operation. On the other hand, they expected the operators to modify their method to take account of minor mistakes made in previous operations. Operators were expected to be on the lookout for mistakes and to try to allow for them instead of compounding them or sending the work back. For example, if a seam was made too wide by one operator this could sometimes be compensated for by taking in less on another seam. There was a reluctance to accept an operator's excuse that any mistake was the inevitable consequence of a previous mistake:

> 'If a girl said to me that the notches were in the wrong place, I would suggest to her that as an experienced machinist she should still know how the job should look when it was finished. That's where I'd expect experience to come in. She should make the garment as she knows it should be made.'

The ambiguity was a consequence of the fact that by and large the foremen had originally been apprenticed tailors and had learned to 'make through' a whole suit. They had not really accepted that whenever a manufacturing process is broken down into small operations, standardization of method becomes critical. This was probably the remoter cause of the problem of quality.

A more immediate cause was felt by management to be the absence of a satisfactory device for influencing the performance of operators. The search for a mechanism that would make the girls 'quality conscious' was a constant preoccupation of management and supervision. The competence of the operators was not in doubt. As one of the Quality Control Department staff commented:

> 'We can produce an excellent garment. All you have to do is tag on a label "For Special Attention". The same people will do the job. The only thing is that they know that at the end of the line it's going to be seen by one of us. That job will be of the standard Mass-Bespoke would want. . . .'

In theory all faulty work was returned to the operator responsible. For a variety of reasons, this did not always happen. Sometimes mistakes were not detected until later on in the production process by which time other things might also have gone wrong, making it difficult to identify the original fault. Furthermore, where there was ambiguity about which of the operations was the source of error, foremen might refuse to accept a garment back for alteration from a subsequent section in the production process. One foreman said that he had made himself very unpopular by refusing point blank to take work back if he thought his section was not responsible for the mistake. He explained the reaction he provoked when he took a garment to the foreman who, in his view, was responsible:

> 'A lot of jobs were coming back to my section that should never have come back. . . . I had a lot of trouble with other foremen because I'd refuse to take them back. . . . It got around that I had a bad attitude, but these people also forget that it's their attitude. Their attitude as soon as they see me coming is defensive. . . . They put a brick wall up against me and say it's not theirs before you can show them a job.'

Another reason why operators did not always have their faulty work returned to them was that sometimes foremen felt that operators were not competent to put it right or that they would take too long doing so, thus jeopardizing the completion of production targets. A few foremen also admitted to being afraid of upsetting their operators if they gave them back too many alterations. Consequently, mistakes were often put right by someone other than the person who had made them, either by an alteration hand, or another operator, or a member of supervision. Two-thirds of the operators interviewed said that they were expected to put right other operators' mistakes, and many members of supervision spent a considerable amount of their time doing alterations themselves. One foreman explained his predicament as follows:

> 'In my job I'm *supposed* to see that the work's going through even. Keep the colours in the right order you know. But what I *do* is get stuck in. You get told not to do alterations and things like that—give them back to the girls. But I take it and do it myself. A girl'll tend to rip the whole coat apart and get the machine to sew it up when a few hand stitches would have done. So it's quicker for me to do it. And then sometimes if the girls are pressed, I'll rip a coat myself and sew it. Sometimes the management come round and say, "You shouldn't be doing that." But I think it's a bit tongue in cheek. They expect you to do it.'

From the point of view of getting the suit completed satisfactorily it was immaterial whether faulty work was put right by the operator who had made the mistake or by someone else. But only the returning of garments to the operator concerned could influence her performance in the future. Operators working on a payment by results system lost earnings while reworking substandard garments, and quite apart from any financial penalty, by having faulty work returned to them they received feedback information about their errors, with the consequent possibility of learning from their mistakes. However, the potential influence of this procedure on performance was severely undermined by the existence of the alternative procedure for adjusting substandard quality, whereby faults were put right by someone other than the operator concerned. This inevitably reduced the deterrent effect of any financial sanction for bad work, for operators were well aware that even if their work was faulty, retribution was far from certain. It also reduced the value of any feedback that did take place, for operators had no way of knowing whether borderline work was not returned to them because it had been just good enough to pass inspection or because someone else was putting it right.

Thus, although management felt that some device was needed to make operators quality conscious, the way that faults were handled in practice had a directly opposite effect.

Rectification of faulty work was not, of course, confined to alterations. Some faults called for new cloth to remake part of a garment which had been 'killed'. Also cloth could be lost—collars and pocket flaps were notorious for disappearing. The need for replacement cloth could have resulted in production delays as well as proving a source of embarrassment to production foremen, since no stocks of cloth were kept at the Factory. However, it was the practice in cutting suit lengths off the bale at the central warehouse to allow a few extra inches in order to make it easier for the cutters to get a suit out of the cloth. It was considered that the wastage of cloth involved in 'cutting long' rather than 'cutting short' was compensated for by the reduced time taken by the cutters marking and cutting out their 'lays'. This practice of supplying the Factory with slightly longer lengths than was absolutely necessary enabled many spoiled jobs to be put right without attracting attention to mistakes. Sometimes it might be several weeks before a particular pattern of cloth recurred; in that case it might be necessary to send back to the central warehouse. But usually the same patterns of cloth recurred sufficiently often to provide the Factory with a supply of spare cloth. If a large piece of cloth—say a sleeve, or part of a jacket body—was damaged or 'killed', then it was necessary to try and 'fiddle' a new part out of a lay, perhaps by combining several lengths of similar cloth to do this. (The need to do this was reinforced by a directive issued by the Factory management during the period of the research that foremen were to stop sending back to the central warehouse for more cloth.)

Another impediment to the satisfactory control of quality was the difficulty already referred to of setting precise quality standards. The lack of clarity was reflected in several ways. Only one out of the sixteen inspectors interviewed felt confident that she always knew whether or not to pass a garment. Three-quarters of them said that they were liable both to pass garments which were later rejected by someone else, and to reject garments which were considered satisfactory either by the operator concerned or by the foreman. Nearly a third of production operators interviewed felt that they were given back work which in their view should have been passed. When this happened, the operator could either show the garment to a member of supervision, who might pass it, or else send it down the line again and hope that this time it would slip past the inspector. There was certainly confusion in the minds of both inspectors and operators about what constituted satisfactory work.

The main reason why quality standards were not made clearer was that knowledge of them was also believed to be part of a tailor's craft. A tailor knew what was a 'good suit' and supervision, with a tailoring background, considered further specification of standards superfluous: 'Quality standards are something which tailors know.'

The extent to which quality standards were left implicit was reflected in the way inspectors were trained: 'You can't put old heads on young shoulders. You teach by experience. You show a new inspector by saying "This is good. This is bad. Come to me if in doubt." '

However, foremen did not derive their ideas about quality only from their knowledge of tailoring. Even though each foreman had his own concept of what constituted a 'good suit', he did not always use this as a criterion in making decisions about whether or not work was satisfactory. Foremen learned through experience on the job what was likely to come back from subsequent sections or from Final Passing and what was not. For example, foremen had discovered that mistakes which matched did not matter: if both sleeves hung slightly wrong, if both jacket pockets were higher than they should be, or both jacket vents longer. Errors of this kind were part of the foreman's concept of a satisfactory suit, one that would probably get by Final Passing and be acceptable to the customer.

THE CONFLICT BETWEEN TIME AND QUALITY

The fact that there was inherent flexibility in quality standards, resulting from their being implicit rather than explicit, together with unambiguous definitions of delivery dates led to a situation where quality was more likely to be sacrificed, when there was conflict between it and delivery dates. Several foremen regarded the relaxation of quality standards as inevitable if production targets were always to be reached:

> 'You've got to rush it through. You let things go. If they're really bad, you've got to make them right before you can let them go. Some things will just come back. . . . You try and get away with the little things.'

In many kinds of manufacture the conflict between time and quality has cost implications which complicate things further. This was not the case at Mass-Bespoke, as the extra time taken to make a suit well rather than badly was insignificant. Operators may have been tempted by the system of payment by results to rush things through but there was no inherent clash between quality and production targets.

The main conflict between time and quality occurred when it came to making decisions about whether or not faults were serious enough to warrant alteration. Making alterations to garments—especially when seams have to be unpicked—often takes far longer than the original operation. Sometimes to get at the mistake it is necessary to unpick the work of subsequent operators which then also has to be done again. As a result, decisions about whether or not to rectify faults were often based on whether there was time available for doing alterations.

Pressure of time was also the main reason why members of supervision helped out with alterations rather than return them to operators, thus reinforcing the impression that quality standards were erratic. Pressure of time also resulted in unco-operative and sometimes acrimonious relationships between production foremen and encouraged them to try and pass the buck in order to avoid faulty work being returned to their section for alteration. This buck-passing reduced still further the amount of feedback operators received about the standard of their performance.

The difficulty of balancing the conflicting demands of altering substandard work and meeting delivery dates had led some members of supervision to feel that they were trapped in a vicious circle: because they spent so much time doing alterations they had no time to supervise the work and to prevent it going wrong in the first place. One of the Quality Control staff commented:

'I think the machinists on the floor have the feeling that they're just not watched. If a supervisor or one of us go and stand, we'll rarely see a bad job being done. . . . It points to the fact that supervision is not strong enough. . . .'

In his view production supervision's involvement with alterations was the main barrier to improving quality, and he had been trying to persuade them to accompany him around their sections to look at the work being done:

'They don't like it. They know while they're walking round with me their alterations are piling up. . . . They're so imbedded in this at the moment that we couldn't expect them just to drop it . . . . We're going round trying to encourage them to spend a quarter of an hour in the morning and in the afternoon looking at the work on each section. It's laughable when you think of the amount of work going through.'

Because of the other factors involved, however, it was unlikely that closer supervision of the work would by itself have answered the 'Q' Factory's quality problems. Furthermore, there was little doubt that in according overriding importance to meeting delivery dates rather than quality, managers and supervision believed that they were in line with top management policy. A phrase widely used at both managerial and supervisory levels in the factory was: 'You get one kick for quality but two kicks for production.'

The maintenance of flexibility in quality control standards was therefore of paramount importance to Factory personnel at both supervisory and management levels. It shielded them from getting two kicks for both production and quality. This would have been a possibility if performance in the sphere of quality had been detectable and public in the same way as that of delivery, or the choice of corrective action had not been in the hands of the production foremen themselves. This was appreciated by the Factory Manager who was aware that his right to have the last word in quality matters was a key factor in getting work through the Factory. It was very largely for this reason that all inspectors in the Factory were responsible to production foremen and not to the Quality Control Department:

> 'I would consider putting the inspectors under Quality Control once we get on top of our quality problem. But as things are at the moment, if we let Quality decide what should be passed, production would come to a standstill.'

CONCLUSIONS

This Chapter has set out what appeared to be the major problem of managerial control in the Mass-Bespoke Factory. In terms of the framework presented in Chapter 3 the situation was one in which control was fragmented, resulting in a conflict between time and quality objectives. Moreover, the mechanisms relating to the control of both time and quality appeared to be inadequate. In the case of the time controls, the problem seemed again to be one of fragmentation; one control procedure being incompatible with another. As far as quality controls were concerned, the failure appeared to lie in the inadequacy of the adjustment mechanisms influencing operators, and in the lack of explicit standards.

Reference was made earlier in the chapter to the difficulty experienced in assigning Mass-Bespoke to any of the technical categories developed as part of the research programme. Interestingly enough, the same uncertainty about the nature of the production task appeared to underlie the control problems. The fact that the majority of the products were still made to order for individual customers meant that the values of the Mass-Bespoke organization remained those of unit production; the firm's success being closely linked with its expertise in selling and development, that is, styling activities. As a result, the production activities had suffered from a status point of view and had received less top management attention.

This had led to a situation where although the hardware of standardized production had been installed—the firm being progressive and innovative in this respect—the less tangible aspects of the technology, that is the body of ideas which expressed the goal of the work, its functional importance and the rationale of the methods employed, had not been adjusted to this hardware.

Again referring back to Chapter 3, the fact that the firm had moved up the technical scale to the point where the design of the system was becoming separate from its operation was not sufficiently recognized. It is not suggested that the firm could do without its tailoring expertise, but what was needed was to utilize this expertise in the planning and standard setting area of the business rather than in the direct production supervisory hierarchy, where the traditional attitudes of 'knowing a good suit' and of modifying later operations to compensate for earlier mistakes could create problems. What appeared to be needed was an expert in production organization and control who, by skilful use of the tailoring expertise available, would establish the logic of garment manufacture and adapt it to the new production process.

A particularly satisfying aspect of this piece of research was that a dialogue developed between the researchers and the firm through which the problems referred to in this chapter became more explicit. As a result, changes have been made that will enable the research workers to take a second look, focusing on the effects on the system of these changes.

JEFFREY RACKHAM

7 Problems in Meeting Delivery Dates: Time Control and Variation in Product Range

In the previous three chapters broad descriptions were given of the way that management control was exercised in three firms of widely different types. These descriptions attempt to explain the total system—to provide an overall picture of all the control systems and the interplay that takes place between them. This chapter, although also based on a tracer study, concentrates in more detail on a narrower front. One particular mechanism of control is described and an assessment made of its effectiveness and of its implications for the total system of managerial control.

Madingley, like Hollington already described in Chapter 4, is one of the manufacturing establishments of a large industrial complex operating in the electrical engineering and electronics fields. It will be remembered that one of the main conclusions reached as a result of the Hollington study was that the control system was not entirely appropriate for the type of production. It was designed to cope with more variety and uncertainty than in fact existed; the reason being that the control system was basically the same as that operating throughout the whole organization, whereas the production technology in this particular manufacturing unit was at the most standardized end of the firm's product range. Madingley, which was much more representative of the main stream of the firm's production has already been briefly described in Chapter 2, where it was shown that in comparison with other firms studied it had a high degree of variation in product range.

Although much of what was said about the Hollington control

system is also a description of the Madingley system, the latter had some unique features. These had been introduced to some extent at least in a deliberate attempt to cope with the extra uncertainty in the production operations. The set of procedures that is the subject of this chapter was a case in point and was not in operation at Hollington.

This set of procedures was related to one aspect of the control of time. The activity concerned was called order control, and the primary agents in the transactions involved were the personnel of the Order Control Section.

THE SETTING OF TIME TARGETS

The Order Control Section had three tasks that could be separated theoretically; first, it was responsible for the creation of an overall time plan for the production and related service functions that made up the manufacturing process; secondly, it had to ensure that information could be collected on the basis of which this time plan could be periodically reviewed; thirdly, it had to revise the plan as deemed necessary.

The phrase 'time control' has been used frequently in this book; in the industrial vernacular, time control is 'seeing that delivery dates are met' or 'trying to achieve targets'. This implies that there is a statement, assumption or general idea about the dates at which products or batches of products are to be ready for despatch and that activities are geared to these time targets.

Firms vary considerably not only in the extent to which time targets are made explicit and communicated but also in the degree of realism in their target setting process. One of the well-known problems for production management in the kind of industry in which Madingley operates is that the setting of delivery dates is usually part of the bargaining process between firms and their customers. Sales or commercial managers responsible for the bargaining process rarely have to accept the responsibility or take the blame if delivery dates are not met, and there is therefore a tendency for the bargains made to be somewhat unrealistic from the start.

Moreover, at the early stages in the time control process, in this type of industry the delivery date may be months or even years away and the achieving of that target therefore depends upon the satisfactory completion of a considerable number of successive and intermediate steps. Commitment to a delivery target thus further

K

implies commitment to targets for these intermediate steps, each of these targets being more or less strictly limited by the overall delivery target and by each other.

The creation of an overall time plan therefore involves making a series of estimates of these limits based on previous experience of the material and human characteristics of the production system. Within the limits of the overall delivery target, there may or may not be considerable room for choice in the detail of the plan. It may be found, however, that the time estimated for the various stages cannot be made to conform cumulatively with the delivery date. The choice then is either to produce a plan which is merely fiction or fantasy, or to ensure conformity by manipulation of the constituent targets or by alteration of the overall target. If the overall target is altered this fact may or may not be communicated to the customer at this early stage. But at least the task set for production management is consistent and feasible, and it can be argued that the customer will suffer less in the long run than he would if the production management were set standards which were known to be impossible to meet.

ORDER CONTROL PROCEDURE

In some firms time plans operate as mandates or instructions and sanctions are closely associated with them. In Madingley the functions of the Order Control Section were seen in a somewhat different light. The job of the Section was limited to the circulation of information about what programme would be feasible, so that those whose function it was to issue instructions in various areas—production management and supervision for example—would know what instructions would be appropriate from the point of view of the time plan. Work allocation remained in the hands of line supervision. The major part of this information was circulated before the production of any particular order began, and the basic document used was referred to as the Pre-production Progress Report or P.P.R. Sheet.

For every order, a series of P.P.R. Sheets was issued as the plans became firmer. Each order was given a P.P.R. number which became its primary means of identification throughout the Works at all stages of planning and production.

The exact details of the way the P.P.R. Sheet was used varied from order to order. The first estimates made in the creation of the time plan, and the way they were knitted together, sometimes turned out to approximate closely to the final commitment, and sometimes diverged considerably.

As indicated already, this study of order control was part of a wider tracer study and the way that the Order Control Section operated was examined in relation to a particular order that was being followed through the system; this order was for 200 VHF receivers, and was generated by the Aeronautical Division. The Company was divided into a number of divisions as well as a number of manufacturing units, each division being concerned with the design and marketing of a group of products. The various units provided manufacturing facilities with different, although overlapping, capacities. When a division wanted a product made, it placed an order on one or other of the units, subject to an overall maintaining of the distribution of work by the Central Office Production Control Department.

The first information received in the Order Control Section about this order was informal, indefinite and at a point in time about a year before the products were formally commissioned. This information was, however, something more than rumour. The man in charge of the Order Control Section had been told by the Production Controller, his immediate boss, that a VHF receiver was being developed in the Aeronautical Division, and if put into production would probably be made at Madingley Works. A quantity estimate was also given, together with 'confidential brief details' describing the sort of thing the receiver was expected to do. A P.P.R. number was issued, and Order Control raised a P.P.R. Sheet, Issue A, for circulation to the following people and departments:

1. Works Manager.
2. Purchasing Officer.
3. Test Superintendent.
4. Production Superintendent.
5. Production Controller.
6. Ticket Issue.
7. Estimating (first issue only).
8. Methods Superintendent.
9. Order Control Section.

This was dated March 1960.

This P.P.R. Sheet of March 1960, was unspecific and of a preliminary nature. This was indicated in two ways. First, whereas the successive issues were distinguished by numbers, this Sheet was called Issue A, and only subsequently were Issue 1 and Issues 2 to 7 raised. Secondly, the P.P.R. number, normally a four-part number, each part conveying a different class of information, was only a two-part number at this stage.

As soon as a P.P.R. Sheet was raised, the product became an item on the agenda of the P.P.R. Meeting, held once every four-week period, where its progress was discussed, new information brought up and appropriate details updated by the issue of a further P.P.R. Sheet.

The first re-issue, Issue 1, came seven months later, dated Week 44, 1960, the period covering the end of October and the beginning of November. The P.P.R. number had by then been given as a full four-part number and the following information was included on the sheet:

Order expected approximately	*Feb./Mar.* 1961
Delivery required	*Period* 1/62
Tooling quality	2000
Probable batches	200

Issue 1 was circulated to the same people and departments as before.

Issue A and Issue 1 represented the first appearance in the paper work of the control system of the products being traced and the interesting question from the research worker's point of view was what purposes or function these Issues served. What happened as a result of their circulation and would anything have been lost had they not been circulated at all?

It was observably clear that nothing of any real significance happened as a result of these Issues. They constituted no authority for anyone to start doing anything. Moreover the information contained in them was too indefinite and superficial to provide a basis for anyone to make plans as to how they might proceed should such authority subsequently be given.

But had they any purpose other than that of initiating action? Did they encourage production management to think ahead for example or had they significance as a mechanism for keeping people informed? If the latter, were they circulated merely because of the current ideology that emphasizes the importance of 'keeping people informed' or was the information considered useful in itself? The answers to these questions again appeared to be in the negative; as far as could be seen these Issues made little impact as pieces of information. The people to whom they were circulated were too busy with more pressing and immediate problems to pay much attention to them.

The generation, as opposed to the circulation, of this information did serve one purpose. It provided a focus for filing the various pieces of information about the new development that began to trickle in from this point onwards. For example, the Methods Section began to receive drawings; and it was helpful for the staff of that Section to have some means of relating the drawings to the relevant product and so build a picture of what the finished article was going to be like. The mechanism of the P.P.R. Sheet did, however, seem unwieldy for fulfilling this purpose alone and the impression was obtained that the paper work of the control system in Madingley was to some extent created for its own sake; it had a life of its own, quite separate from the products to which it related.

Generally speaking, therefore, the circulation of Issues A and 1 appeared to be of doubtful benefit; the marginal utility of getting information early being offset by the increase in the complexity of the paper work system. There is a tendency to judge the effectiveness of a firm's communication system by the amount of information communicated. Of course it is possible to have too much as well as too little information, and by overloading the system to reduce the impact of the essential communication.

It was recognized in making this judgement that the particular batch of products being studied may not have been typical of the product range as a whole. It was possible to envisage a situation in which some action would have to be taken at a very early stage to provide the necessary production facilities, and the fact that the circulation of the early issues automatically brought the products on to the agenda of the P.P.R. Meeting meant that a mechanism existed for initiating such action. Discussions suggested, however, that this happened very infrequently.

Six months after the circulation of Issue 1 the Order Control Section received a copy of the first formal document relating to the tracer product, the General Registrar or G.R. This document was a request from the Aeronautical Division to the Company for authorization to spend money on the production of the receiver. The Order Control Section was required to indicate on the G.R. whether Madingley was able to provide the necessary production facilities. Approximately one week later, in Week 11, March 1961, the Order Control Section received the Master Works Order

(M.W.O.) which indicated that a formal order had been given by the Division to the Works. The G.R. documentation was part of the financial control paper work of the Company and external to the Works. The M.W.O. therefore was the first piece of paper that factory management regarded as an instruction to produce. It was only at this stage that the Works could take positive steps to put the production machine into operation. The Methods Section began to scrutinize the drawings to plan how the product was to be made, to create a unit breakdown and layout and to calculate the number of 'generations' going to make up the final product. (The manufacture of a product at Madingley consisted of a sequence of operations which *either* altered material *or* combined one or more parts together into an assembly or sub-assembly. In the terminology used at Madingley the final product emerged from what was referred to as the first generation assembly. Sub-assemblies used in this first generation assembly were produced by the second generation assembly and so on. Most products made at Madingley had up to five assembly generations. This particular VHF receiver involved seven.)

This information was then passed by the Methods Section to the Order Control Section so that a time plan, based on the generation numbers, could be formulated. The Order Control Section used certain rules-of-thumb in formulating its time plans. Departments and sections were given target weeks when their part in the overall procedure was expected to be complete. This was calculated as follows. Scheduling was expected to be completed one week after the Methods Section had passed its information to the Order Control Section. Stock Control then had two weeks to deal with the order, the Purchasing Department was allowed the next three weeks and production was scheduled to start eight weeks later.

Then for each generation, the piece of equipment requiring the largest number of operations was taken as a yardstick and the production times were estimated on the basis of two operations per week. The earliest assembly generation started four weeks after production started, and a four-week gap was allowed between each generation. The target date for the completion of testing was four weeks after the completion of first generation assembly; and delivery was scheduled for four weeks after test.

THE TIME PLAN FOR THE TRACER PRODUCTS

Right from the outset, difficulties arose in relation to the tracer products. For some time after receiving the M.W.O. the Order Control Section was unable to take any further action. This was due to the fact that the Methods Section were held up because there were no drawings available. The drawing office was part of the divisional organization; thus the initial hold up was outside the control of the Works.

During the thirteen weeks after the receipt of the M.W.O., the order's progress was considered at successive P.P.R. Meetings, further details trickled in, and the P.P.R. Sheet Issue 1 became well scribbled over. Then in Week 24 (about the middle of June), Issue 2 was raised; this confirmed that the order had been received, and embodied a 'Standard Provisional Time Plan'.

It is interesting to note that the time which elapsed between the receipt of the G.R. and the receipt of the M.W.O. was about a week; the giving of authorization to spend money on production appeared to be no more than a formality. On the other hand the delay between receipt of the M.W.O. and the Issue of P.P.R. Sheet 2, when things could get started, was three months. During this three month period, the Order Control Section and the Methods Section had both taken short-cuts, in trying to reduce the delay as far as possible. The Methods Section's short-cut was to start on their breakdown of the product before receiving as large a proportion of the drawings relating to it as they would have liked. The Order Control Section's short-cut was to miss out a stage in the normal procedure by going straight to the 'Standard Provisional Time Plan'. The normal procedure was to issue first a 'Provisional Time Plan', and then,when all drawings had been received,'Standard Provisional', then 'First Run' and 'Repeat' plans. Right from the outset, therefore, actualities failed to keep up to targets and before production had actually begun, the Works was operating on the assumption that short-cuts would have to be taken if the delivery date was to be met. Both the Methods and the Order Control Sections felt constrained to go ahead with their part of the procedures before they had as much information as they would have liked. The going ahead before being really ready was reflected at almost every stage in the process. Production departments, for example, also found themselves in the position of being asked to start producing sub-assemblies and assemblies before they had all the bits and pieces necessary for completing the job.

It was surprising to find the Works organization taking these short-cuts and making special efforts to overcome delays originating in the Division, particularly as the separation between the responsibility for negotiating delivery dates and that for producing the goods on time usual in this kind of industry was formalized in the case of Madingley by the organizational separation between the Works and the divisions.

Two factors were of importance here. The first was that the different manufacturing units were to some extent in competition with each other and the divisions were the customers. The second was that Madingley and the Aeronautical Division were on adjacent sites, and as a result there were face to face contacts between the personnel of the two organizations. The Order Control and Methods Sections being at the initiating end of the production process were involved in these contacts. The impact lessened as the products moved through the manufacturing processes.

It could not be said in this case, therefore, that the delays in the system were occasioned by inadequate liaison between sales and development departments on the one hand, and production departments on the other.

Going back to Issue 2 of the P.P.R. sheet, this was raised in the middle of June 1961 with the delivery date still specified as the end of Period 1 in 1962. Thus there remained only eight four-week periods in which to complete the process right through planning, producing, test and despatch. The 'Standard Provisional Time Plan' in Issue 2, however, estimated that ten or eleven periods were needed for the total process.

Issue 2 was the first document in which the time standards for the tracer product were set. It was intended to provide a basis upon which all departments likely to be involved with the production of the order could begin to plan their part of the process.

But even at this starting point, the document was self-contradictory, showing an estimated delivery date some ten weeks after the required delivery date—both dates being left side by side on the Sheet, and producing the impression that failure was inevitable.

Furthermore, this inevitable ten-week failure was likely to become an even more serious failure. As all the details of design were not yet known, the information needed for the creation of a complete time plan was not available, and the chances were that the time plan that had been created would turn out to be even more wrong, beyond the inconsistencies already inherent in it.

Doubt has been thrown on the value of circulating Issue A and Issue 1. Was there a better case for circulating Issue 2 ? Was there any value in making plans on the basis of standards which start off by being inconsistent, and are likely to become utter nonsense?

The fieldwork of the research was centred on the movement of the products through the manufacturing process and it was all too easy at that stage to say that even at the time the plans were made and the targets set, the planners ought to have realized that they were utter nonsense. What had made them nonsense was by that time fairly clear. The planners had assumed, firstly, that the information they had in June 1961 was all there was to get, and secondly that their rules-of-thumb were sufficiently accurate to provide a fairly realistic forecast of the progress that might be expected.

The second assumption was probably justifiable, although it does not necessarily follow that these rules-of-thumb provided a satisfactory planning tool or technique. But the first assumption was so wrong that any inaccuracies in the techniques used for planning became insignificant. The information available was inadequate for the purpose for which it was being used, and the planners really knew that this was so. They had had dealings with the same designers before, and knew that the first order for new equipment always encountered difficulties and delays. They knew that the receiver concerned was in the forefront of advances in engineering, and that the discovery and removal of the 'bugs' that would inevitably appear in it could not possibly be accomplished within the weeks and fortnights allocated by their rules-of-thumb.

They must have suspected that their plans were nonsense; but nevertheless they had written them out neatly on the official paper work (designed by the O and M Section and printed in regulation green), circulated them to representatives of other planning, producing and measuring functions, and waited for the plans to fail. And fail they did.

The extent of the failure of the plans can be seen from the progress subsequent to the issue of P.P.R. Sheet 2. The order continued to come up at P.P.R. Meetings for a further year. After Issue 2 of the P.P.R. Sheet dated Week 24/61, and giving delivery date as Week 14/62, there were a further five issues (see p. 140).

Each of these issues also included the statement that the delivery was required in Period 1 of 1962. The purpose of including this continual reminder of failure is not at once apparent.

Issue 3 put the scheduled delivery date back from Week 14 to

Issue	Date issued	Reason for re-issue	Reason for change of plan	Scheduled delivery date
3	*Week* 25/61	*Provisional time plan for two generations added*		*Week* 22/62
4	*Week* 28/61	*(No change)*		*Week* 22/62
5	*Week* 47/61	*Time plan changed*	*Design changes*	*Week* 25/62
6	*Week* 15/62	*Time plan changed*	*Design changes*	*Week* 31/62
7	*Week* 22/62	*Programme revision* C	*Outside supplies*	*Week* 37/62

Week 22. The reason for this can be traced back directly to the lack of drawings mentioned previously. Prior to Issue 2, the Methods Section had identified five assembly generations in the manufacturing process and the time plan incorporated in Issue 2 was based on this assumption. When further drawings became available, the Methods Section found, however, that there would in fact be seven assembly generations. This new information was passed to the Order Control Section who had to re-formulate the time plan and re-issue this as P.P.R. Sheet 3.

Thus the scheduled delivery date was put back by eight weeks, not because the original design had been changed, but because the full details of it had not been communicated at the outset.

It was, however, design changes originating from the Division when production was under way that were responsible for the scheduled delivery date being put back on the next two occasions, first by three weeks and then by six weeks; these alterations in plan being incorporated successively in Issues 5 and 6 of the P.P.R. Sheet.

Finally there was an alteration of scheduled delivery date from Week 31 to Week 37, because of the failure to obtain materials from outside suppliers according to plan; and this led to the issue of P.P.R. Sheet 7.

Issue 7 was realistic in that in Week 29/62 the order was 'put over to Progress' and in Week 33 was 'put over to Output'. An order was 'put over to Progress' when the first generation assembly was reached. The Progress Controller was given the responsibility for taking a detailed look at the progress on all the items making up the order and had to report on the situation at the next P.P.R. Meeting. If at this Meeting the Progress Controller felt confident that the order would be completed in the next four weeks, it was taken off the agenda of the P.P.R. Meeting and put on to that of the weekly Output Meeting. If he was doubtful, the time plan was again revised or the order kept on the agenda for review at the next Meeting.

The order was therefore completed approximately nine months after delivery was required, the greater amount of the work being already overdue before it actually arrived on the shop floor.

TIME CONTROL AND VARIATION IN PRODUCT RANGE

Readers whose industrial experience has been only in firms in which the production technology is more limited and standardized will interpret this account of the way that Madingley failed to meet the required delivery date on the first batch of the tracer products as criticism of its effectiveness as an organization. Indeed it might be said to provide an excellent example of 'what is wrong with British industry'.

The information has not, however, been presented with criticism in mind. The combined experience of the members of the research team within their framework of the comparative task analysis approach had made it only too clear that in this type of production, problems of time control are almost insoluble. Moreover, the fact that Madingley was not unique in failing to meet its delivery date is demonstrated by the fact that of the twenty-three week delay that occurred after the circulation of Issue 2, six were due to late deliveries from outside suppliers of components.

As has already been pointed out, the firm was operating in an industry in which unrealism creeps in at the outset in the negotiation of delivery dates between the firm and its customers. In addition Madingley was at the least standardized end of the firm's product range. Hollington, at the opposite end, was able to do better from a delivery point of view. Even so this superior performance was not achieved without some strain on the people concerned, and it also weakened the cost control system.

Most important of all, however, the circumstances described above relate to the first run of a new product, and it does not seem unreasonable to suppose that the tribulations experienced arose to a considerable extent from the situation of novelty. The production of 200 VHF receivers involved a complex set of actions, and the choice of these actions, their timing and their sequencing, involved an equally complex set of decisions. And since these actions and decisions were non-standard, in the sense that the problems had not been encountered in any earlier run of the same product, it may be supposed that they involved a high degree of uncertainty. This extra uncertainty was injected into a situation where, even in the case of repeat runs, the complexity resulting from the number of products being manufactured concurrently meant that there were changing priorities involving the reallocation of resources in a relatively unpredictable way.

Expressing this in the terms of the notions of Carter *et al.* (1), decisions in situations of novelty were made on the basis of unsure beliefs, so that the situation was one of 'potential surprise'.

Accepting that the greater the degree of variation in product range and of innovation the more difficult the problem of time control, the question arises of whether the P.P.R. procedure described in this chapter made any contribution to the solution of the problem. As Burns and Stalker (2) have pointed out, this type of production needs an organic form of management, and at first sight it therefore appears unlikely that building one more set of impersonal procedures into the administration system would improve the situation in any way. As has already been seen, the procedure had to deal with changes in information of a quite fundamental nature. At the outset the information was vague and limited in quality. At the end it was detailed and specific; in between the procedures had to take account of both clarification and changes in information.

THE FUNCTION OF THE P.P.R. PROCEDURES

The first point that must be emphasized in the evaluation of the P.P.R. procedure was that it was not intended to operate as a control or adjustment mechanism. There was complete separation between target setting and control and there was nothing that the Order Control Section could do to ensure that the required delivery dates were met. Indeed, when delays were caused either by outside suppliers or by design changes originating in the Aeronautical Division, all that happened was that the target dates were put back the required number of weeks. In other words, although the procedure was carried out primarily through the agency of the

Order Control Section, which was part of the Production Control Department of the Works, it was in no way a control procedure for the Works. It provided no mechanism for comparing the actual performance of the Works with the target set. It was not monitoring the performance of the production departments and, in the light of discrepancies caused by internal disturbances, adjusting the instructions to those departments. In the first place, the disturbances arose from sources external to the production departments—and in some cases external to the Works. And secondly, the procedure was not primarily concerned with monitoring production performance, since most of the activity involved in the procedure took place before the production system started to achieve any output.

The procedure did not enable control to be exercised on the Division either, or on the outside suppliers, since the agents of the procedure were not in a position to give instructions to either Division or suppliers. In some situations the existence of a procedure which made explicit the consequences of design changes for the meeting of delivery dates might have provided an indirect mechanism for controlling the behaviour of design engineers. But as Chapter 4 indicated, this was an organization in which the design element in the work was regarded as the most critical to success and it was therefore unlikely that the problems liable to arise as a consequence would influence the engineers in their decisions to change designs. Indeed the prestige and power of the design engineers may have been an additional, if not the major, reason why both the Methods Section and the Order Control Section tried to accommodate the Aeronautical Division by pushing ahead with the circulation of Issue 2 before the full particulars were known. The Division was not only a customer but also a very powerful part of the total organization. The ethos of the organization ensured that design considerations would inevitably take precedence over delivery considerations. Whether this was a satisfactory state of affairs is impossible to say, but satisfactory or not it would have required a major reorganization to change it.

Accepting that the P.P.R. procedure had no control implications, was it a useful target-setting device? Did it have any function that was not adequately covered by the preparation of the production control schedule for each order in the way described in Chapter 4. Reference has already been made to the fact that Issue A and Issue 1 tended to overload the communication system with information that was too vague and indefinite to be useful. To some extent, therefore, these Issues could be said to be dysfunctional. Was the same true of the P.P.R. procedure as a whole?

The conclusion was reached that as far as the successful accomplishment of the organization's primary task was concerned, the P.P.R. procedure was of marginal significance. The dissolution of the Order Control Section would probably have had little short-term effect on the performance of the Works.

Nevertheless the Section has important social functions and its removal could have serious long-term effects. The first of these functions arise from its boundary position in the Works organization. Madingley Works can be conceptualized as a complete organization in itself or as part of the total system of the Company. In the former case, the Order Control Section had an important role in providing a mechanism for exchanges across the boundary with the environment (3). It was primarily concerned with preparing the Works for environmental change, including design changes and failures of suppliers.

Within the wider context of Company organization as a whole, its function was to assist in the regulation of the relationship between the Works and the Aeronautical Division. The way in which it responded to stimuli from the Division helped to consolidate the superior prestige position of the Division in the way that the Company ethos intended. Moreover, had overall Company management decided that the relationship between the Works and the Division needed to be changed, the Order Control Section would have been available for use as an instrument of change.

It had, however, another important function. In this connection it is necessary to ask why the programme produced by the personnel of the Order Control Section appeared at times to have made so little sense. It might be suggested that they were optimists. But what benefit was there to be had from allowing their optimism to outweigh their estimates of probability? Who were they trying to please or appease? Did they in fact please or appease anyone, either in the short term or in the long term? Did not their optimism result in fact in opprobrium rather than approval?

There could be another and more complex explanation. In situations of more repetition and standardization in the production processes, the main function of a planning or programming procedure is a technical one—to provide for the need to coordinate the multifarious actions that will go to bringing about the total, complex production process. But in situations of a high degree of variety, change, or novelty, the degree of uncertainty or potential surprise with which individuals are faced is such that the programming procedure may in addition have a more important function to perform. This function can be expressed in a number of ways—and may be comprised of a number of constituent factors.

Because of the anxieties that uncertainty is liable to produce, a programme may have value merely because it produces an appearance of certainty. The main function of the P.P.R. procedure may therefore have been to inject order into an unpredictable future. It is also possible that the creation of a time-structure for the future satisfied what Berne (4) has called 'structure hunger', and Allport (5) 'pattern creation'.

If uncertainty provides an excuse for inaction, even a false, hypothetical or interim destruction of uncertainty may have a positive value. It limits uncertainty within bounds that enable individuals to act constructively. The information collected by the research worker about the Order Control Section appeared to provide a useful illustration in miniature of the theories of Durkheim (6) and Kornhauser (7) about the anxiety-reducing functions of societies and social groups.

In situations of uncertainty, even nonsensical plans may be better from this point of view, than no plans at all. The weakness of Issue A and Issue 1 was that they did not reduce uncertainty sufficiently to make action possible, rather than that they were more obviously nonsensical than the succeeding issues.

References

1. Carter, C. F., Meredith, G. P. and Shackle, G.L.S., (eds.). (1954) *Uncertainty in Business Decisions.* Liverpool University Press, Liverpool.
2. Burns, T. and Stalker, G. M. (1961) *The Management of Innovation.* Tavistock Publications, London.
3. *See for example,* Rice, A. K. (1963) *The Enterprise and Its Environment.* Tavistock Publications, London.
4. Berne, E. (1966) *Games People Play.* Deutsch, London.
5. Allport, G. W. (1955) *Theories of Perception and the Concept of Structure.* Wiley, New York.
6. Durkheim, E. (1951) *Suicide.* Free Press of Glencoe, New York.
7. Kornhauser, W. (1959) *The Politics of Mass Society.* Free Press of Glencoe, New York.

R. ALAN HEDLEY

8 Organizational Objectives and Managerial Controls—A Study of Computerization*

THE RESEARCH SETTING

The reason why computerization was of interest in the research being done at Imperial College was implied in Chapter 3. Briefly, the introduction of integrated data processing and the use of the computer for production programming and control are regarded as innovations that push a firm concerned towards the single system and mechanical ends of the two managerial control scales described in that Chapter, and make it possible to obtain a greater comprehension of the state of the production system.

This movement along the control scales is therefore seen as the intervening factor linking computerization with its observed effects on organizational structure and behaviour, and when the opportunity arose to study a computer application, as part of an organizational analysis of a large manufacturing complex, it was welcomed.

This complex, which we have called Division X, was one of six product Divisions of an even larger and more complicated industrial Corporation. Division X consisted of fourteen formerly independent Companies that were brought together in 1958 into six main Company groups.† The new Division was controlled by a Divisional Managing Director, assisted by an advisory board which consisted of the Managing Directors of each Company group together with a number of functional directors.

---

* The framework for data analysis used in this chapter was developed by the author in his M.A. thesis presented to the University of British Columbia in 1966. Some of the data used was collected by Ian Bates, an M.Sc. student of the Management Engineering Section of Imperial College, and by Peter Combey.

† These groups are referred to as Companies 1 to 6 throughout this paper.

Three years after the establishment of Division X the Chairmanship of the Corporation itself passed to a new man who was keenly interested in the use of advanced information-generating techniques. Then in 1962–63, a slight recession which brought a sharp fall in profits, led senior directors to consider more acutely the question of what knowledge and information they needed in order to direct policy in the face of an increasing diversity of manufacturing operations and increasing competition at home and abroad.

A committee founded by the new Chairman recommended that within Division X a break should be made with the previous *laissez faire* policy towards the constituent Companies, and that a move should be made towards a rationalization of resources that might enable the production facilities of the entire Division to be treated as a single system from a planning and control point of view.

In addition to recommending a move to more comprehensive planning, the rationalization policy focused attention on the possibility of standardizing products in a way that would assure the Division of maximum returns from its new ranges of expensive and highly mechanized machinery, while at the same time retaining the facility to produce the very specialized products which many of their customers demanded.

It was felt that the provision of integrated data processing throughout the Division would be a move in the desired direction, since moves towards more planning, rationalization and standardization could be more fully realized with the introduction of a complex computer system.

However, the history of computerization in the Corporation goes back beyond the formation of Division X. In 1956 the Director of Research and Development on the main Corporation Board suggested to the Board 'the very considerable potential importance . . . of getting involved in the use of computers'. He persuaded the Board to set up a research project with fairly wide terms of reference, to determine where computers would be useable to the best advantage and what organization should be set up to deal with them.

A project team was set up which worked on these problems from 1956–59. In 1957 the main board authorized the hiring of an IBM 650 computer for three years for research purposes. It was to be used experimentally and did not have to justify itself in terms of

L

revenue. Initially the project team visited a diverse selection of manufacturing Companies within the corporate structure to ascertain the possible areas of application. The members of the team decided that the manufacturing Companies which were then being brought together into Division X presented the most promise.

In 1960 the project team presented a report to the Board stating that there were advantages in the use of a computer within the Corporation and recommending an initial application in Division X. The report also recommended that owing to the complexity of processing required and the sheer volume of work, the right approach would be to install a central computer as large and as powerful as could be financially justified, rather than a series of smaller computers that would perforce be restricted to relatively simple tasks. The report included a recommendation on the type of machines to purchase (IBM 7070 and 1401). The report was adopted by the Board, and the Companies in Division X were asked by the Board to give their full co-operation.

The team began work on the development of computer programmes for all the Company groups in Division X. Since production control was recognized to be the essential foundation of an ultimate integrated system, the original plan was to computerize the complete manufacturing operations of each Company, from the planning of work schedules and the ordering of raw materials to the determination of wages and the printing of customer invoices at the time of despatch. In addition, the computer would be used to analyse costs and sales, and to plan future progress.

As this chapter will show, progress was slower than expected, partly because of the complexity of the operations to be controlled and partly through lack of acceptance. The early attempts to base computer programmes on existing manual methods proved abortive.

It was only when the first programmes were run in 1963 that the full extent of the problems involved in attempting to apply integrated data processing to the production and marketing of the products of Division X was realized. Computer application was then limited to two Company groups, in an attempt to concentrate the effort in a more limited field.

In 1965 a team was set up to rewrite the programmes. On the basis of this experience the Computer Director wrote a report saying that more hardware was needed and proposing the purchase of an IBM 360/50 'real-time' computer with direct 'land-line' links to IBM 360/20 computers located on various manufacturing sites. The main Board considered this report and committed itself to the necessary expenditure in 1968.

THE RESEARCH METHOD

The field study of this computerization was carried out between October 1965 and March 1966. During that period, therefore, there was direct and first-hand observation of what was happening. The past history of the development was obtained in part from its documentation and in part from intensive open-ended interviewing with senior management in each of the major organizational units—the Computer Unit, the Division and the Companies. This included all executives at 'director' level, all senior functional executives who maintained the Division/Company communication links and the senior systems analysts of the Computer Unit. The breakdown of the total number of interviews is given in Table IV.

Table IV *Number of people interviewed*

	Division	*Companies*	*Computer Unit*	*Totals*
Directors	9	47	1	57
Other executives	10	31	2	43
Totals	19	78	3	100

THE RESEARCH FRAMEWORK

As indicated above, this study of computerization is part of a much longer term programme of organizational research in the firm under review. In time, therefore, it will be possible to collect information relevant to the central theme of the research now being undertaken at Imperial College: that is, on the effects on organizational structure and behaviour of radical changes in the system of managerial control. This chapter deals only with the introduction of the computer; it covers the ten-year period during which the imprecise organizational objective of 'getting involved in the use of computers' progressed to the point where the firm committed itself to a third generation 'real-time' computer for the purpose of achieving integrated data processing throughout the fourteen manufacturing Companies in Division X. This chapter shows, too, how the situation was made more complex by the fact that divisionalization, involving an ever-increasing measure of centralization of control over the manufacturing complex was simultaneously under way.

THE RESEARCH DATA

(a) *The search for an organizational objective*

As we have seen, the initial acceptance of the idea of computerization by the Main Board appears to have been due to a combination of circumstances.

The general industrial trend towards more effective use of resources, accompanied by the development of new management tools and techniques, had resulted in a 'need' for increased sophisticated measurement and comparison; while the trend within the organization towards more product, process, market and organizational standardization and rationalization, plus the inclinations of the present Chairman to 'establish systematic consolidation ... through all advanced information-generating techniques available' were additional factors in the Board's approval of 'getting involved in the use of computers'. The Board felt that the hiring of external consultants to advise them on how this could be done would not be very useful as it was doubtful whether at that time anyone with the necessary experience and knowledge was available. It was decided, therefore, to recruit qualified systems analysts, programmers and machine operators as they became needed and were available, and build up an internal project team.

The task of this project team was to explore alternative areas for computerization, at the same time devising methods for their implementation. The team was also expected to win general approval of computer technology and of the specific proposals contained in its report. Some of the more important alternative applications that the project team considered, and the reasons for their acceptance or rejection, were explained by the Computer Unit Director as follows:

(i) *Computerize accounts.* This alternative was considered and rejected because it would not fully utilize the complex data processing equipment that the Board had agreed to hire in 1957. Also, the Computer Unit Director stated that benefits from computerizing accounts are few. 'There is very little advantage in the speed-up achieved and few clerks are saved.'

(ii) *Computerize stock control*. This alternative was rejected as not being the central problem. As an ancillary project it would be considered at a later date.

(iii) *Computerize production control*. As the Computer Unit Director said in a speech to the senior management of one of the Companies in the Division: 'The real way to make money with a computer is to go into the production control field. The labour displacement is small in this area, but using the computer substantially enhances the chances of reducing work in progress, improving delivery records, reducing stock inventory, etc. One can make a substantial set of savings, but only in return for substantial investment. If one can crack the production control problem—the hardest of all—all the rest follows.'

The project team investigated all manufacturing Divisions within the Corporation with production control in mind. It rejected Divisions where there were mainly standardized mass production plants, because production control problems did not seem to be acute in this technical area. Division X, however, manufactured batches of products mainly to customers' requirements. Any type of order was accepted within the limits of the existing plant. Each order therefore, was planned, costed and loaded separately. There were also in the Division a number of fairly similar Companies from a technological point of view. Thus the production control programmes devised in that Division would, it was felt, be applicable not to just one, but to all Companies.

Even though it is difficult to establish how full and how accurate this information collected about events that were from five to eight years passed was, this historical description of the introduction to the idea of computers, and of research into using them in this Corporation does seem to illustrate a concern for the *feasibility* and *acceptability* of proposed objectives. The initiating interest group, in this case the computer team, after gaining approval for its project, started to develop first a possible and then a workable and operational proposal to present to the Board. They did this by *'searching out'* various alternative courses of action to: 1. provide the most 'satisfactory' application; 2. specify the reasons as to why alternative courses would not be as appropriate, and 3. establish a priority among alternatives in case the first one proved unworkable. They also attempted to communicate the idea both of integrated data processing and of the possibility of defining the 'logic' behind the scheduling of the manufacture of the Division's products to Company and Divisional management.

The project team discussed the various alternatives in the report which it produced in 1960, specifying in detail the feasibility of computer application, and proposing initial application in Division X. The report indicated the type and organizational setting of the computers required, and stated that the overall objective of the computer application in Division X would be to provide integrated production control for all the manufacturing Companies, in accordance with a stated time schedule.

The proposals in this report were accepted by the Main Board, and they endorsed their approval of these new objectives with a 'request' for all Divisional and Company personnel to co-operate fully with the newly formed Central Computer Unit in its application of integrated production control for Division X.

The project team chose, quite deliberately it seems, to concentrate on the most difficult area of computer application. Whether this was entirely owing to the fact that this was seen as the area in which the greatest return could be obtained on the effort and money invested or whether the complexity made it irresistible as a challenge it is impossible to say.

From a communication point of view, however, there is no doubt that it would have helped considerably if success could have been demonstrated in a simpler and more manageable application before moving on to production control. The fact that the communication and the way in which it was communicated was not wholly acceptable to, and therefore not endorsed by, Company and Divisional managements undoubtedly had important implications which were evidenced throughout following events.

(b) *Consolidation of the proposed objective*

The request from the Main Board for co-operation was the point at which the Companies became directly involved in the computer application and the Division became responsible for its coordination. Immediately, three broad areas of functional responsibility became visible. The Computer Unit, with its task of devising programmes to computerize and thus integrate the complete manufacturing operations of each Company, represented a predominantly *technical* interest; the Companies, with their obligation to apply these programmes to their operations without jeopardizing existing commitments, represented a strong *manufacturing* (production and marketing) concern; and the Division, whose job it was to lay the groundwork for a successfully integrated control system and maintain an adequate return on investment for the Division as a whole, represented a *coordinating* function.

Thus the Companies, which until 1958 had been on a largely autonomous footing, were now faced with intervention from two sources. Firstly, the creation of a body of divisional executives all seeking information from the Companies was resented, and even resisted by some Company managers; and secondly the formation of a central Computer Unit, with further powers of intervention, represented an instrument through which the greater centralization of control implied by divisionalization could be implemented.

An added complication was that the Division, with its specialized function of providing coordination and integrated control of the Companies, was ambivalent in its interests and values. On the one hand it saw itself as representing the apex of an ultimately integrated system of control, while on the other, the emotional involvement of Divisional personnel with the Companies from which the majority of them had been drawn led to the rejection of this concept and to a tendency to operate as a service centre, helping Companies to achieve their individual objectives.

Against this background of emerging interest groups, the Computer Unit attempted to work out a production control programme for each of the operating Companies. This proved to be more difficult than had been anticipated. Company executives' reactions are illustrated in the following comments:

'The decision had been made that it would be best to computerize only one kind of production operation and specifically production control. Production control was thought to be the core or the key and from this everything would follow. It was recognized that if it were mastered, all else would come easily. Unfortunately, this first hurdle has not been overcome. At the beginning, things worked reasonably well. We were asked to provide *general* rules for making our products. It was only when the computer started feeding back that we found we were in a "helluva" mess.'

'No-one had tackled the programming of the manufacture of our kind of product on a computer before, so to start with it was a very difficult job. . . . There is a lack of knowledge of what we are actually doing. There are lots of cases where we don't know.

We can only work by trial and error. It's very difficult to simulate "expediency" on a computer.'

The staff of the Computer Unit quickly realized that—as one of them put it:

'There were no general rules for manufacture, and without them it was not going to be feasible to store in the computer. There would be no use in storing the method related to every single product. One had got to find the general logic behind it.'

Inextricably interwoven with the technical problems was the inevitable and natural resistance to change of any sort, particularly resistance to 'external examination'. The fact that the computer personnel were sponsored from above, that is, from the Main Board, was also a barrier to their acceptance.

The initial problem of not knowing this 'logic of manufacture', together with the fact that the Computer Unit's attempt to approximate the manufacturer's rules-of-thumb on the computer had failed, suggests that the 'perceived' feasibility of the computer project differed from its 'actual' feasibility. This initial failure of the Computer Unit to formulate a feasible and acceptable objective seems to have been largely responsible for the conflict and pressures that followed to modify the objective.

(c) *Conflict and pressures to modify the objective*

It was in 1963, after the first programmes had been run, that the various conflicting views were articulated. Company executives were the most vocal of the people concerned, especially those in the Company in which the application had begun and was most concentrated. Initially, a few managers from each of the Companies had been made responsible by their Company Managing Directors for co-operating with the Computer Unit in its review of the various production control procedures. These managers had also to ensure that production was kept going, and when computerization of technical planning and selection of raw materials proved to be only partially successful, they found themselves obliged to institute manual controls to control the mechanical control system. They complained to their superiors who in turn brought their problems to the Company Managing Directors.

This cadre of executives, formerly very powerful, and still extremely influential, participated on the Divisional Board as members, but had no direct control over it. At the time when the

Company Managing Directors took up the complaints about computerization, they were also engaged in waging a war against the decreasing autonomy of their Companies, and against the increasing responsibilities being given to the functional directors on the Divisional Board. Therefore it must be realized that the conflict over computer installation took place in a wider context of conflict.

The Computer Unit admitted a relative failure but remained undaunted in its belief that the general logic of the production processes must and could be identified.

Company criticism was of four main kinds:

(i) *Authority without responsibility*

Company management felt that the Computer Unit was either not willing or not allowed to take responsibility for the impact of its actions on production results. They felt they had no alternative but to co-operate with the Computer Unit, but were still judged by the Division and Main Boards on their current manufacturing operations. In other words they were faced with another major variable that could significantly affect their viability but over which they were given little or no control. They felt that the Computer Unit should be made responsible in what they called 'pounds, shillings and pence terms' so that it might temper some of its more radical and costly ideas.

(ii) *Insufficient consideration and knowledge of Company conditions*

Closely allied to the above set of criticisms were the Companies' claims that the Computer Unit was not sufficiently cognizant of Company conditions, and in many cases did not attempt to increase its knowledge. Many Company executives genuinely believed that there were too many variables in the production processes for manufacturing operations to be computerized, and that the speed of throughput was too high, and the detailed information required impossible to produce within a reasonable time period. Also, they felt that the mass of alternatives that had to be dealt with, such as cancellations and schedule alterations, meant that amendments could not be reflected in the programme quickly enough.

On the commercial side, marketing managers maintained that the only way to get business in a very competitive field was to juggle discounts to different customers. The computer introduced an inflexibility in this respect which they were not willing to accept and with which they could not cope.

(iii) *Insufficient planning*

From where they were viewing the application, many Company executives thought that the approach of the computer people was insufficiently planned. There was no provision for people leaving the project and no training programme to ensure the continued effort to apply the computer to manufacturing operations. Also, some executives felt that there were not enough people initially engaged on the project, and those that were were not of sufficiently high calibre.

(iv) *Insufficient liaison*

The last main criticism of the computer application, and one about which the Computer Unit Staff and the Company executives were able to agree, was that there was inadequate liaison between them, and a damaging lack of communication caused largely by the specialization of function and the internalization of subgoals. Other studies (1, 2, 3) too, report findings that suggest a relationship between the degree to which members of two groups share norms, values and/or superordinate goals and the ability of the two groups to communicate and co-operate. One study goes further, suggesting that 'the greater the contrast in values and norms between two groups, the greater the tendency for those groups to reduce their interaction with each other' (4).

In this case, as suggested above, the difference in values revolved around the Computer Unit's *technical* objective to introduce a centralized control system and the Companies' largely *emotional* reactions to what they saw as a loss of individual control and discretion to the Computer Unit. The Companies' anxiety was not entirely without substance. The following conclusion made in one of our earlier reports of work in this firm is relevant (5). What tended to happen in the absence of definition was that the people responsible for systems analysis made policy decisions about the various controlling factors almost without being aware of doing so. There was therefore the danger of long-term decisions being made in terms of their appropriateness to system design rather than in relation to more fundamental criteria. Thus real control tended to shift to the systems designers.

During the processes so far described, Divisional organization was relatively unformulated and the Division's reluctance to involve itself in the internal problems of the Companies prevented it from intervening in the conflict. Only belatedly did it enter the arena, when to some extent its position had been strengthened. The Companies were beginning to prefer interference from the Division to loss of discretion for the Computer Unit. They bargained a loss of autonomy for an increase in support. Thus the Division assumed responsibility and changed the state of affairs by limiting computer application to Companies 1 and 2. The Managing Director, advised by his functional directors, decided that the Computer Unit would be more likely to arrive at the core of the production control problem if its focus were narrowed.

This action thus brought to an end attempts to realize the objective of achieving integrated production control for Division X without the desired results having been achieved. Instead, a deeper search was started by the Computer Unit to try and ascertain the logic behind manufacturing operations, and the Division also started a search to develop an organizational environment more conducive to the achievement of the original objective of computer application.

(d) *The search for modified objectives*

The Computer Unit began its more detailed second period of search on the assumption that the development of more precise methods of manufacture was a necessary prerequisite of an integrated production control programme. What the systems analysts had to devise was a logical system for scheduling the manufacture of products, the existing system being too pragmatic and empirical. To do this they had to talk to the production managers and their staff in Companies 1 and 2. To use one of Homans' (6) assumptions, this increased interaction enabled both the parties involved to improve their 'association methods'.

A more tangible result of this question and answer process was the construction of a series of procedure manuals which ultimately formed a basis for training Company executives.

By the end of 1964, the Division had become much more involved in computer application. As indicated already, the failure to intervene earlier had been largely owing to the traditional autonomy of the Companies. There was also, however, a lack of experience and understanding of what computerization of the kind being attempted really meant. The early confidence of the Computer Unit staff in their ability to implement an integrated control system had led to the false assumption that this was merely a technical and straightforward matter. Conscious of its earlier failure, it was now with a sense of urgency that the Division attempted to devise some proposals for a successful implementation.

The Managing Director of the Division stated one of the problems to the investigators:

'One feels that the failure has been the insufficient involvement of top management in the computer exercise—both here at Divisional Headquarters and at the Companies. We have been leaving things far too much to the Director of the Computer Unit. He's been conducting a mathematical exercise, and we've been leaving things for him to put together. We found out too late that top management *must* be involved for the thing to be a success. It wasn't the Computer Director's fault; it was the failure of top management to realize that the computer is just as much the responsibility of top management. We didn't realize the implications quickly enough.'

But before it could develop specific proposals, the Division first had to ask itself in general terms what it was trying to achieve in the computer application. To quote the Managing Director of the Division again:

'All of us are worrying at the moment about getting uniform information systems in the Companies which will tell us at the centre what's going on, so that we can redistribute orders. It will show up the inefficiencies between Companies, something I suspect some of the Companies are worried about.'

The next task was to determine *how* to achieve this objective. Having recognized that the failure of the Computer Unit to gain acceptance at Company level had proved to be one of the main stumbling blocks previously, he saw this as the first problem to tackle. A number of steps were taken.

First, divisional management proposed that there should be more involvement in the project on the part of senior Company personnel. More of the responsibility for implementation and more control over implementation should be assumed by the Companies and less by the Computer Unit. To ensure that this involvement would be regular rather than sporadic, it further suggested the formation of three Company working parties whose prime responsibility would be the implementation of the computer programme. These working parties would collaborate with the Computer Unit.

To gain more acceptance of the project, these working parties were chaired by functional directors from the Divisional Board because, as one director commented:

'... the Computer Director. . . is very much of a red rag to a bull to many Company people. . . . He is a very sound man, but there has to be someone between him and the Companies, from whom they will "take it". There has to be a "front man", but a man who has to believe in what he is talking about.'

Thus another bargain was struck; the surrendering of some control over applications by the Computer Unit in return for increased acceptance.

As well as attempting to make the Computer Unit people and their project more acceptable to the Companies, the Division also faced the problem of 'selling' its own function to these previously quasi-independent manufacturing Companies. Hoping that it would help on both counts, the Managing Director commissioned the Director of the Computer Unit to lay on two- or three-day courses for middle management from both the Divisional and Company organizations together. These covered subjects ranging from the basic principles of computers to detailed information about the computer applications within the organization. It was also suggested that both the Computer Director and some of the Divisional directors should make day visits to the Companies in an attempt to explain the *raison d'être* and in this way gain the necessary endorsement. These proposals were agreed and implemented by the Divisional Board.

The various committees had been set up by the end of 1965 and in the same year the Computer Unit announced that it had successfully concluded its search for the basic laws of manufacturing the products of Division X.

(e) *Stabilization of the modified objectives*

As far as the Computer Unit was concerned, the next phase of the application was the rewriting of its complete suite of programmes for Companies 1 and 2 based on the 7070 computer.

The formation of Company teams to formulate 'precise systems objectives' was generally viewed by the Company managements concerned as 'a good thing'. As well as making specific people responsible, it also broke the whole job of computerization into more manageable tasks. For example, upon receipt of more detailed terms of reference from the Company working parties, the Computer Unit could set up a number of project teams to design the requisite computer programmes. A Company 1 executive stated that this more formal liaison 'helped to communicate difficulties and ease the strain and tension'.

In Company 2 the response was even more enthusiastic. A special department called 'Computer Liaison' was set up with a manager and one full-time assistant. These two men worked in close collaboration with the seven computer staff who were specifically concerned with the Company 2 application. As well as this Department, a special team of three was set up to be responsible for the writing of a second computer programme. These three men (Material Control Manager, Assistant Sales Manager, and Assistant Planning Manager) were from the most affected departments. According to their Managing Director:

> 'This team is considering every minor detail that will go into the programme. They have now completed this detailed examination and there are between 100 and 200 items still to be resolved. We are now concerned with decisions as to whether we include them in the programme but try to modify them, delay the programme until they are resolved, or modify our original objectives in the light of these difficulties.'

Changes were also made in the structure of the Computer Unit. It reorganized itself to fit more easily into the 'functional' pattern established in the Division and the Companies. Whereas the Computer Unit analysts had been grouped together on the basis of the Company in which they were working, they were now regrouped according to the type of project on which they were engaged. The Company Director said that this was to allow for 'more cross-fertilization of ideas and approaches among people doing the same sort of project in different firms'.

The Computer Unit was certainly more acceptable to the Companies at this stage than it had been previously and there was more collaboration. The reasons for this were obvious. The first and most important was that the original stumbling block in the technical inability to define the parameters of manufacture seemed much more likely to be overcome.

In Company 1 the situation on the 7070 at this time was that the computer was producing between sixty and seventy per cent of the technical plans after being fed with vetted and standardized information from the customers' order by the Sales Department.

In Company 2, there was a slightly higher degree of success. The active involvement of the Division had also had the desired effect. The Division executives had very much the same basic approach to computer application as Company management. As a result they attempted to tackle the problems in a way that fitted into the existing organizational framework, unlike the systems analysts who had attempted to redesign the systems to accommodate the problem. The use of the existing organizational framework meant that established role and status relationships did not have to be disturbed and use could be made of the familiar communications network. But increased acceptance was not complete acceptance, and there were several factors that still created difficulties.

There were a number of technical problems still to be overcome. The reason why over thirty per cent of the jobs were still manually planned in Company 1 was said to be that if a job was needed quickly on the shop floor, too much delay was caused by sending it to the Computer Unit. The manual planners were therefore operating alongside the Computer Unit. If they could foresee their jobs being usurped by the computer this may well have led to negative reactive behaviour, since it would be easy to refrain from sending a job to the Computer Unit when not strictly necessary, in order to produce a low figure in the 'percentage of jobs planned by the computer' column of the periodic report.

The problem of scheduling and loading was a very difficult one in this Company. Of the 3000 customers, 13 absorbed approximately eighty per cent of the total output and every effort was made to satisfy these customers at the expense of the others. Also among the remaining 2987 some were more important than others and some more important at one period of time. The commercial policy adopted for this type of system thus presents a great problem for computer application, so that there was here a very real conflict between subgoals within the organization.

There were also some organizational problems. One was the place of the Computer Unit in the Corporation structure. At the outset it was set up under the auspices of the Main Board, the Research and Development Director of the Corporation being directly responsible. When the computer project team made its initial report in 1960 it was decided that because its entire operations were to be undertaken within Division X, the responsibility for its direction would also lie in the Division. Consequently, control over the Computer Unit was given at that time to one of the Joint Managing Directors of Division X. When he left Division

X in 1964 to manage another Division, the other Managing Director allocated responsibility for the Computer Unit to his Financial Director. A few months before the conclusion of the research reported on here, direction over the Computer Unit was again switched, this time to one of the Joint Managing Directors on the Main Board. The Financial Director of the Division, however, retained his functional link with the Computer Director and still assumed responsibility for the computer application within the Division.

This chequered history had a number of consequences. In the first place, the continual shunting of responsibility for the Computer Unit, even though for ostensibly 'valid' reasons, was thought by those lower down to denote either a lack of active involvement in its installation, or a lack of knowledge of how such a project should be handled, or an unwillingness to accept the responsibility for a project with such pervasive implications—or a combination of all of these factors.

Whatever the reasons, this action, or lack of it, resulted in uncertainty, tentativeness, and even anxiety lower down. One executive in Company 2, which was in fact the Company where most progress had been made said: 'A lot of people have been fence-sitting, paying lip-service to the computer. If it works and is recognized at the top they will be all right, otherwise there may be some trouble.'

A second factor still causing problems was that although the Division had got the Companies more involved in computer application, no specific guidance had been given about how the handling of integrated data processing should be fitted into the Company structure. This resulted in a wide variety of organizational patterns designed to accommodate the computer. In Company 1 the responsibility for the computer application was assumed by the Chief Industrial Engineer who reported directly to the Company Managing Director. In Company 2, the responsibility also lay with the Chief Industrial Engineer, but he reported to the Financial Director. When a third Company became involved in computer application, the Financial Director took control and he was responsible to the Company Managing Director. The differences in Company arrangements provoked reactions. There were some inter-Company communication networks and managers in one Company felt that they should have the responsibilities of their counterparts in other Companies. Thus the way was open to factional disputes and 'power plays' among various interest groups, each intent upon gaining control over that particular Company's installation. As long as responsibility for the computer was seen to be in doubt, the question remained open at various managerial levels as to who was in fact going to assume control. If the responsibility for the computer application had been firmly established and allocated at Corporation, Division and Company levels, questions of illogicality and justification would not have arisen so frequently and from so many quarters.

(f) *The start of implementation*

Although the activities described in the last section together represented considerable progress in stabilizing the modified objectives, the ultimate success of the computer application was by no means secured. However, as far as the relationship between the Division and the Companies was concerned, it appeared that the modified objectives were moving smoothly towards implementation, for the impression was obtained that, largely due to the efforts of the Managing Director, assisted by the functional directors, a workable and acceptable relationship was at last being nurtured.

The main organizational analysis research was by this time well under way and the research team was acting as a catalyst in this change process. The climate of the new relationship was well expressed in a comment made by one of the Company directors on the Divisional Board:

> 'The Managing Director may be individually responsible for the Division but it doesn't mean that he acts in an authoritative way; he's not a dictator. It's the difference between a "human relations" approach in which you tell the chaps and keep them in the picture, and a 'human resources' approach in which you assume you are dealing with a group of *intelligent* human beings who have different experiences and views which it is worth plumbing because they may affect your decision.'

This implies that the Managing Director did neither want nor expect a unified, completely harmonious Divisional structure. He expected, for example, Company Managing Directors to present their own cases very strongly—'this is their job!' However, he did want to achieve an organizational environment in which these same senior Company executives related their Company interests

M

to overall Divisional interests. A comment made about the Divisional Board by one of the Directors was illuminating:

'It seems to me that the Divisional Board may be working towards becoming more than an information disseminator in that people are beginning to know each other better, to know more about what's going on, to think of the Division more as a Division, and of the Divisional Board as something which is not a forum for defending one's Company position (which it used to be apparently). Now people are beginning to feel rather that they are *members* of the Divisional Board. Perhaps they still have to sell it to their subordinates in their Companies.'

This last sentence is a significant one. At director level a bargain was undoubtedly in the making. The Division, by allowing Company Managing Directors to involve themselves on a wider 'divisional' spectrum gained a commitment in the establishment of uniform controls throughout the Division. Acceptance of these controls had not yet been achieved at lower levels of management in the Companies nor had the lower levels of divisional management yet learnt how to apply them in as tactful a way as possible. The conflict associated with the changing Division/Company relationships had now been transferred lower down the hierarchy.

The fact that the Division/Company relationship at the middle level of management was an important ingredient in the acceptance of the computer application is illustrated by the differences that have been referred to between Companies 1 and 2.

One reason for the greater acceptability in Company 2 lies in the origin of the two Companies. Company 1 was one of the original four firms who were members of a federated alliance in 1919. From this time forward it had maintained a powerful and influential position, becoming by far the largest of the six Company groups within the Division, and it was steeped in a tradition of autonomy that had been encouraged for forty years. Company 2, on the other hand, was a new Company conceived by the present divisional management. Born from a merger between two departments of two other Companies, its management, although promoted from these Companies, was nevertheless recruited by the Division. From its beginning Company 2 had been a 'Division X Company'. Because of the problems involved in setting up a new Company and because it did not have a previously established tradition of autonomy, Company 2 had at every management level a more intimate relationship with divisional Headquarters than did Company 1. Also, because of this closer relationship, it had been more involved in 'divisional' projects of which computer application had now become a major one.

Both Computer Unit and divisional staff commented on the differences in the nature of the management in Companies 1 and 2. A typical comment on Company 2 was: 'They are a lively group of people, used to change and altogether they have a very good attitude towards the computer applications.' The same person said of Company 1: 'This is a curious Company dominated by conservatives. They have very tight rules and are very formal in their relationships with each other, being always careful to see that they are not treading on anyone's toes. They like to have all the strings in their own hands.'

The divisional directors became increasingly aware of how important the selection, placement and training of managerial staff was in the establishment of a good Company/Division relationship. They recognized that the growing acceptance of the Division as the organizational unit for the purposes of career development was an important element in the process of divisional control. Suddenly, however, the slow movement within the organization towards implementing the desired directions was disrupted by an event which triggered off a whole series of activities. This event was an announcement that the Main Board had approved of additional expenditure in 1968 for new equipment, 'which offered faster operating speeds and a larger storage capacity than the existing IBM 7070 and 1401 computers, together with the additional benefit of real-time processing'. We must now look at the events leading up to this announcement, which had been going on simultaneously, while the modified objectives were apparently being smoothly consolidated.

(g) *The shift towards real-time processing as an objective*

The Computer Director himself played the major role in initiating these events. Success with computer application had so far been only partial; the problems of establishing the logic of the manufacturing task appeared to have been overcome, but there was still a long way to go before production programming by computer was complete. He foresaw, however, that if progress continued to be made, the existing computer capacity was going to be fully loaded in 1968. He also felt that the problems encountered in Company 1 could only be solved by 'real-time' computing.

The way in which he presented his case, in a report to the Main Board, showed that he was aware that the proposal reflected a fundamental change in the system of control in Division X. In terms of the concepts set out in Chapter 3, what the report dealt with was in fact the likely consequences of a movement towards the mechanical, single-system category of control.

His report also reflected the development of divisional organization, for implicit in the case for the purchase of the new equipment was the assumption that the major focus of managerial control was going to shift from the Companies to the Division, and that the production facilities within the Companies would eventually be programmed as a single system of resources. In the light of current developments in computer technology he recommended the purchase of a 360/50 computer which he said was 'now commercially available and enables all the known defects of the present system to be overcome'.

A schedule for the real-time data processing applications was also contained within the report. Because of the huge backlog of information, Companies 1 and 2 could be 'integrated' by September 1968. Company 3, because of the similarity in its production procedures even though it had relatively little contact with the Computer Unit, was booked for a few months later. Companies 4 and 5 and a soon-to-be-built plant of Company 1 were scheduled for a year after that. Company 6 was not mentioned. Some difficulty was envisaged with Company 5, for there were still unknowns in its manufacturing process which made a technical investigation necessary in this Company, but otherwise it was anticipated that transfer and application should take place smoothly and with perhaps only a minor revision of the time schedule.

The Computer Unit Director seems to have got his report accepted with relatively little difficulty and it is interesting to speculate on why the Main Board made the decision. Several contributory factors can be identified.

In the first place, it must have been difficult for Board members without a great amount of specialist knowledge to argue for or against the case that only the characteristics of a real-time computer system could make feasible the objective of integrated data processing for the fourteen diversely distributed manufacturing

Companies of Division X. To the uninitiated the technical advantages of a machine that could accommodate the equivalent of seventeen to twenty of the Computer Unit's programmes at one time, process enquiries immediately and transmit the result almost instantaneously to an external station, irrespective of the task on which it was at that moment engaged and without any intervention by an operator, must have been irresistible.

There was also the point already made that industrial organizations do get satisfaction from having a reputation as trend setters in the business world. In fact, during the period of the present study, an industrial columnist wrote a full two-page report on the firm which discussed the many attributes responsible for making it a leader in the industrial field. Both the present and proposed computer applications were seen as contributing to this state of affairs. The report became naturally enough a talking point in interviews and general discussion. Although there was a reluctance to accept the article at its face value—it was described as 'the usual journalistic mixture of truth and half-truth'—it did seem to make many of the executives interviewed see the computer application in a more favourable light. Thus, as well as increasing the general prestige of the firm, the press report had the added effect of making the computer project more acceptable.

Also contributing to the acceptance by the Main Board was the fact that there had been a commitment to integrated data processing since 1960. As the new machinery was presented as essential to this objective, the pressure of the prior commitment was a major factor in the acceptance of the Computer Unit Director's report.

Another contributory factor was the organizational position of the Computer Unit at that time. The report was presented during the period when the Unit was directly responsible to one of the Joint Managing Directors of the Corporation and the actual creation and formation of a specialized organizational unit for the computer had given it considerable significance in policy formulation.

This was particularly so since new ground was being broken and the way in which problems were formulated could exert an influence on policy decisions. It could be argued, for example, that the Main Board in making its decision was accepting the most articulate set of proposals, rather than what was necessarily the most appropriate course of action for the organization at that time.

The propensity of the Computer Unit staff to write reports also provides a partial explanation as to why its recommendations were accepted. The individual or group that recognizes, explains, and even provides a potential solution to a problem has an important voice in the way in which the problem is formulated and in the extent to which it is communicated to others in the organization (7).

The contrast between the Computer Unit with its custom of writing reports that spelt out specific procedures, and the Companies with their protestations that 'it is impossible to summarize fifteen years of highly specialized and idiosyncratic manufacturing experience on a computer' came out very clearly.

Whatever the factors influencing the situation, however, the Computer Unit Director got his plans accepted, and he and his staff began the consolidation process of rewriting the programmes for the 360/50 computer.

(h) *Renewed conflict and objectives*

The immediate effect of the Board's decision to advocate real-time processing was to re-arouse anxiety and hostility, and a conflict situation arose which had not been completely resolved at the time this paper was written. The Company and Divisional critics of the new proposals found it difficult to accept that the hardware was the limiting factor in the computer application.

One Divisional executive went so far as to question the contention that 'we have really run out of capacity on the present computer'. The reaction from some of the managers in Company 1 where, as indicated above, the introduction of the computer had run into the most difficulty, was one of amazement—'that this should even be contemplated before any real achievements had been made'. One manager interviewed thought that the Computer Unit people had reached a situation where they believed that the only way to advance was through the purchase of new hardware. With each new hardware recommendation they had promised Utopia, whereas in reality only strictly limited gains had been made on both the 650 and 7070 computers. The Board's decision re-inforced the 'them and us' attitude: the Computer Unit was referred to by one of the more articulate of the managers inter-viewed as a 'super-technocrat civilization, an ivory tower of well-paid young men'. He added: 'We could simulate the introduction of the 360/50 real-time system on the 7070 computer and see who wins.'

Several of the other executives interviewed, in addition to those employed in Company 1, suggested that this Corporation, like many others, had a desire to 'keep up with the Joneses', the purchase and utilization of a computer being regarded by the outside world as an indication of progressive management thinking. They feared that the new purchase was an extension of the attitude: 'First buy a computer and then decide what to do with it.' This criticism was the main crux of the problem, and the point around which most of the conflict revolved was whether a computer should be purchased and a system then devised to fit it, or whether a system should be devised and a computer then found to accommodate it.

The staff of the Computer Unit maintained that this question had no significance, for they said that the machine and the system could not be separated, the two were absolutely bound up together:

'Whatever machine you use, it has limited facilities, so you design the system within those facilities. The technical limits of the machine dictate the type of system you can put in. When you get a machine with better facilities you can design a better system, always assuming you know enough about the system to improve it.'

So to Computer Unit personnel it was not a question of whether or not to buy a real-time computer, but *when*. The advocates of new purchase in 1968 (and they would most certainly appear to be the stronger group) stated that enough had been learned in the ten years of computer application to finally determine the parameters of product manufacture, and they were confident that existing problems would be eliminated by real-time processing. Therefore, a transfer to the new machinery would seem advisable as soon as it could be handled. The proponents of waiting stated that the existing system was being taken as it stood and put on the computer. There had been no basic questioning of the adequacy of the system. A delay in switching to the new machinery would therefore allow for a 'reasonable' search process to take place.

There was an interesting difference in attitudes between Companies 1 and 2, and those Companies that were now being brought into the computer net for the first time. This was linked with the fact that the Division had become more firmly established and there was more central control than there had been at the time of the first computer exercise. In Company 1, as the quotations given above show, the hostility was directed towards the Computer Unit. There was less hostility in Company 2, but here too the Computer Unit was the target.

In Companies 3 and 4, however, computerization was seen as an instrument of increasing central control. Company 3 was certainly more prepared for the change than either Company 1 or Company 2 had been. A lot of work had been done on formulating a theoretical basis for manufacture, the progressing system had been rationalized and a system of priorities in respect of customers' orders worked out, so that managers were relatively optimistic about computer application. What did worry them, however, was the attempt that was to be made to standardize the approach over all the Companies. They objected to the 'bulldozing' on to their Company of policies arrived at on the basis of Companies 1 and 2. The stress on the individuality of the Company might have been caused by the fact that it genuinely did have different problems, but its manufacturing processes were very similar to those of other Companies, and it drew on the same labour market and on similar sales markets. It was, however, the most individualistic Company in Division X, it was the only Company whose name was a household word, and it was obviously reluctant to be drawn into an integrated control structure with standardized procedures across the whole Division.

Company 4 also showed hostility towards Divisionalization, remaining impassive about computerization. In this case, however, attitudes were probably based on the relatively small amount of knowledge and experience of computerization existing within the Company. As one manager pointed out: 'They don't really care about the computer yet. They have a job which takes all their time and the computer to them is a long way away on the horizon.' The Division, on the other hand, was already a reality and demands were made on them for information through which divisional control could be exercised.

The new wave of hostility to the Computer Unit which followed the commitment to real-time processing was handled sensibly by the Division, although as the following quotation shows, divisional management also had its doubts and anxieties:

'This is one of the big issues for the future, and the way we handle it could make a lot of difference to our effectiveness as a Division in the next five years. Are we making a mistake with this "monster"? Although people discuss problems such as this as problems, it is almost impossible to take the emotion out of it. There is a lot of worry and fear surrounding this anthropomorphism.'

The Division was also aware that organizational changes at both Division and Company levels and realignments of power positions would inevitably follow computer application.

The fact that social science research workers were studying the computer application became important at this juncture, for not only did their research reports mean that the Divisional management was more fully informed about the reactions of Company management, but the reports also provided a basis for the discussion of the problems with Company Managing Directors at the Divisional Board.

The line taken by divisional management at these meetings was to accept responsibility for the mistakes that had been made in the early stages, but to say that such a large investment in time and money was now at stake that every effort must be made to achieve the 1968 target. Successful computer application became a major 'key task' of the Division, and the Companies accepted this commitment, if not with enthusiasm, at least with good grace.

A new search process was also begun to find a way of defining the relative roles of Company and Division and to formalize the relationship between them.

When this chapter was written it was too early to conjecture at the success of the application, and its feasibility is still not proven. Nevertheless, the fact that the attempts were never abandoned throughout this long stay is in itself a measure of the Division's success in establishing itself.

Commentary

It became evident during the course of the present study that it was possible to interpret the events observed, at least partially, by adopting two fairly obvious assumptions. First, that as an organizational objective becomes more *feasible* (that is, workable and operational), it gains increasing acceptance from organization members. Secondly, that the more *feasible* and *accepted* the objective becomes, the more control will the initiating group assume over its direction.

In gaining acceptance, however, the initiating group usually has to sacrifice some of its control over the formulation and/or implementation of the proposed objective. This introduces the concept of bargaining as an objective setting and realization device.

March and Simon (8) in their work on organization theory, devote much discussion to the nature of organizational goals and their relation to the decision-making processes adopted to achieve various courses of action. They propose that if goals are accepted by relevant members and groups of members as desirable and feasible, problem-solving techniques will be used to arrive at various courses of action. However, if goals are not deemed either desirable and/or feasible by individual organization members, persuasion will be invoked in the decision-making process. And finally, if groups of members still do not evaluate goals as desirable and/or feasible, then bargaining will predominate in the decision-making process.

March and Simon specify further that because of the potentially disruptive effects of bargaining as a decision-making process that

> 'almost necessarily places strains on the status and power systems in the organizations ... almost all disputes in the organization will be defined as problems in analysis, that the initial reaction to conflict will be problem-solving and persuasion, that such reactions will persist even when they appear to be inappropriate, that there will be a greater explicit emphasis on common goals where they do not exist than where they do, and that bargaining (when it occurs) will frequently be concealed within an analytic framework'.

Although March and Simon assert that each of the above predictions appears eminently testable, they can cite no corroborating evidence, and it is hoped that this paper, therefore, by relating the data collected to these propositions, will enable some assessment to be made of their usefulness.

The setting and realization of an organizational objective can be conceptualized as a cyclical process consisting of three phases: search, consolidation and conflict/change or change/conflict.

Search is the process of identifying the alternative courses of action and their consequences, and attempting to arrive at a 'satisfactory' conclusion;

Consolidation is the process whereby a proposed objective becomes relatively stabilized and formalized as a result of interest group and subgoal formation;

Conflict resulting in change or *change resulting in conflict* is the process whereby the existing balance of costs and benefits is so disrupted that conflict occurs and change follows, or where internal or external events lead to changes in the established relationships sufficient to incur conflict.

The process is recurring, for conflict/change can lead, not to resolution of the problem or realization of the objective, but to a further period of search through which the original objective is defined more precisely, made more feasible or increasingly elaborate. Moreover, the cycles are not necessarily discrete, they can overlap or occur simultaneously.

In the preceding sections the processes relating to the adoption of computer applications have been described chronologically as far as possible, but if overlaps are taken into account, it is possible to identify three discrete cycles in the events studied. These are represented broadly in Table V, while a more detailed analysis is presented in Appendix I.

If we now compare similar processes in each cycle, some interesting trends emerge. For example, each of the succeeding search processes became more explicit and well-defined. The focus of search narrowed appreciably as did the time it took to complete each search process. The energies devoted to ascertaining the feasibility of the objective became more focused. In Cycle 1, several possible kinds of computer application were explored, while in Cycle 3 only the feasibility of various detailed aspects of one project was examined. Furthermore, the emphasis of search became less concerned with the possibility of the objective and increasingly involved with its workability and operationality. Referring back to the March and Simon (9) hypothesis, it is interesting to note that in this case the perceived workability of the objective seemed to generate greater pressure for its acceptance than did its actual workability. Even now the actual workability of the integrated data exercise is still not proven. In Cycle 1, the Computer Unit's attempt to base programmes on existing manual production control systems proved abortive, yet the Main Board accepted the proposals contained in the report because it assumed that these proposals were in fact workable.

The secondary search process directed towards the identification of the appropriate relationship between Companies and Division moved in a similar direction and played a considerable part in the ultimate acceptance of computer application.

A comparison between the consolidation phases of the successive

Table V *Cyclical components of events studied*

		Organizational processes	Events	Section in narrative
Cycle 1	Search	1956–59. *The search for an organizational objective—'getting involved with computers'.*		(a)
	Consolidation	1960–62. *The development of computer programmes in the Companies.*		(b)
	Conflict/Change	1963–65. *Conflict and pressures for change due to unsuccessful use of existing manual production control systems.*		(c)
Cycle 2	Search	1964–65. *Search for a logic of manufacture: search for organizational structure appropriate.*		(d)
	Consolidation	1965. *Cautious compiling of information for revised programmes.*		(e)
	Change Conflict	1965. *Realization that present equipment is becoming overloaded due to search process, Cycle 3. Criticism of new real-time plans.*		(f) (g) (h)
Cycle 3	Search	1965. *Research into problems of data processing leading to recommendation to acquire a 'real-time' computer.*		(g)
	Consolidation	1965–? *Management computer courses: rewriting programmes*		(h)

cycles is also interesting. In Cycle 1 we note the formation of three specialized functional groups—the Computer Unit, the Division and the Companies. Because of the nature of their specialized tasks and due to their histories of origin, these groups form specialized subgoals. The Computer Unit concerns itself almost exclusively with the technical problems involved in the application. The newly established Divisional executives, although their sympathies are to a large extent with the Companies, nevertheless attempt to establish a Divisional structure in which central integrated control is possible. The Companies, steeped in a tradition of conducting their own independent operations, present resistance to the notion of central control. As we proceed through the cycles, there is a growing realization of the state of affairs by the Division, and an attempt by it to bring these subgoals more into line with one another. This involves the bargain of allowing Companies more control over the formulation and implementation of the computer project in return for an increase in commitment and involvement in Divisional operations.

What does this study show about conflict and change processes in industrial organizations? There is a tendency in some business communities, as well as some social science circles, to think that conflict is something to be avoided. The present research suggests, however, that conflict should not be avoided but should be reckoned with and anticipated. Conflict can imply change, just as change can (and usually does) imply conflict. It is these processes that provoke new development; in this case, the development led to new search processes each with a narrower and more precise focus. In the development of this organizational objective, conflict resulted in increased efforts to discover the basic 'laws' of manufacturing the Division's products, and produced an involvement that was previously lacking in senior Divisional and Company managements.

A final thread that runs through this chapter is that the very slow start of the attempt to achieve integrated data processing may have been due to the fact that concern was limited to the definition of objectives rather than focusing on the problems of objective setting and control simultaneously. The study shows how closely the two are linked. The tighter the control aimed at, the more precisely must an objective be defined; similarly, the more precisely an objective is defined, the tighter the control possible.

References

1. Ronken, H. and Lawrence, P. (1952). *Administering Changes*. Harvard Business School, Boston.
2. Seiler, J. (1963) Diagnosing Interdepartmental Conflict, *Harvard Business Review*, **41**, Sept.–Oct.
3. Sherif, M. (1957–8) 'Superordinate Goals in the Reduction of Intergroup Conflict', *American Journal of Sociology*, **63**(4).

4. Seiler, J. (1963) Toward a Theory of Organization Congruent with Primary Group Concepts, *Behavl Sci.*, 8(3).
5. Woodward, J., Combey, P. G. and Hedley, R. A. (1966) Unpublished confidential report on organization of Division X.
6. Homans, G. (1950) *The Human Group*. Routledge & Kegan Paul, London.
7. Dill, William R. (1962) Administrative Decision Making, in Nailick, S. and Van Ness, B. H. (eds.), *Concepts and Issues in Administrative Behaviour*. Prentice-Hall, Englewood Cliffs, New Jersey.
8. March, J. G. and Simon, H. A. (1958) *Organizations*. John Wiley, New York.
9. March, J. G. and Simon, H. A. Op. cit. (See Ref. (8) above.)

PETER COMBEY

9 *The Setting of Objectives in an Electronics Firm*

On Tuesday, August 13th 1963, a heavy rectangular object was lifted on to a lorry outside the despatch bay of a modern factory near London, and driven to the laboratories of a research organization thirty miles away; a routine delivery from a manufacturer to a customer. Three people watched the product leave the factory site: two stores labourers and the author of this Chapter. To the labourers, who had spent the previous two hours manœuvring it into place on the lorry, the departure of the consignment marked the end of just one more loading job. To the author, who had spent the previous seven months observing the manufacturing organization edge gradually towards this moment, the despatch represented the culmination of one of the tracer studies referred to in Chapter 3.

For several reasons, this study was particularly difficult to carry through to completion. The organization in which it was carried out, Electra Ltd., had been radically restructured shortly before fieldwork began and a great deal of political manœuvring was going on while data was being collected. Moreover, the subject of the order chosen as tracer was an extremely complex product, and the order itself was cancelled three months after the fieldwork started making it necessary for the author to select another subject for study and repeat many of his initial enquiries.

It would obviously have been impossible within the limitations imposed here to present the complete findings of such a complex research assignment. For the immediate purpose it was necessary to select an aspect of the study which was self-contained and interesting but which would also add to the general picture being built up in this book. The aspect chosen was the setting of objectives.

The assumption was made in Chapter 3 that manufacturing organizations may be described in terms of four sequentially related kinds of activity: objective-setting, planning, executing and controlling, referred to collectively as the control cycle. This implies that control is exercised within the framework set by the objectives determined in relation to organizational tasks. It follows that the nature of the control process is likely to be influenced by the extent to which objectives are made explicit at the outset and modified subsequently under the pressure of circumstances. In Electra Ltd. the research worker soon discovered that the objectives which had been set in relation to his tracer were neither explicit nor stable.

This lack of precise and fixed objectives was found to have considerable implications for the exercise of managerial control. For example, it meant that the people responsible for executing policy were required to use a great deal of discretion when interpreting their mandates, and to be flexible in their approach; both made the evaluation of achievement extremely difficult. It was decided, however, that for the purposes of this chapter these implications would be largely ignored, and attention centred on the objective-setting process itself; the aim being to try and identify some of the factors that can be important in determining the character of that process in organizations and the way in which they interact over time. In the case of Electra Ltd. these factors proved to be many and complex.

The product selected as tracer was a computer which would measure seven feet by seven feet by three and a half feet and contain over 100 000 resistors, capacitors, brackets, etc., assembled in almost thirty types of modular configuration. But it became apparent early on that the computer would not only be large and intricate. It would also be a complicated amalgam of three kinds of content, each with its own design history extending back between two months and three-and-a-half years before research began. There was the so-called 'standard module' content, which consisted of a number of sub-assemblies designed to perform basic computing operations, and distinguished by the fact that they could be sold individually in their own right; the 'coordinating module' content another set of sub-assemblies designed mainly to link up the standard modules and control their operation but unsaleable except as parts of computers of the tracer type; and thirdly the 'customer' content, a proportion of the computer which was determined by the specific requirements of the customer. Detailed study of the way objectives had evolved in relation to these different kinds of content showed that their histories were significantly interrelated. The development of the customer content could not be adequately appreciated without knowing something of the development of its coordinating module content. Similarly, the development of the coordinating modules could not be understood without some knowledge of the development of the standard modules.

The technology was batch production in the sense that the order chosen as tracer was one of a series of orders for computers of the same general type being dealt with by the organization during the period of the research. Although these orders called for similar combinations of the standard and coordinating modules, they varied considerably in customer content. The impact of these other orders on the progress of the tracer was obviously something that had to be taken into account, and this was an additional complicating factor.

Extending the historical perspective of the study, it was discovered that the standard module and coordinating module content of the tracer and its fellow orders were not unique sets of designs. Each design was the latest version of a type of computing equipment that the firm had been making for over six years. To appreciate why and when these designs evolved it was necessary to trace them back to their origins. This led to an examination of the development within the firm of a group of people concerned with computers, and this in turn brought into focus the objectives of the firm as a whole.

But the significance for the tracer's evolution of both this product group's objectives and the objectives of the firm became apparent not only through probing into its direct line of ancestry as a product. The rapid expansion in the activities and influence of this group within Electra Ltd. between 1959 and 1963, and the radical reorganizations of the firm during this period had also had a shaping effect on the tracer product after the development process had got under way. Evidence came to light suggesting that in this type of industry changes in objectives at the level of the firm and its sub-units can have an effect on the pattern of product development.

Finally, it became clear as the fieldwork proceeded that any study of the evolution of objectives at these three levels—firm, sub-unit and product—would also have to take account of the

N

influence of personal objectives. The electronics industry has a reputation for attracting colourful personalities. Some of these have not found it easy, when the charismatic stage of development has passed, to adjust to a more bureaucratic and formalized organization. As this reconstruction of the evolution of objectives in respect of the tracer product shows, Electra Ltd. is no exception to this rule.

THE GENESIS OF THE STANDARD MODULE CONTENT

In the early stages of the development process, the setting of product objectives was very closely linked with personal goals.

Towards the end of 1959, a junior engineer working on the initial design of computer modules, came to the conclusion that it was time he left Electra Ltd. and set up his own business. Several considerations influenced his decision. He believed that an electronic engineer's creative life was short, and that at twenty-six he was probably at his peak of performance. More specifically, he had always wanted to be his own boss and two and a half years with Electra Ltd. had not altered this ambition. In his early days with the firm, he had been encouraged by its permissive organizational philosophy to think that he might get what he wanted within the Electra organization, for since 1954 it had been the policy of top management to create subsidiary Companies around distinctive and promising new product fields under a Holding Company umbrella. Several such Companies had been set up, and bright young men had been induced to join the firm by the promise of 'a directorship, almost unlimited funds and a pretty free hand'. Some of these Companies were still extremely small in 1959—they were described to the research worker as 'tribes consisting of more chiefs than braves'—but they all had clear-cut identities and substantial autonomy, attractive virtues to ambitious product-orientated engineers operating within the apparently more impersonal and restrictive framework of a function-based Company (Electra Research and Development Ltd.).

In 1959, however, divisions of the present Company began to be set up rather than new Companies. The reason given for this change of policy was the control problems of a multi-corporate organization, and it seemed that there might be less scope in the future for individual expression and advancement. A divisional structure was built up around the activity with which Brown (the engineer already referred to) was most closely identified, and he began to prepare seriously for a move out of the firm by working privately on the design of a number of basic interrelated computing modules.

Within a short time he had sorted out most of the logic underlying the development of the modules and started fitting them into a linking system of control. During the spring of 1960, however, while talking informally to Alexander, a senior colleague who was mainly responsible for the entry of Electra into the computer field, he let slip some of the ideas he had been refining at home. In his own words:

'It happened quite accidentally during one of the odd little conversations a number of us were getting involved in around that time about future development policy. The specific topic we were concerned with was the scope available for improving an existing "standard module".

I seem to remember that I was dying to talk to someone about what I'd been doing by that time, for two main reasons. My primary objective in life has always been to design fantastic circuits and when I've succeeded I want to share my excitement with other people who can appreciate what I've done. I had also reached a stage when I wanted to clarify some of the ideas I'd not sorted out to my own satisfaction. Hitherto, when this had happened, I had always tended to talk to other members of the Computer Group to get their slants on the problems.

Once I started talking I found that it was difficult to stop. It would have been embarrassing if I'd stopped short and tried to cover up. Anyway, Alexander displayed considerable interest in what I said and asked a lot of pertinent questions.

If Alexander had ignored my disclosure when I blurted it out I would almost certainly have left Electra and nothing that has happened subsequently would have been quite the same. As it was, he immediately allocated some of his development budget to me so that I could think through my ideas in Company time, and then began sounding out other members of the Group about the pros and cons of manufacturing the new design.'

The Computer Group consisted of six people whom it was customary to involve in formal and informal discussion about computer policy. In addition to the two engineers Alexander and Brown, there was a third engineer, who since joining the Company in 1958 had become increasingly identified with computer systems engineering, and three people from the Commercial Division of the Company.

The most senior commercial member of the Group was the Computer Sales Manager, a man who had a technical background in electronics as well as a great deal of field experience as a salesman of Electra's other products. He was the first specialist salesman to join Alexander in the very early days of the computer activity with the object of promoting its initial designs. Since then he and Alexander had fought hard each year to obtain the maximum allocation of Electra's development funds to computers. He was at this time probably Alexander's closest confidant, and was beginning to build up a reputation as a skilful negotiator and intuitive interpreter of market trends. Both he and Alexander were making it plain to their superiors that they were looking for broader responsibilities than were then available in the computer field.

The other two members of the Group were sales engineers, recruited by the Commercial Division because of their experience in computer application, and expected to act as a counterweight in design matters to their less commercially-minded colleagues in the Research and Development Division. When Alexander first approached other members of the Group with Brown's preliminary specification for the new module the salesmen argued against proceeding with its development.

They had four main objections, the first two being characteristic of the arguments that develop between sales and development departments in this kind of innovative industry. These were that on the whole they were satisfied with the existing module; if inelegant, it was at least out of the troublesome development stage and selling reasonably well. Moreover, although the new specification might significantly reduce the cost and bulk of the module, the customer would not buy it unless its operational characteristics were as good as those of the current module.

The other two objections illustrated the differences between design-orientated and market-orientated engineers. One was that radical redesign of this module would probably necessitate the redevelopment of other closely interdependent standard modules. The other was that the part of the range most in need of refurbishing was the coordinating system into which these modules fitted, rather than the standard modules themselves. The recent entry into the European and U.K. markets of a major American competitor was very likely to undermine the market for Electra's existing range of computers. It was essential to start preparing to meet this challenge if they were not to be forced to give up computer manufacture altogether.

Alexander countered. In his view the new American competition could be met in the long term only by radical redesign of the Company's products, beginning with the basic modules, and Brown's specification provided an excellent starting point.

It is important to stress that neither side was arguing from totally rational premises. The sales people were piqued by the realization that a junior engineer had produced a 'really staggering improvement' at a time when they thought they had the initiative. On his side Brown, having decided to stay with the Company, was anxious to see as much as possible of his original work translated into reality:

'Having in effect thrown in my lot with the Group I naturally wanted *my* ideas to be accepted and used. If they eventually proved to be economically successful it would do me a lot of good in relation to my position in the firm; if they failed of course I'd probably have to leave. . . .'

On this occasion the arguments from the Research and Development side won the day. It was agreed, reluctantly as far as the sales staff were concerned, that Brown should go ahead. Very soon afterwards he deliberately 'leaked' an idea for another standard module on which he had also been working privately. This time, because of the success of his earlier design, permission to pursue the development was obtained without difficulty.

GENESIS OF THE COORDINATING MODULE CONTENT

During the summer of 1960, while standard module development was under way, the Sales side suggested incorporating the new designs in an altered version of the Mini-Mac, the smallest computer in the existing range, sales of which were beginning to decline. Other designers in the Research and Development Division had brought complementary sub-assemblies to a relatively advanced stage, and there seemed to be a possibility of an exciting and very competitive replacement. The engineers accepted the logic of the proposal but expressed doubts about the time schedule proposed. After discussion it was agreed, however, to aim to have the new machine ready for display at the Computer Exhibition in November 1960.

Early in September the salesmen put forward another proposal based on the forthcoming availability of the new 'standard modules', and a formal meeting of the Computer Group was convened to consider it. In an attempt to fill a gap in their range of equipment, the salesmen were reverting to their earlier idea of redesigning the coordinating modules, and on this occasion they were supported by Brown. His extra-mural activities had included sorting out a new 'optimum' set of coordinating modules, and he wanted an opportunity to translate it into working form.

The combined case was a persuasive one, and it was accepted by the meeting. A list of twenty-one characteristics that the new computer ought to embody was drawn up after a free-ranging discussion. The wording of the list was not precise. It included such phrases as '. . . some form of digital display. . .', '. . . simplified control logic . . .', '. . . the price would probably be . . . .'

Moreover, although two of the sales people present at the meeting claim they recall Alexander's indicating that initial development of the new machine would take 'about a year', the minutes make no reference to a deadline for the completion of a prototype. According to Brown: 'It was all a bit vague, but this was inevitable because none of us knew precisely either what we wanted or what was possible.'

The meeting ended with Brown being asked if he would agree to take charge of the 'follow through'. He undertook to rough out some alternative configurations incorporating his colleagues' suggestions as a basis for further informal discussion.

THE DEVELOPMENT OF THE 'ECONOMICAL COMPUTER'

Between October 1960 and July 1961, the development of what soon became known as the 'Economical Computer' went ahead in fits and starts. Brown was unable to concentrate for long at a time on the problems involved in its construction because of crises elsewhere which required his attention. In November 1960, for example, he was called in to resolve problems that had arisen during the final assembly and testing of the first prototypes of his standard module designs and of the new Mini-Mac, to try to meet the Computer Exhibition deadline. This deadline was not met and the first public demonstration was deferred to another Exhibition in January 1961.

In February, Alexander got wind of a massive potential market for a 'toy' version of one of the new modules and he asked Brown to give priority to designing a modified specification to suit the customer's requirements. This occupied several weeks.

Finally, in May, Brown began to get requests for engineering assistance from the draughtsmen and production planners concerned with the firm's new factory (Factory A) some distance away. The modules and the Mini-Mac, which had been successfully presented in January, were being hurried into 'standard' production—in the research worker's terms 'small batch' production—to meet the demand before it evaporated. Travelling to and from Factory A, to help with the resulting problems, became a regular feature of Brown's working life in the summer of 1961.

It was not possible to find out in retrospect how far Brown discussed with either Alexander or other members of the Group the implications of these short-term crises for the longer-term commitments to the development of the Economical Computer. Available information suggests that during this period Brown was given more discretion than hitherto over the allocation of his time to the various elements of his work load. One reason for this was that towards the end of 1960, the 'flood of persuasive inspiration' which had emanated from him earlier in the year reaped its reward in the form of enhanced status. He was made formally responsible for the initial design of computer equipment, and the promotion automatically brought with it more scope for taking personal initiative. Another reason was that Alexander was becoming deeply involved in setting up a new design activity, and had less time spare to supervise Brown.

One consequence seems to have been that developing the Economical Computer was given a lower priority than getting the new standard modules into production. It was customary at that time in Electra Ltd. for the engineer who designed a new standard product to shepherd it through the initial production stage. In any case, not only Brown's own future but also the development of the Economical Computer depended on the success of the new standard modules. When problems arose in connection with these modules, therefore, he was willing to abandon other work and concentrate on their resolution.

The next disturbance came in July 1961, when Electra Research and Development Ltd. moved in its entirety from the premises it was then occupying into part of a new office block recently completed alongside Factory A. Although not publicized as such within the firm, the move represented one more stage in the process of tentative and piecemeal rationalization initiated by top management two years earlier. This process had impinged on the evolution of the Computer Group on two previous occasions.

In 1959 it had thwarted the crystallization of the Group as a semi-autonomous Company. More recently, a reorganization of the Commercial Division had brought about a change in the functions of the salesmen; they were required to deal with other design groups and sell other products. This limited the time and attention they could give to computer affairs.

The immediate effects of the move were that Brown was much more accessible to deal with the problems arising during the production of his module designs, and that the physical act of transporting equipment to the new laboratories gave the sales engineers their first sight of the prototype of the 'Economical Computer' and an opportunity to review Brown's progress. This review caused some misgivings. One of the technical salesmen recalled his initial impression of the prototype in these words: 'It was a very crude, badly engineered lash-up which contained a number of bright ideas, but looked rather empty for a machine we would have to sell with that kind of a price-tag.' Another, seeing the 'lash-up' for the first time, estimated unofficially that the selling price of a production version of the design would be much more than was originally estimated: 'This put the cat among the pigeons! If correct it meant that we were going to be landed with a direct competitor for our existing large machine instead of the hoped-for addition to the range. Given the increasing difficulties we were experiencing in the field trying to sell our large machine, the idea began to dawn that we should invest more money and time in the development of the new design as its successor.'

An informal and intermittent debate about the future of the Economical Computer was carried on in the Computer Group throughout July and August. As a result, by the beginning of September, a policy revision had been made along the following lines. First, the range of component modules to be offered to potential customers would be made wider and more up to date than originally planned (or even envisaged); second, the new machine, now to be known as the 'Electra 100', would be engineered along much more modular, 'meccano-like' lines than the Group's previous computers; and third, in view of these modifications it would obviously not be possible to have a working model of the new computer ready for demonstration until sometime early in 1962.

Alexander allocated more of his development budget to the project, and Brown started constructing another prototype using components 'cannibalized' from the Economical Computer.

ORGANIZATIONAL CHANGE

This was the point reached by October 1961 when the Managing Director of the holding Company formally announced the most radical step taken so far to rationalize the firm's activities. The multi-Company organization was replaced by a two-Company framework.

In Factory B, another of Electra's factories which housed an already centralized medium batch operation, the change had little effect. But in Factory A, which housed all the people and facilities involved in the custom-built and small batch manufacture of complex equipment, this reorganization involved breaking up the largely product-based Companies and regrouping most of the personnel into horizontally organized, function-based divisions under more centralized management.

The most significant effect for the Computer Group was that in the reorganized Company both Alexander and the Sales Manager were promoted. Alexander became second-in-command of a new Research and New Developments Division in Factory A, with six design teams under his direction. The Sales Manager was made a General Sales Manager responsible for the commercial viability not only of computer manufacture in Factory A, but also of three other product groups. Alexander later said that this inevitably reduced the amount of time available for detailed monitoring of computer affairs.

CHANGES IN BROWN'S ROLE

Alexander's promotion meant that Brown had even more discretion than before in the allocation of his time. His enthusiasm for involvement in production problems was waning however. Being now on the same site, he found himself in the last three months of 1961 approached by a succession of production planners, supervisors, inspectors, testers and finally salesmen, about problems arising in connection with 'his' standard module designs: 'At every stage in the manufacturing process and even after despatch, someone would pick on something they didn't like about a module and then harry me until it was put right.'

This he found more and more irritating:

'I learnt a lot about myself during this period. Up until then I'd tended to think that I'd be able to deal with all the minute detail and ignorance of its implications which characterized the quantity-production side of the business; and I'd wanted the experience of dealing with it, not simply because I thought it needed doing properly, but because it might come in handy if I eventually left Electra and set up a firm of my own. But after a hefty dose of "engineering" I was becoming terribly frustrated by the fiddly and argumentative nature of what it involved. It was then that I began to reconcile myself to the idea that dreaming up ideas and playing with crude working models was probably my cup of tea.'

Shortly before the end of 1961 a major crisis involving one of Brown's standard modules became so serious that it was perceived as threatening the future viability of the computer activity as a whole. One of the sales engineers involved in handling the resulting problems in customer relations reported as follows:

'It wouldn't have been so bad if we'd spotted the trouble before sending any of the new modules out into the field. As it was, several of them were despatched to priority customers and we heard about their deficiencies very soon afterwards. But, to make things worse, we didn't hear about these deficiencies from our testers; the first intimation that all was not well came from the customers. They complained about overheating and seizure of modules, and general failure to match up to "spec". It suddenly became apparent that we were moving into a very tricky period in our relationship with the outside world. It was a period which could be fatal for the computer activity as a whole, and damaging for the firm as well. What was at stake in essence was Electra's image as an organization able to fulfil its promises in this field.'

During this crisis, consideration began to be given to whether a different approach was needed to the engineering of computer designs for repetitive production. The salesman continued:

'First, very specifically, we were beginning to get some rather disturbing feedback about the impact of Brown's preoccupation with module engineering on the development of the Electra 100 (the replacement for the Economical Computer). In view of the importance of this new system for the future and the difficulties being experienced by Brown in his role as production engineer, it seemed to us he should be relieved of all but the Electra 100 project and any other initial design work which needed doing; we *knew* he was a brilliant *ideas* man. Now seemed to us an appropriate time at which to start being more sophisticated in the way we productionized our increasingly complex designs. It was no longer justifiable, from our point of view, to assume, as Alexander and other top managers on the "systems" side had done hitherto, that initial design and engineering could be done effectively by the same people. Engineering complex designs into a form which permits trouble-free production calls for special kinds of people, with a certain amount of sympathy for production problems and temperaments able to withstand, but at the same time accommodate, all the vested interests bearing down on them.'

In January 1962 the regular members of the Computer Group held one of their rare formal meetings. Prominent items on the agenda were the module engineering problem and the state of the Electra 100.

The first item to be raised was the state of the Electra 100, and Brown made a statement about what he had achieved so far. He was asked to estimate how long it would take him to get the prototype into a state suitable for demonstration to potential customers, and gave mid-April as the earliest feasible date 'given favourable conditions and no major unforeseen snags'. Pressed further, he agreed that the machine would not be fit for public exhibition before late May, but that the date of the Instruments Electronics Automation Exhibition, due to take place round about that time, was probably a reasonable deadline.

When making these 'guestimates', Brown repeatedly said that a lot would depend on the extent to which he was required to deal with module engineering modifications. After consideration of this second problem it was unanimously agreed that the designer was overloaded with engineering work, and that he should be relieved of it completely to devote all his time to the Electra 100 and other development projects. One of the technical sales engineers (a severe critic of all Brown's module engineering efforts) and four members of the recently formed Engineering Division, were given the job of salvaging what they could from the troublesome module designs.

Had this proposal come earlier, Brown would probably have

resisted it. As it was, it fitted neatly into his reappraisal of his own capacity.

INCREASE IN COMMERCIAL PRESSURE

Up to this point in the history of the 'standard module' and 'co-ordinating module' content of the tracer product, the engineers, in particular Brown, had dominated events. There had been opposition to their ideas at the outset, and spasmodic attempts had been made to exert pressure of various kinds. But this had had relatively little impact. All the circumstances, including the promotion of Alexander and the Sales Manager, the moving of the research organization to the factory site and the widening of the salesmen's responsibilities, had combined to allow Brown considerable freedom.

From the beginning of 1962, not only did Brown's role become less dominant, but also pressure from the Sales side of the organization began to increase.

The first indication of this came in February when Brown asked for a meeting to discuss rumours that ten Electra 100's had been fed into the production programme by the Sales Division, the first standard version of the machine being due off the shop floor some time in August. Brown felt that if this was true, the Division had acted on unreasonable assumptions.

The Sales Manager admitted that he had authorized the inclusion of the Electra 100 in the production programme, but said that in the previous autumn he had been given the impression that the new design would by now be ready for production. Moreover, at the Computer Exhibition held the previous November, his salesmen had put out some feelers about the machine and stimulated a number of requests for quotations from potential customers. One enquiry had crystallized into a virtually firm order for delivery in August 1962.

The Sales Manager admitted to the researcher during interview that these 'facts' had been deliberately introduced into the conversation as a means of putting pressure on Alexander and Brown. As he saw the situation:

'You've got to give engineers a tight deadline to work to or you'll never get anything out of the door. You've got to get some efficiently working models out into the field by hook or by crook to undermine customers' inhibitions or you'll never get your new product off the ground commercially. It's all a matter of balance and judgement. . . .'

Agreement was reached between the Sales Manager and the engineers; the August delivery date would stand if the Sales Manager could persuade his initial customer to purchase the first, crudely engineered, development prototype.

Three months later the Computer Group met again to discuss a report by the Sales Manager about the commercial progress and prospects of the computer activity. The report contained some pointed references to the Electra 100, and these provoked a heated discussion centred around estimates of the new computer's production schedule and production cost, neither of which were considered satisfactory by the salesmen. The schedule included the delivery of the first working prototype in August (as agreed in February) but predicted a ten-month interval before the delivery of the first production version (June 1963). The cost was described in the minutes as 'much higher than envisaged and not at all competitive'.

The salesmen also had criticisms to make of the production schedule. They were concerned that the proposed delivery of the first prototype to a customer, although welcome from one commercial point of view, would deprive them of a demonstration model and the engineers of a vehicle for fault-finding and evaluation. Moreover, the long interval between this first delivery and completion of the first available production version would make it impossible for them to accept an order for several Electra 100s from a customer with whom they were currently negotiating on the basis of initial delivery in December 1962.

Alexander finally agreed that a modified version of the Electra 100—to be called henceforth the Electra 200—would be constructed by Research and Development for use as a demonstration model, and later would be part of the order currently being negotiated.

The next crisis occurred as a result of the Instruments Electronics Automation Exhibition. As one of the technical sales engineers put it:

'The Electra 200 "clanged" commercially with a deafening thud. The prototype looked like an upright piano complete with beer stains, and it couldn't be switched on. It was a miracle to me that we kept any customers interested in it. As it was, the customer expecting the August delivery remained loyal to it as a system, but insisted that we do some re-engineering before delivery; while the second customer suddenly became very cagey about placing a firm order. No one else showed any interest whatsoever. . . .'

The echoes of the commercial failure of the Electra 200 at its first public outing resounded through the firm. A great deal of money had been spent on its development on the assumption that it would prove commercially successful and become the backbone of the computer range for several years. Now the end of its market life seemed to be in sight.

Alexander immediately carried out soundings amongst his colleagues in the Computer Group to see what they thought about the situation. Their reactions were consistent. Everyone felt that a computer with many of the basic characteristics of the first Electra 200 prototype, but more thoroughly engineered and more attractive in appearance was an essential component of the future range. Unless it could be developed very quickly they felt the Group would probably cease to exist.

There seemed no obvious technical reasons why a rescue operation mounted immediately should not be successful. However, Alexander would need money to finance the work and a first-class engineer with a sales and production orientation to lead the re-engineering team. For good commercial reasons, moreover, he would need to ensure that the customers who were still willing to negotiate obtained what they wanted; this too would require money and specialized engineering skill.

THE RESCUE OPERATION

Alexander's request for more money caused consternation among top management. A number of other activities in Factory A were passing through difficult times, and they were also asking for additional finance.

But Alexander argued his case persuasively. He dwelt at length on the considerable contribution currently being made to the Company's annual turnover by production based on the Computer Group's earlier designs, and the impressive growth in the size and profitability of this activity. Finally, he laid heavy emphasis on the crucial importance of the Electra 200 system for the continuance of computer production, and thus for the survival of the Company itself.

He got what he wanted. The next problem was the appointment of a man to take charge of the re-engineering of the Electra 200. The obvious candidate was the technical sales engineer (Evans) who had consistently criticized Brown's efforts, had been proved right by the course of events, and recently shown himself capable of effective module engineering. When offered the job, however, Evans made it clear that he would accept it only if given freedom of action to apply his engineering ideas. After discussion with other members of the Computer Group, Alexander accepted Evans's conditions with their support, Brown being the only dissentient.

Finally, Alexander turned his attention to the problems presented by the need to meet existing customers' requirements, and after further discussion with members of the Group, set in motion a crash programme which involved the production of a number of saleable prototypes of the Electra 200, under another research and development engineer.

In September 1962 the Sales Manager drew up his annual sales forecasts for computers and included among his predictions the re-engineered Electra 200. He did so after consulting Alexander and a number of his subordinates about the likely state of the market for existing and imminently available products during 1963. Soon afterwards, the Sales Manager met the Production Programmer to discuss the optimum production sequence.

At this meeting, a number of technical and scheduling problems arose in connection with the 200 system. Obtaining answers to these problems clearly involved approaching Evans, the new design authority responsible. Evans, of course, was an ex-salesman and an ex-subordinate of the Sales Manager. As far as the latter was concerned, however, he was now in a different reference group, and the Sales Manager was careful to put his own case firmly before recommending that the Production Programmer should contact Evans. He indicated that the Sales Division wanted the first re-engineered Electra 200 computer to be ready for delivery in June 1963.

This was the same deadline as had been attached to the completion of the first 'standard' Electra 100 five months earlier, that is shortly before the Instruments Electronics Automation Exhibition and before the decision to re-engineer the system was made. Selecting it, therefore, represented the application of commercial pressure once again.

Having come into contact with Evans on a number of previous

occasions and observed his formidable debating skill, the Production Programmer briefed himself well before organizing a meeting. He made careful calculations, based on average production times, of the implications of the Sales Manager's deadline, and working back from the despatch date found that Evans would have to start releasing detailed design information in two or three months' time. Even this would be tight and the Programmer's experience of new designs of the magnitude and complexity of the Electra 200 system told him that unless Evans could be persuaded to release provisional information almost immediately, either the deadline would have to be changed or there would be a series of crises.

The Programmer seems to have put his case for advance information persuasively, because Evans began authorizing the release of some provisional parts lists before the end of September and some provisional metalwork drawings during October. He said, however:

'It was much against my better judgement because I had had a bit of experience already of the way in which "provisional" information could scull around on the shop floor long after being superseded. But the pressure from the shop floor was tremendous, and the commercial deadline, while very tight, wasn't totally absurd and there wasn't much point in trying to get it formally altered at that early stage in the game. . . .'

As this account of the events of the spring, summer and early autumn of 1962 has shown, the process of modifying product objectives continued as crises occurred and pressures developed. But whereas beforehand the modification of these objectives had been closely linked with Brown's personal goals, they were now the outcome in the main of what amounted to a bargaining process between the Sales and Development sides of the business, with Sales becoming increasingly powerful in the wake of increasingly demanding market considerations.

REDEFINITION OF COMPANY OBJECTIVES

It was at about this point in time that the customer content of the tracer order first appeared on the scene. One of Electra's European sales representatives proposed to the Sales Manager and Alexander that the Poznan Trade Fair, scheduled to take place in June 1963, would be an ideal setting for the exhibition and guaranteed sales of the first re-engineered Electra 200. The idea was attractive; not least because the fair was sufficiently remote from the home market to permit the re-introduction of the initial refined system as 'a radically new product'. Authorization was quickly forthcoming, therefore, a specification was discussed and agreed, and the engineer who had been made responsible for the crash programme of saleable prototypes was delegated to supervise the computer's assembly.

Between that point and the start of the fieldwork for the tracer study, another series of events connected with the redefinition of Company objectives took place which had important implications for what happened later to the tracer.

Since its foundation soon after the War with a staff of two and a few hundred pounds capital, Electra had grown rapidly, building up to a turnover figure of several million pounds and a staff of well over a thousand. Growth had been the primary objective, and through several takeovers successive owners had accepted this objective and had been reasonably content to let top management run the business in its own way.

In October 1962, however, a report presented to the Chief Executive of the present Company showed that during the first nine months of 1962 there had been a considerable deficit, and that there seemed little hope of significant recovery during the remainder of the financial year.

The Chief Executive acted quickly. He sent for the Electra Ltd. Managing Director, and his two principal deputies, and after questioning them about the problems behind the figures and their prescriptions for recovery, made three decisions.

Firstly, Electra Ltd. from now on would focus on profit rather than growth as its primary objective. Secondly, the existing two Companies would be restructured as one, and thirdly, one of the deputies would be made responsible as Deputy Managing Director for the day-to-day implementation of the general policy of the new integrated Company.

Between October 1962 and February 1963 the Deputy Managing Director was fully occupied in dealing with the problems of reorganization and control. Gradually, however, he began finding time to make 'temporary but detailed excursions into different functions to see how the reorganized management team was approaching the tasks of integration and reform', to 'learn something about the computer side' with which he was not very familiar and 'to see if the approaches now being adopted were appropriate to the profit-first objective'.

o

In the course of one of these excursions he came into contact with the quotation for a very substantial order, involving four re-engineered Electra 200s, which was being handled on behalf of a customer (Customer X) who had already purchased a similar number of saleable prototypes of the 200 series. He made a point of following it through, even to the extent of becoming involved in the final negotiations. According to the Sales Engineer who was technically responsible for them: 'The negotiations benefited from his involvement in that they raised a number of problems connected with the firm's pricing policy and he was able to authorize the necessary adjustments more quickly than would have been the case under more normal circumstances.'

The spotlight was now on the 200 series and in particular on the order soon to be received from Customer X. From now on the pace quickened.

The effects of the reorganization had not been fully felt at the time the tracer study began, but two points were immediately clear to the research worker. The first was that in the Burns and Stalker terminology (1), the organizational structure was becoming less organic and more mechanistic, and the second was that top management was not only doing its best to devise a tighter although still predominantly personal system of control over design and production operations, but also seemed to be aware that in order to achieve tighter control, product objectives had to be made more stable and more explicit.

RESCHEDULING THE TRACER

This movement towards the more precise determination of objectives got under way as far as computer manufacture was concerned in March 1963; the Sales Manager met Alexander, the Computer Assembly Engineer, the Production Superintendent, the Production Programmer and two of the sales staff, to discuss the implications for the existing production programme of five orders for the Electra 200 series (including Customer X's order) which he and his sales engineers had obtained with some difficulty during the previous three months.

The Sales Manager began by listing the delivery dates which had been promised to these customers during the sales negotiations. These were spread at approximately monthly intervals between June and December. Then he invited comments.

The Production Programmer and the Computer Assembly

Engineer, who had both been given an indication of the content of the list beforehand, reacted by pointing out the circumstances that would make it difficult to meet some of the deadlines.

The Programmer indicated that the production programme was behind schedule for a variety of reasons, but mainly because of delays in completing the re-engineering of the coordinating module content of the computer. The earliest the Sales Division could expect the first delivery would be mid-June. Even this would mean a tight assembly programme, however, and it would therefore probably be wiser for the Sales people to re-negotiate the first deadline to allow for delivery at the end of June.

This postponement of the first delivery had two unpalatable implications. It would make it impossible to exhibit the computer at Poznan, because the equipment would not be ready for shipment at the end of May, and it would require the re-negotiation of all deadlines other than the one already agreed for the end of June.

At this point the Sales Manager expressed considerable frustration. He conceded that the Poznan scheme must now be abandoned but resented the cavalier attitude being shown towards commercial problems. Electra's leading competitor was currently offering a guaranteed three-month delivery of not very dissimilar computers, and if he was forced to adjust all his promises now by as much as a month, Electra Ltd. might lose some of the orders. Could not the Assembly Section 'double up' and start producing computers in parallel instead of in series as at present envisaged? Could not the Production Department rush through the first few modules from the present batches as soon as they were ready to enable the Model Shop to begin fitting and cableform manufacture 'that little bit earlier. . .'?

The discussion raged to and fro as a number of alternative ways of dealing with the problems were considered. Eventually, it was decided that the Poznan order should definitely be cancelled and its module allocation transferred practically *en bloc* to newly acquired orders. The delivery of the first completed Electra 200 would now go at the end of June to the customer with whom that date had been negotiated. This the factory would aim to complete in the middle of June. A second delivery should be promised for a fortnight later, and would actually take place two weeks after that. The third delivery, which would be the first of the second series of four computers ordered by Customer X, should be promised for the end of July and given absolutely top priority in line with the Managing Director's express wishes.

It can be seen that a bargaining process was still going on, but now there was a powerful force coming down on one side of the scale.

The decision to cancel the Poznan order had implications for the research worker, as well as for the personnel of Electra Ltd., since it obliterated the tracer that he had been following closely for three months. A choice lay open to him; he could select a completely new tracer, or follow the standard and coordinating modules that were to have gone into the Poznan computer into the order or orders to which they were to be transferred.

In the event, it was decided to transfer the modules almost entirely into the first Electra 200 making up Customer X's second order, and it was therefore appropriate for the research worker to pursue the latter course.

LAST MINUTE MODIFICATIONS

In May 1963, two months after this special planning meeting, a routine meeting of people involved directly in the assembly of Electra 200 computers was held to review progress on the sequence of outstanding orders; and the new tracer was 'raised' as an imminent work load for the first time. The meeting was distinguished from the others described in this chapter by the fact that the discussion focused not on strategic problems like the basic design of the computer or the overall shape of the production schedule, but on operational problems likely to affect the achievement of the objectives laid down in March. Doubts were expressed by one or two people about the realism of the deadlines attached to the tracer; these were waived aside, however, and the original dates re-emphasized strongly although it was accepted that work might have to be done on it after delivery. Thus, although right from the beginning of the assembly process the order began to run slightly late, there was no longer any doubt of what the time targets were.

This did not mean the product objectives had stabilized from a design point of view. During the eight weeks prior to delivery they were modified on numerous occasions, albeit usually to a small extent, in response to a galaxy of unforeseen circumstances. For example, in the light of his experience with the Electra 200s already installed on his premises, Customer X insisted that Electra should design and make a new cooling system and fit it into the tracer before it was delivered. A series of design changes to the coordinating modules of the 200s was sparked off during the assembly of the two computers immediately preceding the tracer in the production queue, and this not only made necessary technical modifications to the tracer's modules but added to the delays already accumulating for other reasons; this in turn encouraged the Computer Assembly Engineer to adjust the schedule.

In view of the history it was somewhat surprising that these product modifications did not lead to any radical change in the time target for the tracer product, particularly when towards the end of the manufacturing process it became apparent that Customer X had lost interest in the rapid delivery of the computer.

But by this time, on the organizational objectives level, the accommodation of the customer was no longer the main consideration. Time was now much more closely linked with money and it was left to the Deputy Managing Director of Electra Ltd. to provide the final time target—one which had important implications both for the computer activity and for the firm (2). Quoting what he said during a 'Deliveries Meeting' held on Tuesday, 6th August 1963:

'We don't half need the tracer in this period's figures, not just because without it the computer activity will be £20000 down on its target, but because our performance as a whole looks a bit sick. . . . Even if we deliver it next *Monday* (author's emphasis) we'll invoice this *Friday* and thereby squeeze it into the figures.'

On *Tuesday*, August 13th 1963, the tracer was lifted on to a lorry outside the despatch bay of Factory A. . . .

COMMENTARY—THE EVOLUTION OF OBJECTIVES

Because of its complexity, this story of the way that objectives evolved in relation to the tracer product has been difficult to present briefly or clearly. Readers with knowledge of the manufacture of complex electronic equipment will detect in this chapter many signs of a concern for clarity of exposition rather than for absolute accuracy of description. The account is patently incomplete, but enough information has been given to make it possible to highlight some of the features of this study that are significant in the context of both this book and the development of organization theory generally.

The data makes it very clear that 'objective-setting' is not always the simple and self-contained element in the control process implied in Eilon's cyclical model referred to in chapter 3 (3). In this study, objectives related to the technical, temporal and financial aspects of a product emerged initially in a vague form, changed several times during the gestation process in the light of experience or altered circumstances, became increasingly specific under various kinds of pressure, and only after many months crystallized to the point at which it became possible for the product to be delivered to its customer.

One of the most interesting aspects of this study centres on the implications of this evolution of product objectives for the other kinds of objectives relevant to the functioning of the organization. As suggested at the beginning of this chapter, these include what might be termed the overall organizational objectives, the some-times vague, sometimes very specific, statements of intent, formulated in relation to the direction of the organization as a whole, usually by the Chief Executive, or by one or more members of the top management team; the sectional objectives of the different reference groups within the organization; and finally the personal objectives—the more or less specific goals set for them-selves by individual members of the organization.

In the terminology of the ideas and concepts presented in Chapter 3 and illustrated in Fig. 3 Electra has provided an interesting contrast to the firm described by Klein in Chapter 5. In 'Four' Works there was complete separation between processes of designing and operating the production system. In Electra Ltd. there was a complex interaction between those processes, an interaction that at times amounted to total overlap. Another important difference between the two firms was that whereas in 'Four' Works product objectives remained stable over a long period of time while organizational, sectional and personal objectives revolved around other aspects of organizational function-ing, in Electra Ltd. the interactions between these various objec-tives resulted in new or modified product objectives.

The significance of this last point becomes clearer if the informa-tion presented in this chapter is compared with that presented in the preceding one. Hedley too (see Chapter 8) was concerned with objective-setting inside an organization and with the interplay between different personal and sectional interests. In the firm he studied, however, as in 'Four' Works, product objectives remained stable and the fact that some of the people and groups involved in the introduction of the computer had to ensure that there was a steady and continuous flow of products from the factory complicated the situation for them. In the long term it was probably inevitable that if the change in the system of control was successfully carried through, product objectives would have to be modified to fit the new system. In the short term, however, the bargaining process developing around the new system was not allowed to interfere with the current production task.

One of the outcomes of carrying out a tracer study in a firm like Electra Ltd. was the accumulation of a tremendous amount of detailed information about the objective-setting process which could be developed to a much greater extent than has been presented in this chapter. It would have been interesting, for example, to elaborate on the reciprocal relationship between the different types of objectives in the situation, or to show how the processes of information exchange, sounding, lobbying, bargaining, mediation, conciliation, arbitration and even coercion, become important at different points in the evolution of the objectives.

Fascinating as it was to study, the dangers of a situation in which current product objectives were so closely tied to other kinds of objectives were all too obvious. There were times during the field-work when it seemed that nothing was ever going to get to the point of being delivered to a customer; there were other times at which it became doubtful whether what might eventually be delivered would be what the customer originally wanted. This led the research worker to consider once again how an organization can be structured to operate effectively in such an innovative sphere. His impression was that the answer to the question may be even more complicated than is implied by Burns and Stalker (4).

The general if somewhat marginal shift of Electra's organizational structure towards the mechanistic end of the Burns and Stalker spectrum which began towards the end of 1962, appeared to have varying impacts on people working in different parts of the organization and at different points in the total manufacturing process. The changes in control procedures, managerial styles and philosophy associated with this shift were accepted and assimilated fairly readily by those associated closely with the more stable and routine module assembly activities. But they encountered resistance and stimulated evasive tactics among individuals and groups working on the less stable and less routine aspects of modular design and development and 'systems build'. This suggests that it may be necessary to adapt the structure of an organization to 'fit' the varying nature of the work which has to be done at different points in the manufacturing process and that more or less mechanistic arrangements may be appropriate simultaneously in different functional areas.

An organic system was undoubtedly appropriate in the early stage of the development activity, but this case study suggests that had the organizational structure of Electra Ltd. not become more mechanistic, in particular more authoritarian and less consultative, not only would the tracer have been less likely to leave the factory when it did, but also the whole computer activity could have been threatened.

References

1. Burns, T. and Stalker, G. M. (1961) *The Management of Innovation.* Tavistock Publications, London.
2. This is a clear instance of what might be called 'goal substitution'; cf. 'goal displacement' as described by Philip Selznick (1943), in An Approach to a Theory of Bureaucracy, *American Sociological Review*, 8(1), and 'goal succession' as described by Peter Blau (1956), in *Bureaucracy in Modern Society*, Random House, New York.
3. Eilon, S. (1962) Problems in Studying Management Control, *International Journal of Production Research*, 1(4).
4. Burns, T. and Stalker, G. M. Op. cit. (See Ref. (1) above.)

ROSEMARY CROMPTON
DOROTHY WEDDERBURN

10 Technological Constraints and Workers' Attitudes*

In 1965 the authors of this chapter were collecting data about the attitudes and behaviour of industrial workers on a large site belonging to a major national Company. This was part of a wider study to compare the attitudes of manual and non-manual workers to differences in their terms and conditions of employment. The Seagrass site consisted of a number of distinct Works, employing widely differing technologies and producing a number of different products. When the attitude data was analysed differences were found between the Works. These appeared to be associated with differences of technology. The association was such as might have been predicted from the earlier work of industrial sociologists such as Blauner (1) and Woodward (2). Operators in continuous flow process production plants were generally more satisfied with their jobs than were those working in a machine-minding setting.

At this point one of the authors moved to Imperial College and became involved in the discussions being conducted around the research results presented in the present volume. It was therefore decided to try and use the concepts presented in Chapters 1 and 3 to explain the differences found at Seagrass. As will be seen later the labour force in the three Works on the site to which this chapter refers was relatively homogeneous in terms of social characteristics and orientation to work, and thus it seemed reasonable to look for explanations of the differences in attitudes within the

* Based on material fully reported in Dorothy Wedderburn and Rosemary Crompton, *Workers' Attitudes and Technology—a case study*, Cambridge University Press, forthcoming, 1969. The study was financed by a grant from the Social Science Research Council to the Department of Applied Economics, Cambridge.

work situation itself. The first step, therefore, was to examine the nature of the differences in the constraints and facilities arising from the technology and from selected aspects of the administrative systems in the different Works. Secondly, the consequences of these constraints and facilities for the operators were examined. Thirdly, an attempt was made to identify the effects of the differences in the system of control in the three Works upon the tasks of the operators and the role of first line supervisors.

THE SEAGRASS SITE

At the time of the research Seagrass was a large site of about 900 acres on which were employed over 10000 workers. The site had been continually developing over the last seventeen years. On it were five main and distinct Works. All of them were chemical Works but they produced commodities ranging from petro-chemicals, which were the raw materials of further chemical processes, to yarn and staple fibre—the raw materials of the textile trade. The individual Works were managed by separate Product Divisions of the Company to which the site belonged. Some Divisions controlled Works located on other sites, and in every case the Divisional Headquarters was located off this particular site.

The pattern of production and marketing in each Works was the responsibility of the Division concerned and in one sense therefore it seemed as though various Works on the Seagrass site belonged to separate firms. But all Divisions were governed by the overall economic policy of the Company (for example, decisions about large-scale capital expenditure were taken at Company, not Divisional level) and, most important for the present discussion, the Company's basic labour policy was applied throughout the site. This policy was planned and negotiated with the appropriate trade unions at Company level. Thus the Company bonus system, the Company job grading system, and the Company pay levels, were uniformly applied. There were informal opportunities for some bending of such Company policies to suit local circumstances, although considerable importance was attached centrally to the maintenance of uniformity. The responsibility for the application and coordination of this common labour policy rested with one of the Divisions that had a Works on the site. This Division was also responsible for the administration of the site and for the provision of common services to all the Works. The individual Works were therefore operating against a common background of policy and services; this had particular significance for the study of the attitudes and behaviour of the operators in the different Works.

THE PRODUCTION SYSTEMS IN THE THREE WORKS

Three of the five Works on the site were selected for further study. In 1965 the smallest, Works A, employed 392 general workers, who with few exceptions were working continuous shifts. Within the complex which made up Works A there were eight separate and physically distinct plants which between them produced twelve different products. Works A was an example of a 'pure' continuous process Works, within the terms of Blauner's definition (3): 'There are no recognizable machines and very few workers visible. . . . The flow of materials; the combination of different chemicals; and the temperature, pressure and speed of the processes are regulated by automatic control devices.' The plants on this Works ran continuously for a year or more.

All of the products of Works A were liquid or gaseous and were piped away. Except when sampling, the operators never saw a raw material or an end product. Over two-thirds of them were engaged in tasks which involved the monitoring of equipment, the reading of dials and charts and the adjustment of valves or furnaces. These tasks were performed in the control room of the plants, or outside among the structures of pipes and columns. A group of ancillary workers, tradesmen's mates, riggers, slingers, laboratory testers, etc., serviced the different plants. About a quarter of the output of the Works was piped to other Works on the site, and about forty per cent was sold to Works belonging to the parent Company but located elsewhere; the remainder was sold on the market.

Works B was also selected as a continuous flow chemical Works, but further study revealed certain differences from Works A. Works B consisted of five distinct plants concerned with production. In four of these plants the process was continuous in the sense that raw materials (which were obtained from Works A) were fed in at the beginning of the process and there was a continuous flow of product at the end. In Works B the product was solid in a granular form and a number of variations on the basic product were produced. Changes of product could result in the whole process stopping and restarting: this could happen as often as once a week. Moreover, owing to the nature of the process, more frequent minor unscheduled stoppages could occur. The fifth plant on Works B manufactured a different product from the other four, but in 1965 accounted for only five per cent of total employment in the Works.

There was a large finishing and warehousing section where the Works B products were graded, bagged and packed prior to sale. Most of these sales were to customers outside the Company although the Company remained the Works' largest single customer. The total number of general workers employed in Works B in 1965 was 670—and as in Works A most of them were working shifts. Nearly half were engaged on the chemical process, a quarter in the finishing sections and a quarter in ancillary jobs as in Works A. In the warehouse the job consisted mainly of filling, bagging and loading. At the end of the chemical process, men operated machines for chopping the polymer, whereas the men on the chemical process itself were engaged in monitoring jobs of a kind very similar to those performed by the operators in Works A.

Both Works A and Works B were handling highly inflammable materials. Therefore, strict safety regulations had to be enforced to control smoking and the wearing of protective clothing as well as the way in which maintenance operations were conducted. Failure to comply with these regulations could result in dismissal.

Works C was distinctly unlike either Works A or Works B. The production began with a chemical process, which manufactured twenty varieties of a product, in form not unlike that produced in Works B. The main chemical process involved the use of eleven similar trains of equipment, each train operating on a batch basis with a batch cycle of approximately six hours. Consecutive runs of the same variety could be made for a week or more before change-over. The solid product was chopped and bagged, as in Works B, and some marketed at this stage. But the major part continued for further processing either in the filament yarn or staple fibre section of the Works. Here the product was extruded and spun into yarn. In the staple fibre section, the yarn, once processed, was drawn and chopped into short lengths, and the fibre was despatched to the customer in large bales. In the filament yarn section the spun yarn was also drawn and wound on bobbins on frames similar to those in use in the cotton industry. The resulting bobbins passed through a fairly large inspection section before despatch. Between fifty and sixty different types of staple fibre, and eight different types of yarn were marketed. Variations in product, particularly on the filament yarn side, could, as will be shown later, have considerable impact upon the nature of the operators' work.

Works C was the largest of the three Works. In 1965 over 2200 general workers were employed in the Works, and most were shift workers. Eighteen per cent were in the chemical process section. Many of the tasks here were of the monitoring kind described in Works A, but there were also jobs such as machine-minding at the chopping and bagging stage. A fifth of the general workers were in the staple fibre section and nearly half in the filament yarn section. Here the jobs were machine minding and thus machine paced. In the draw twist area of the filament yarn section for instance, the operators had to string up the machines, patrol them, and doff the bobbins when they were full. The remaining jobs in Works C were of an ancillary kind, as in Works A and Works B.

DIFFERENCES OF ATTITUDES AND BEHAVIOUR BETWEEN THE THREE WORKS

A sample of fifty general workers in each of the three Works was interviewed about their attitudes to various aspects of their employment situation.* These attitudes can be discussed under five main headings: attitudes towards the Company as an employer; towards senior management on the site; towards immediate supervision; towards the job itself; and towards pay and fringe benefits. The detailed questions and results are presented in the main report of the survey. The object of this chapter is to summarize and pinpoint the most important areas of similarity and differences between the three Works studied.

(a) *Attitudes towards the Company*
In their attitudes towards the Company as an employer there was little difference between the workers in the three Works. In all three emphasis was placed upon security (both of employment and of maintenance of income through fringe benefits) as being a good feature of employment at Seagrass. Criticisms were of bad management in a general sense and of the impersonality of the organization. The people interviewed were not asked to rate the Company as an employer by comparison with other employment. Therefore there is no simple means of summarizing whether the general attitudes to the Company were 'favourable' or 'unfavourable'. But, by and large, it can be said that, despite some very real and vocal criticism,

* The main survey material also included general workers in the other two Works on the Seagrass site, as well as craftsmen. But the discussion in this chapter relates only to general workers in Works A, B and C.

there was an underlying degree of contentment and indeed positive enthusiasm shared by all three Works about some aspects of the Company as an employer.

(b) *Attitudes towards senior management*

The three works were also alike in expressing considerable dissatisfaction with management/worker relations in general. However, we found that many more of the men in Works A actually had contact with a member of senior management than in the other two Works and there were correspondingly more complaints that there was too little contact with management from Works B and Works C.

When asked for suggestions for improving management/worker relations, however, men in Works A and Works B were alike in putting most emphasis upon face to face contact with management on and off the job. They said they wanted more mixing socially, less status consciousness and more visits by management to the shop floor. These suggestions were also made by some of the men in Works C, but there the critics put emphasis on the need for easier *access* to management—not necessarily by visits to the shop floor— and for better communications generally.

For purposes of comparison with other research the question was asked:

> 'Here are two opposing views about industry generally. Some people say that a firm is like a football side—because good teamwork means success and is to everyone's advantage. Others say that teamwork in industry is impossible—because employers and men are really on opposite sides. Which view do you agree with more?'

Willener (4) has suggested that this question reveals whether men see employer/worker relations in fundamentally 'oppositional' or 'co-operational' terms. Only a little over half of the Works C general workers answered in 'teamwork' terms compared with about four-fifths of workers in Works A and Works B. In this area, therefore, some differences in attitudes were already emerging.

(c) *Attitudes towards supervision*

These differences were carried further by a study of the men's attitudes towards their immediate supervision (in most cases the assistant foreman). In all three Works, personal relations with the supervisor were said to be good. But in Works C nearly half of the sample said their supervisor lacked authority, whereas only seventeen per cent in Works A expressed this view. Similarly nearly half of the men in Works C compared with only nineteen per cent of the men in Works A said the right men were not chosen as supervisors. The attitude of the men in Works B fell in between. In discussing the qualities needed in supervisors, only a third of the Works C men mentioned personal qualities of leadership and the ability to organize whereas more than two-thirds of the Works A and B respondents emphasized these qualities.

(d) *Attitudes towards the work task*
A similar pattern of contrast was found between the views of the men in Works A and those in Works C in relation to the job itself. On this occasion the attitudes of the men in Works B fell much closer to those of the men in Works C. Nearly three-quarters of Works A respondents found their jobs interesting compared with only thirty-nine per cent and twenty-six per cent respectively in Works B and Works C. A large majority of Works A men said that there was nowhere else on the site or plant where they would prefer to work. But some groups in both Works A and Works C expressed a preference for another job either on the site or within their own plant.

(e) *Attitudes to pay and fringe benefits*
A matter of prime importance for any worker and one which may well colour his other views of the job is the level of pay. On the Seagrass site a system of job appraisal was operating which allocated each job to a category from zero to fourteen. These categories carried an hourly differential above the basic rate. The distribution of job categories in a Works was dictated by the technical process itself, and some Works carried a higher proportion of high category jobs. At the same time, although a bonus norm of twenty-seven per cent of basic pay was operating in all the Works, certain groups of workers were able to earn above this, while in other cases earnings could fall below this norm because of variations in the opportunity to earn bonus. The opportunities to work overtime and extra shifts also varied from time to time between Works. In the period immediately before the fieldwork, overtime working had been markedly higher in Works C than in the other two Works. It was therefore quite possible for the distribution of earnings to vary between the Works.

In fact this was the position at the time of the research. Earnings in Works A and B were very similar. About a third of the men in both Works were earning more than twenty pounds a week, and rather more than a half between seventeen and twenty pounds. In Works C, however, twenty-two per cent of the men were earning more than twenty-five pounds per week and thirty per cent between twenty and twenty-five pounds. Not surprisingly, therefore, we found that men in Works C were less critical of their pay than men in the other two Works. Works C men more often than men in the other two Works, tended to express the view that there were no other firms in the neighbourhood which would pay more. These differences between the Works did not appear in attitudes to the other economic aspects of employment, i.e. the Company pension and sick pay schemes, the terms of which were highly approved by men in all Works.

Differences in Behaviour

In Chapter 1, six categories of overt behaviour are identified. It is difficult in an attitude survey to collect evidence to enable examples of behaviour to be classified and compared by this system. Attention has most often been directed to the category of constraint-evasive behaviour because here certain measurable indicators are often available, although their precise significance may be disputed. It was possible to obtain figures for comparing the turnover rates, absentee rates and incidence of industrial disputes for the three Works. As far as turnover was concerned, there was little difference between the Works, and they all shared in the general rise which applied to the Seagrass site in the period 1964–66 and which coincided with a general improvement in the employment situation in the area. As turnover on the site rose, absenteeism declined. But absenteeism was consistently higher (over the period 1964–66), in Works C than in Works A and Works B. As for industrial disputes, apart from a general overtime ban in operation for from two to three months in the period 1964–66, Works A and Works B had none which affected the production workers. Works C not only shared in the overtime ban but in addition had nine walk-outs most of which were centred on bonus issues.

SUMMARY OF ATTITUDES AND BEHAVIOUR

As the data has shown the main contrast in attitudes and in the limited aspects of behaviour that could be studied was between the pure continuous-flow process Works, Works A, and the batch production Works, Works C. The differences centred not on the general attitudes towards the Company or management in general, but upon the supervisory system, the work task and the extent to which the samples in the two Works took a co-operational or a conflict view of the firm. Moreover, Works C personnel showed a higher absentee rate and a greater proneness to indulge in grievance activity than those in Works A. Somewhat surprisingly Works B fell between the two extremes. As a Works with a large element of chemical process production, a simple relationship between technology and attitudes would have led us to expect a closer resemblance to Works A. The men in Works B certainly took a co-operational view of the firm more often than Works C men, but they were closer to Works C in their views about the lack of interest of their job and in their criticism of supervision.

THE BACKGROUND OF THE MEN IN THE THREE WORKS

It was important at this point to see whether the differences of attitude and behaviour could be attributed to differences in the workers' prior orientation to work rather than to variations in the actual work situation in which they found themselves (5). Different groups of workers, it has been argued, expect different satisfactions from work, and have a different ordering of these satisfactions. The ordering is influenced to a considerable extent by factors external to their current work situation. These may include the nature of the local community, the values transmitted to the worker by his family and his social milieu, his own experience of social mobility, etc. To the extent that a worker has any choice of employment, it is presumed that he will select that occupation or job which most nearly satisfies his personal order of needs. Thus there may be a process of self-selection through which workers with similar needs converge, and this could itself then be reflected in different patterns of attitudes and behaviour within a particular organization. On the other hand, differences of attitude and behaviour may reflect differences in the extent to which expectations are more or less satisfied by different work situations.

One indirect indication of the existence of different expectations from work could be the extent to which the social characteristics of the workers in the three Works differed (6). Differences of background between the three groups did exist but were very limited. Between seventy and eighty per cent of the total sample had lived in the area all their lives and between thirty and forty

P

per cent had never moved outside the immediate locality in which they were born. The general area in which they were living could be characterized as a homogeneous working-class area. A network of kin and friends had played its part in bringing the men to work on the site. The area had fared badly in the depression of the 1930's, and until the middle sixties the unemployment rate was twice the national average. Most workers, therefore, either directly or indirectly through their families and neighbours, had probably had experience of what unemployment meant. This could account to a large extent for the emphasis that all respondents put on the importance of the 'security' that they felt the Company offered. The tradition of trade unionism in the area was strong and the Seagrass site had something of a reputation within the Company as a 'militant' or 'difficult' site, although, as will be seen in the main report of the study, the general workers here were possibly less responsible for this reputation than were the craftsmen.

There were some small differences in the age distribution of the sample between the Works. The proportion of respondents who were over forty-five at the time of the interview was similar, about thirty per cent. But Works C had thirty-five per cent below the age of thirty compared with only seventeen per cent in Works A. Because they were on average younger, more Works C men had dependent children, and were buying their houses with a mortgage. On the other hand, the distribution of the samples by length of service was very similar. Previous job experience was also similar. Two-thirds had been in semi-skilled or unskilled manual jobs before coming to Seagrass. One small difference was that twenty per cent of the Works C sample, compared with seventeen per cent of Works B and thirteen per cent of Works A, had last been employed in white-collar or supervisory jobs.

Thus there were some differences in social characteristics between the samples in the three Works. However, from our evidence it seems unlikely that they arose as a result of men with particular sets of characteristics selecting for themselves particular jobs in the different Works. This would have involved two stages of job selection; first coming to work on the Seagrass site at all; second obtaining work in a particular Works.

There is no doubt that many men 'chose' to work at Seagrass because of the security the Company offered, although until shortly before the survey the general choice of jobs in the area was, as already indicated, extremely limited. The development of the Seagrass site was in itself an important extension of job choice. However, the chances of the men coming to the Seagrass site and being able to choose which of the Works they wished to be employed in, had been very slight until recently.

From the beginning the Company had used a system of common recruitment to site employment for general workers. Once recruited the men went to a labour pool from which they were then selected for one particular Works. In theory, therefore, a man could not present himself at Seagrass saying: 'I wish to work in Works A rather than in Works C.' It appears that of late, however, a man wishing to go to a particular Works would be unlikely to be turned down if he were at all suitable.

Until about 1963, however, there was a buyers' market for labour and there was little pressure to deviate from the labour pool system. As the recruitment of labour has become more difficult, there has been a tendency towards direct recruitment to an individual Works. For example in the period 1960–64 an average of twenty per cent of new recruits to Works A, thirty per cent to Works B and forty-five per cent to Works C came from direct recruitment. But despite this trend, the bulk of the labour force, at the time of the research, had come via the labour pool and its common recruitment policy.

The theoretical policy of the labour pool was to send men from it, in turn, to fill casual vacancies, or for interview for a vacancy in a Works with a view to permanency. The Works had their own rudimentary systems of selection. For example Works C did not normally accept men over thirty-five for the filament yarn section because it was felt that manual dexterity decreases with age. On the other hand, they tried to get men with rather higher levels of intelligence for the chemical process areas. Works A might test an applicant for his ability to do simple decimal calculations by asking him to calculate odds on horses, on the principle that if he could do that, he could also read the panels in the control room. But in practice, according to management, few men had been rejected. Many of the sample were not aware that they had in fact ever been on the labour pool complement because on recruitment they had been sent to a Works and had stayed there permanently.

Thus in practice there was some element of selection. But this was not exercised so much by the men themselves as first by the foreman of the labour pool selecting men for interview by the Works, and subsequently by Works management. For instance the younger age of the men in Works C was largely to be explained by the selection policy of management.

DIFFERENCES IN ORIENTATION TO WORK

Different social characteristics may be indications of the existence of differing expectations from work. As Goldthorpe (7) has suggested, young men with families to support and mortgages to meet may be more concerned with pay levels than older men. However, some more direct evidence was obtained of the sample's orientation to work. Respondents were asked to name the three most important things which in their view made a job a good one. In all three Works good physical working conditions came first, and money second, both being a long way ahead of other factors. The reasons given for coming to work at Seagrass confirmed the view that the men in all three Works were alike in what they wanted in their jobs. At least forty per cent gave 'security' as their reason for taking the job. Interestingly, however, more of the Works A men went to Seagrass because it was simply 'a job' or for the money, while more Works C men went because of the prospects or because Seagrass was 'a good firm to work for'.

Similar proportions in all three Works had generally favourable attitudes towards their union and participated in elections for union officers and attended branch meetings. Nor was there any evidence that Works A or Works B men were more achievement orientated than Works C men. The men's assessment of their chances of promotion were similar in the three Works, and similar proportions wanted promotion. Thus the differences found between the Works in the 'co-operational' or 'conflict' view of industry do not appear to reflect any basically different orientations to trade unions or to promotion.

From this data it appeared that the men in all three Works were primarily concerned with the 'extrinsic' rewards from work. In terms of security and good working conditions they seemed to have found what they wanted at Seagrass. In terms of money, however, it was Works A and Works B men who were disappointed, yet they were the workers who displayed more favourable 'shop floor' attitudes and behaviour. Works C men, who were most satisfied in terms of money, were the dissatisfied group in terms of both job interest and supervision.

These external characteristics of the labour force have been discussed at some length in order to explain why the further analysis was concentrated upon an exploration of those aspects of technology and of the control system which might be linked with the differences of attitude and behaviour which had been found.

Although it is not disputed that external factors like age and degree of family responsibility play a part in influencing work attitudes and behaviour, the difference between the men in the three Works cannot be adequately explained in this way. The size of the sample restricted the amount of analysis possible but attitudes to supervision and job interest within the three Works were examined in relation to two broad age groups. Nonetheless between the Works differences remained. Within Works there were some differences between the two age groups—above and below thirty. The more critical attitudes of the men in Works C were common to both age groups and conversely, the greater degree of satisfaction in Works A was felt by both age groups. This seems to suggest, therefore, that in this case age was not very important in influencing attitudes. On the other hand, it is possible that the greater financial responsibilities of the Works C men did play a part in explaining the behaviour which arose out of their expression of greater dissatisfaction. It seems possible that failing to find any intrinsic satisfaction from work, the maintenance of a satisfactory position on pay became doubly important; hence the number of walk-outs by the Works C men over bonus disputes. The converse would be that in Works A, although the men were also primarily concerned with pay and disappointed because they judged it to be relatively low, in the absence of family pressures they found interesting work and satisfactory supervision adequate compensation, at least temporarily. To examine this possibility further it was necessary to explore the characteristics of the technology and the control systems operating in the three Works.

THE TWO LEVELS OF THE TECHNICAL SYSTEM

THE TECHNOLOGY

Studies by sociologists and psychologists (8) in identifying those elements of the work task which are likely to be linked to the expression of favourable or unfavourable attitudes, were used in the analysis of the differences in the constraints and facilities afforded by the technologies of the three Works. The most important elements identified were the variety of tasks the operator had to perform, the degree of discretion he had in the performance of the tasks, and in the pace of work, the amount of freedom of movement away from and around the work position, the possibilities of social interaction with other operators on the job, the operator's perception of the responsibility of the task and the physical working conditions in which he carried out his job.

Workers in all three Works had been alike in saying that the most important aspect of a job was good physical working conditions. In general the workers in all three Works had compared their physical working conditions at Seagrass favourably with their earlier industrial experience. But in fact the different work tasks were carried out in differing physical conditions even within the same Works.

The most pleasant working conditions were undoubtedly to be found in Works A. Operators in the chemical process areas were less fortunate, marginally in Works B and certainly in Works C. This was not because of any difference of standards but because the nature of the process, and the greater variety of products being manufactured in Works B and Works C dictated these differences. Most of the workers operating in a machine-minding setting had more noise to contend with than most chemical process operators. The spinning and draw twist operators in the filament yarn section of Works C had the most unpleasant working conditions. These men were working in clean surroundings, but the atmosphere was humid and the noise of the machines so great that to communicate with one another was very difficult. Thus the variations in physical working conditions were of such a kind that they could clearly contribute to the satisfaction we found in Works A and to the discontent in Works C.

There was little doubt that the operators in Works A were carrying out the kind of tasks that other social scientists have considered contribute to satisfaction on the part of the operators. It is true that some writers, in discussing the effects of automation, have suggested that tasks which require the monitoring of dials, etc., are very boring. But the operator in the control room in Works A had a number of monitoring tasks to perform, and some discretion as to precisely when and in which sequence they were performed. Moreover, when all was going well and there was no breakdown, he had great freedom to vary the pace of work, and to move about. As one assistant foreman interviewed said: 'That's one thing about working here, you're not tied to the job like on an assembly line—a man can take a smoke or a break if he wants it.'

Much has been written about the chemical process operator's

sense of responsibility for the maintenance of the process. Although there is no direct evidence of this in the attitude survey results, indications of this feeling were obtained from general observation and discussion. The men in Works A were more conscious of their identity as chemical workers than the other workers on the site. They were more interested in the idea of a chemical workers' union because, as they put it: 'each trade should have its own union'. They also placed more emphasis upon the importance of adequate training for the job, which suggests that they took some pride in their technical competence. All men in Works A were trained to do two or three jobs so that continuous operation could be ensured in case of sickness, accident or holidays. In addition there was always the possibility of training for more jobs and for higher category jobs when vacancies occurred, and a few exceptional operators would be familiar with as many as twelve jobs. This not only enabled the men to understand how their work fitted in with that of other people, but it also offered prospects of betterment, within the limits of the job category system on the Seagrass site.

But why did the same considerations not apply to chemical operators' tasks in Works B and Works C? The actual work of monitoring and recording was the same, and there were also some possibilities of promotion to more responsible higher category jobs. But in both Works B and Works C the chemical operators had less discretion to vary the time or the pace at which they carried out their tasks, and they had less freedom of movement. The chemical process in Works B was far more complicated than that in Works A and it demanded more constant attention from the operators since a greater number of variables had to be controlled. At the time of the fieldwork increasing automation was putting even more pressure on the operator. Equally important in Works B and Works C, the more frequent changes of product allowed less discretion for the chemical process operator. For example a change-over on a plant in Works B could mean that operators were moved temporarily to another part of the plant. This interfered with the development of their routine and rhythm of work. In Works C the chemical process was less fully automated than in either Works A or Works B, and the operator had to perform transfers semi-manually and at specific but variable times according to the nature of the product. This limited both his discretion to vary the order and his freedom of movement.

Furthermore there are different ways in which freedom of

movement and opportunities for social interaction may be provided
by different technologies. An illustration is supplied by comparing
two other groups of workers, those in the warehouse of Works B
who were packing and bagging the product, and the filament yarn
inspectors of Works C. The work in the warehouse, unautomated
at the time of the fieldwork, was completely routine and unskilled.
Men filled, sewed and palleted sacks of the product on moving conveyor belts. They had some control of their pace or work within
the limits set by the belt, but there was no variety in the way in
which the tasks could be performed. On the other hand it was
possible to stop the lines altogether so that all the men on a shift
could take a smoke or a meal break together.

In the inspection department in Works C the work also appeared
extremely routine. Each bobbin of yarn had to be held up to a
bright light to inspect for flaws, weighed to check it was the
correct size, wrapped in tissue paper and then packed in boxes.
There was room for the operators to develop a special, although
limited, skill which enabled them to detect flaws, unnoticeable
even to other experienced men in the Works. But social interaction was limited because the operators were sitting in partly
enclosed cubicles. Nor was there any variety in the job. On the other
hand, individuals could vary the pace of their work, and in particular could build up banks of work so that they could start late or
finish early. Here too, it was possible for the men to stop work
together for breaks.

Without doubt, the jobs which scored lowest on almost all
elements listed in the first paragraph of this section were those in
the staple fibre and filament yarn area of Works C. In the staple
fibre area the extruded molten polymer was passed continuously
through a series of machines which stretched, crimped, dyed and
finally chopped and baled the yarn. The operators controlled these
machines. In the spinning area there were three basic jobs—the
pack operator (the man handling the polymer), the spinner and the
doffer. Some variety had been introduced by rotating the men
between the three tasks, so that they spent four weeks spinning,
two weeks doffing and one week as pack operator. Incidentally,
this meant a higher job category for the men in this section because they could do three jobs. The men worked as a team and
there was some social interaction on the job. On the other hand,
the machines were running continuously except when the product
was changed, or there was a breakdown, and so they could not be

left unattended. A small degree of flexibility was allowed because the pack operator was able to build up a reserve and this enabled him to relieve other members of the team occasionally. But by comparison with the chemical process operators in all Works, there was little discretion or freedom of movement. The processing side of the staple fibre area was very similar, except that here the men on the three main jobs, the baler operator, the cutter operator, and the draw frame operator, were not rotated. These jobs were positions on a limited hierarchy of increasing skill, through which men could be promoted.

Freedom to interact socially, to move around and to vary the pace of work was lowest of all, however, in the filament yarn area of Works C. In both the spinning and draw twist areas continuous close attention to the routine operation of machine tending was required if the quality of the product was to be maintained. For instance, if one of the holes in the spinneret was feeding through an irregular thickness of yarn this had to be detected immediately, otherwise the fault might not be discovered until the yarns came to be knitted or dyed. The pace of work of the spinner was therefore dictated by the pace of the machine and by the nature of the product, that is finer or coarser yarn. He patrolled his machine, doffing the bobbins at precisely defined times to ensure constant and correct weight. He was isolated from other operators and had to be continuously on the alert for mishaps. Once he had become a trained spinner there was no other job to which he could be promoted.

The work in the draw twist area was very similar and the same factors applied. There was no freedom of movement. It was necessary to be constantly on the alert for breaks in the yarn, and to doff and restring the bobbin. The draw twist area was made up of a number of rooms in each of which about forty men worked. The quality and type of machine varied between the rooms, and at the time of the fieldwork the shifts were rotated between the rooms, in order to even out the opportunities for working on the better machines or better qualities of yarn. This meant that the men did not necessarily know who would take over from them at the end of the shift. In this situation it was easy to succumb to the temptation of doffing the bobbins early. This could lead to the next bobbin becoming over full and to the jamming of the machine at the beginning of the next shift, an added source of irritation for the operators. There were no job rotation or promotion possibilities for the men in the draw twist area.

Combining the physical working conditions and the nature of the work task, the contrast in attitudes between Works A, where most of the men were chemical process operators, and Works C, where most of the men worked in the filament yarn and staple fibre area, was not surprising. A frequently expressed view was that the monotonous work in the textile area of Works C, with its overwhelming demands for surface attention and its restriction of movement, was really 'woman's work'. In fact women were not employed only because of the legal regulation of shift working.

The important differences in the requirements of the production tasks in Works A and Works C were the product of their very different technologies. At a more detailed level of examination, important differences in the production tasks of Works A and Works B could also be identified, which might provide an explanation of the apparently deviant position of the Works B men in their attitude to the interest of their work.

THE CONTROL SYSTEM

But what of the control system defined as in Chapter 3? The control system at Seagrass was not studied in the same detail as in the firms to which the previous chapters relate. But operators are most likely to be concerned with the mechanisms which are devised to check on the quantity and quality of their output. It was decided therefore to select for special study the bonus system and the quality control system and study the impact of these systems on operators in the different Works.

The bonus system

In the terminology of this book, bonus systems can be regarded as impersonal administrative mechanisms of control over quantity and/or quality of production. As such they are generally most effective in manufacturing situations where the operator himself can influence these two variables. Of course, even in such situations they do not always have the desired effect, for operators may not respond in the expected way to the incentive offered. Moreover, other features of the administrative system, formal or informal, may work in the opposite direction and erode the expected effects of the bonus system. But in many branches of the chemical industry the technical process itself and the design of the plant, rather than the operator, controls the rate, and, to a large extent, the quality of production. Thus the way in which a bonus system operates is closely linked to the technology.

The bonus schemes at Seagrass conformed to a Company pattern, and covered such diverse activities as the individualistic inspection operations in Works C, where the pace and quality of work depended entirely on the operator, and the essentially teamwork process-controlled tasks in Works A. A multi-factor bonus scheme had been introduced shortly before the attitude survey. It was based upon calculations of inputs of measured work together with allowances for other factors such as quality of output. Where appropriate, bonus was awarded on a group basis and, by agreement with the trade unions concerned, the 'norm' or standard rate of bonus earnings was set at twenty-seven per cent of a man's basic earnings in his particular job category.

The consequences of the bonus system upon the level of bonus earnings and upon the weekly fluctuations in earnings varied considerably according to the nature of the technology. This is illustrated by the experience of three different groups of workers; the chemical process workers in all three Works, the men in the warehouse of Works B, and in the inspection groups in Works C, and finally the machine operators in Works C.

In Works A the bonus team was a group of chemical process men (between two and four) working under an assistant foreman. These men could be operating either a plant, or a discrete part of a plant. The main elements of the work were the reading of dials, making adjustments, etc. Bonus levels could vary between bonus teams, although such variations did not always appear justified to the men because the differences between the inputs of measured work were imperceptible to them. But in any case the variations in bonus were small both between groups and from week to week. Bonus earnings were not related to output and in cases of breakdown a 'lieu bonus' was paid. Thus a common general source of criticism of bonus systems in process production—that the pay is lowest when the men are having to work hardest, as they do when a breakdown occurs—was avoided.

In the chemical plants of Works B variations in bonus payments between different groups of operators had been eliminated by treating all the plants as one bonus group, thus the same bonus was paid to all operators. For the same reasons as in Works A, bonus payments in the chemical area of Works B showed little variation from week to week.

The chemical area of Works C had a system of bonus payments rather like that in Works A—men were organized in bonus teams operating different parts of the plant. In this batch chemical process some effort was made to control the quantity of output by basing one part of the bonus calculations on the number of batches produced. However, the actual speed of production of batches depended more on the nature of the product and the process, and only marginally on the speed with which an operator could turn valves to empty tanks, and clean them out, so that the weight given to this factor was relatively small and fluctuations in bonus earnings, although perhaps greater than in Works A, were also small.

In the warehouse and finishing section of Works B, each shift constituted a bonus team. The main criterion for bonus payments was the number of bags packed per shift. The operators in the warehouse could control the rate of production by their pace of working, and therefore had a high degree of control over their bonus rate, and so it could rise above the twenty-seven per cent standard. The inspection area of Works C had a bonus system very similar to that of the warehouse and finishing section of Works B. Bonus was linked to output (that is the number of bobbins inspected) and the bonus group comprised the number of men working on a particular shift. The rate of production depended entirely on the individual operators and, as in the warehouse and finishing section of Works B, bonus earnings above the norm were not uncommon.

The biggest variations in bonus arose, however, in the staple fibre, and more especially, the filament yarn areas of Works C. In the staple fibre section the two main areas of production—spinning and processing—constituted two bonus teams. Movements, cleaning, amount of output and quality were taken into account when calculating bonus rates. Men would therefore lose bonus if the machines broke down, or if faults arose in the quality of the product. On the other hand, the constraints of the production system (that is the rate at which the machines were running) did not allow upward variation above the standard of twenty-seven per cent. In practice, because of the large size of the bonus teams in this particular area, losses often tended to even themselves out. Thus, although there was more weekly variation in bonus than in any of the chemical process areas, the variations were still not excessive.

In the filament yarn area, output and quality were again important components of bonus calculations. In the spinning area the bonus team was the shift team. Variations in the product presented the operators with different kinds of problems. Fine yarns were more likely to break, but heavy ones had to be doffed more frequently. Other variations also affected the bonus. It was the frequent changeovers of the machines from one type of product to another that had most effect. Production credits could be lost on the changeover shift while men on the next shift could gain despite the fact that they did not have to work as hard as the men who had changed the machines.

In the draw twist area a man's bonus group was determined both by the particular shift on which he was working and by the product he was making. So the size of a bonus group varied between one man and twenty. The complex system of rotation from room to room already referred to, had been introduced in an attempt to distribute fairly access to both 'better' machines and better bonus paying products. But bonus earnings could still vary considerably and they were particularly sensitive to the faults of the individual operator.

Thus the bonus in Works A and, to a large extent in Works B, was insensitive to the demand of the production system, and varied little. Within the main areas of Works C it was fairly sensitive not only to the efforts of the operator but also to the variety and type of product. Despite these differences the majority of the operators in all three Works were critical of the bonus scheme and almost as many critics were found in Works A as in Works C. The main criticism was the inadequacy of the method of calculation, and in particular that the bonus did not give enough weight to what the men considered to be the most important things, like the volume of production. But although the men in all three Works were critical, it was only in Works C that the bonus system became an issue around which grievance activity developed. This may have been due to the fact that the bonus varied most in the staple fibre and filament yarn sections of this Works, and it could be lost through technical difficulties as well as failure on the part of the operator. It could also vary as a result of the system of rotation between the rooms in the draw twist area, and as a result of changes in the product. Here was a situation where the men were performing a monotonous and restrictive task, and where they felt little sense of cohesion with the rest of the Works, but strong cohesion with the men on their particular shift. When this was combined with the difficulties of bonus fluctuation it was not surprising that the fluctuations were seized upon as issues for dispute and as a basis for considerable pressure from the operators upon management.

Some of the characteristics and behaviour of the draw twist operators in Works C called to mind Sayles' 'erratic' work groups (9). Their overall level of grievance activity was high, their participation in union activities was high, and there was low evaluation of their performance by management. The draw twist operators did not work as a team, however, nor were their jobs highly rated by other operators, except in terms of pay. But the tasks were extremely central to the total operations of Works C, they were homogeneous, there was a certain solidarity among the men on the same shift and there were few opportunities for promotion to other jobs. What is perhaps particularly interesting is that since the research was undertaken there has been a reorganization in the Works which has reduced the sensitivity of the bonus system and there appears to have been a considerable change in the behaviour of the workers in that they are now much less militant. It must be pointed out that 'quick conversion to good relationships with management' is, according to Sayles, another characteristic of 'erratic' groups.

The quality control system

During the years immediately before the fieldwork, Works A and Works B were both concerned with increasing the quality specifications of their products. This had an effect on the operators in both Works, in that they were working within continually narrowing limits. The nature of the quality control system, however, differed considerably between the two Works. In Works A it was mainly built into the production system, in that dials showing the continuous analysis of the product were to be read as an integral part of the operator's work. If the continuous analysis showed that the quality of the product was veering outside the prescribed limits, the operator concerned had to adjust his equipment to bring the quality back within the limits. Increasingly stringent quality specifications meant that the operator had to make adjustments more frequently, as the area of 'slack' in the production system was systematically eliminated. More detailed quality checks carried out by the laboratories were communicated directly to the operator. He acted on these results if necessary and, if he encountered any serious difficulties, called on his supervisor for help.

The situation in Works B was quite different. There was no built-in system of quality control on the continuous process plants of Works B. The results of regular quality tests by the laboratories were communicated to the supervisor and not to the operator as in Works A. This was both because of the nature of the chemical process, and because of the variety of products made in these plants. It was the responsibility of the supervisor to remember and to understand the quality specifications of the many different products, and to take the necessary steps by issuing instructions to correct the process if necessary. Comparing the two Works one might say that Works A was a classic example of the operator's task becoming the 'control of control', and of control being almost completely mechanical. In Works B, differences in the chemical process, combined with the variation in products, made such mechanical control difficult. There was a well-developed impersonal administrative system of quality control in which the supervisor played an important part, and this had profound consequences for his role and his relationship with the operator.

The quality control system in the batch chemical area of Works C was very similar to that in Works B. The results of tests by the laboratories were communicated to the supervisor, who acted on the results, and if necessary instructed the operator to vary the process. But in the filament yarn and staple fibre areas of Works C there were two ways in which quality could be affected and controlled. The degree to which the process was operating smoothly in a technical sense was important in producing the required characteristics in the yarn and fibre. Quality was also affected by the way in which the operator did his job, for example doffing his bobbins at the right time, or avoiding putting greasy fingers on them. A sophisticated sampling system was used to produce charts of variations in aspects of quality. These charts indicated visually the limits within which it was acceptable to deviate from the standard. On the basis of information provided by this sampling method, it was the supervisor's responsibility to decide when and whether action was needed to rectify the quality of the products. He might also take action on the basis of direct communication from the quality control section. As has been indicated, the individual bobbins of yarn also went through a further stage of inspection, when they were visually examined and weighed.

A familiar situation in much of manufacturing industry is conflict between producing the required quantity of goods of sufficient quality at the right time. In Works A this conflict did not arise because control of quality and rate of production were built into the plant and the rectification process to control quality was clearly defined by the technology. The position was similar in the chemical plants of Works B and Works C, and again there was little conflict between quality and quantity. Moreover, there was little relationship between these types of control and the individual operators' bonus earnings.

Although quantity was given priority in the staple fibre and filament yarn areas of Works C, production had to stop or output be rejected if the product was of insufficient quality. This affected bonus directly and meant that at least for the operator, the conflict between quantity and quality was a very real one. The supervisor was, therefore, called upon not only to respond to the quality control system by taking the necessary steps to rectify the process, but also to prevent faults by the individual operator, and to see that this conflict was resolved in a way acceptable to the standards laid down.

In Works A control over quality broadened the responsibility of the operator and encouraged a 'teamwork' relationship between supervisors and men because they worked together to solve the technical problems posed by the system. But in Works C control over quality resulted in close supervision and increasing pressure on the operator from the supervisor. These differences, therefore, in the working of both the bonus system and the quality control system in Works A and Works C helped to increase satisfaction in Works A but decreased it in Works C. Moreover, the quality control system in Works C operated through the direct action of supervisors and this also affected the relationship between supervisors and men with consequences for the operators' attitudes towards supervision.

THE ROLE OF SUPERVISION

Bonus and quality control systems are often regarded as examples of impersonal administrative controls. But as Chapter 3 suggests, these systems may be mixtures and can be administered at two levels. They may be impersonal in the sense that the rules are laid down in advance and the results measured or judged by persons or departments on the periphery of the authority structure of the organization. At another level—the adjustment mechanism level—however, feedback can be personal. It is made through the normal authority structure (that is via the first line supervisor) who has both to maintain quality by instruction to the operator, and to justify the bonus payment when it is in dispute. One consequence of advanced automation is the elimination of the personal feedback element and the direct communication of the results of the controls to the operator. This was the situation in Works A and to a lesser extent in Works B. The design of the process in these Works was such that unlike Works C the main control over quantity was incorporated in the design of the plant. The retention of the bonus system in these plants appeared to reflect the desire by the Company to maintain a common wages policy for a site where different production systems were in operation side by side. Control of quality was also built into the plant in Works A, but not in Works B. In other words quality control in Works A had become largely mechanical, but in Works B it remained administrative and impersonal as it did, of course, in Works C.

Other aspects of control systems are also affected by automation. One which has been touched upon above is the planning and sequencing of operations. In Works A this was also built into the design of the plant. But in Works B and Works C the changes in the type of product meant that the supervisor was personally responsible for decisions about the length of runs, and for the allocation of labour and resources. In other words, there was again more personal intervention through the authority structure.

This appears to support the suggestion made in Chapter 3 that the mechanization of control has profound consequences for supervisors' tasks:

'Line managers and supervisors increasingly cease to concern themselves with the day-to-day problems of production operations and function primarily as adjusters and supplementers of the control processes.'

What does this imply for the role of supervisors in the different Works? Has it any bearing on the wide variation in attitudes of operators towards immediate supervision?

The men known as assistant foremen on the Seagrass site would probably in many firms be called chargehands. A change of title and status in Seagrass had occurred a year or two before the attitude survey was undertaken. This regrading was in itself likely to have caused some stresses and strains, for the then existing chargehands were not necessarily of the right quality to fill the new role. But these men were certainly regarded by the operators as the first line of supervision. The relationship between the operators and the supervision varied in the three Works. In Works A the supervisor worked in a team with his men to maintain the flow of production. He was the person immediately called on when anything went wrong and close co-operation was needed during emergencies. Also in Works A the number of men supervised by an assistant foreman was never more than four, and was more often two or three. To revert to our earlier discussion about freedom of movement for the operator, it was easier for him to take a break because a supervisor could keep track of this small number of men and the organization of the work could be more informal. In fact in Works A the assistant foreman was seen by management both as a 'leading operator' whose *work* was essential to maintain the process, and as a leader and controller of labour. However, for the purpose of analysis, what is important is that the operators in Works A also saw the assistant foreman as being in a position of authority. Even so it was only in this Works that the foreman figured at all prominently as the person with whom operators would consult if they had problems with the calculation of bonus, or complaints of any kind. In the other Works it was the assistant foreman who was usually approached. In Works A, therefore, contact between the operators and both the assistant foremen and foremen was close.

Blau and Scott (10) have suggested that where the assembly line organizes the work process, that is, where there is some mechanical control of planning, the typical pattern of interaction is that the worker approaches the foreman when he needs help or supplies rather than the foreman making demands of the worker. This influences the foreman's behaviour even when he does have to make demands on the worker. His trouble-shooting role encourages him to seek improvements by offering advice to the workers rather than by issuing commands. This is even more likely to be the case on a continuous process plant like Works A.

Another related aspect of this kind of interaction between supervisor and operator is the influence it has upon the operator's perception of the source of the authority which the first line supervisor exercises. Gouldner has identified two fundamentally different criteria for the legitimation of authority—authority based on technical knowledge and experience, and authority based on incumbency in office (11). The men in Works A described the qualities of a good supervisor as first and foremost powers of organization and leadership, followed very closely by good knowledge of the job. Over eighty per cent of them thought their immediate supervisor was able to deal with their questions and problems, and their satisfaction with their supervision stemmed from this recognition of technical superiority, leading them to say that their supervision was adequate and that in general the right men were chosen as supervisors.

In Works B, however, the supervisor was more of an administrator and organizer than a co-worker with his subordinates. He was the channel by which quality was controlled and frequent changes of production meant that much of his time was taken up with organizing production changes and reallocating men. To these characteristics of his supervisory role, which were determined in part by the chemical nature of the process itself and in part by the variety of products, must be added the fact that a deliberate management decision had been taken to decrease the number of supervisors in the chemical process areas of Works B in order to enlarge the job of the operator. The assistant foreman in Works B, therefore, was much less available to give help. The fact that he was supervising more men also made it more difficult to allow freedom and flexibility in respect of informal breaks. There were more men for him to keep an eye on. He was still relied upon, however, to help in solving problems and in dealing with emergencies. The men in Works B seemed on the whole to accept that their supervisor had enough authority to answer their questions and deal with their problems. But in Works B nearly twice as many men as in Works A thought that the wrong people were chosen as supervisors, and they were far more critical of the amount of discipline exercised over them. It must be borne in mind in this connection that strict enforcement of safety regulations was necessary.

In the chemical area of Works C, the general role of the supervisor was very similar to that of the Works B chemical area supervisors. It was in the staple fibre and filament yarn areas of Works C that it differed to the greatest extent. In these areas a very large part of the supervisor's job was the organization of production. Supervision would be called upon to help if technical difficulties did arise, but the work of individual operators had to be closely supervised and monitored in order to maintain full production and quality. A number of important changes in the supervisory structure in Works C have taken place since this study was made. At that time the men, but not the assistant foremen, in the draw twist area were rotated between rooms, with the result that the supervision was not able to build up a continuing relationship with the men.

As already indicated, in this area bonus earnings were sensitive to the amount produced, so that the operators were likely to be very critical of any technical failure on the part of supervision to keep production running. Indeed, as no complex chemical reactions appeared to be involved, an experienced operator might feel he understood the mechanical limits of his repetitive tasks as well as his supervisor. The men in Works C thought the most important quality for supervisors was to know their job, and yet they were the most critical of their own supervisors' ability to deal with their problems. Thus the operators here looked to technical competence to legitimize the authority of the supervisor and felt that legitimacy derived in this way was lacking in some cases.

One difference between the three Works which has been touched upon in this discussion of the role of first line supervision relates to the size of the work group controlled by one assistant foreman. In Works A the average number of operators working under one assistant foreman was about three. In the chemical areas of Works B and Works C, the work groups were larger, varying between eight and twelve men, while in the staple fibre and filament yarn areas of Works C, one assistant foreman was responsible for up to fifteen men. In the warehouse of Works B and the inspection area of Works C about twenty men worked under one assistant foreman. Even where other elements in the task are the same, the larger the number of men a supervisor has working under him, the more difficult will be the social control of individuals and the greater the need to rely upon bureaucratic rules. In Works A, the size of the group controlled by an assistant foreman was small enough to allow for a high degree of personal flexible control and the granting of correspondingly greater discretion to the operator. In the warehouse and inspection areas some collective freedom could be granted because the process could be stopped and started at the discretion of the supervisor. But in the staple fibre and filament yarn areas not only was the process continuous but the number of men under the control of one supervisor was such that he could not easily allow any flexibility.

SUMMARY AND CONCLUSIONS

This discussion has been concerned with material collected from one case study and for this reason alone it would be dangerous to generalize from the research results. However, as a case study it has a number of special features which may enable a contribution to be made to the current debate about the role of technology in influencing attitudes and behaviour in the work place. First, the study has covered the operation of different technologies against the background of a common Company policy and geographical location. Secondly, the evidence suggests that the three Works employ labour forces that are homogeneous in their social background and orientations to work. In this situation it seems reasonable to suppose that, with the reservations referred to earlier in this Chapter, most of the variations of attitudes and behaviour within the different Works can be attributed to technological factors.

The emergence of this link between technology and behaviour on the Seagrass site is not interpreted as an indication that socially determined expectations of workers are unimportant in the total picture. Nor does it even imply a particular view about the most useful explanatory variable. Although this chapter—as the book does generally—supports the view that for a research method which relies upon comparisons, technology is a useful variable with which to start to classify and compare organizations rather than the social characteristics and orientations of the labour force, it does not imply a particular theoretical standpoint. Indeed, a totally satisfactory explanation of industrial attitudes and behaviour requires an understanding of the dynamic interaction of within work and ex-work variables.

Another important point illustrated by the detailed study of the technology of the Works on the Seagrass site is that few organizations have a unitary technology. The admixture of the warehousing and packaging section in Works B with the chemical processes themselves led to a lower degree of expressed job interest in this Works as a whole than would have been expected from a 'pure' chemical process works. In Works C, on the other hand, the presence of a chemical process area tempered the degree of criticism voiced by the people working in the filament yarn and staple fibre processing areas.

The inclusion of Works B in the further study proved invaluable, however, for another reason concerned with the classification of technology. In the early general discussion with management it was suggested that the chemical process in Works B was similar to that in Works A. The first general observation of the work tasks of the chemical process operators in Works B confirmed this impression. But further study revealed that the variety of products manufactured, the nature of the chemical process and the resultant system of control in Works B had profound consequences both for the work task of the operators and for the role of the supervisors.

Woodward *et al.* in their discussion of the nature of technology in Chapter 1 have said:

'Because of the complex nature of the relationships which connect the technology of a firm with its structure, it is likely that some, but not all, characteristics of technology will be reflected in organizational structure or in industrial behaviour.'

Those that are so reflected were described as salient. In the case of Works B three salient features can be identified—first the solid nature of the final product which meant that it had to be handled before being marketed, second the variation in the product range, and third the complexity of the chemical process.

Variety of product was also a salient characteristic of the task in Works C where it also had profound consequences for the character of the work role of supervisors. Because of this variety, in both Works B and Works C, unlike Works A, the supervisors had to be concerned with the organization, planning and sequencing of production. In Works C, however, variety also had considerable consequences for the ease or difficulty of the operator's task and via this, his bonus earnings.

The final point to emerge from this study has been the importance of taking into account not only the nature of the production processes but also the administrative system or rationale of the way production was organized. Differences between the Works in expressed job interest were reflections of objective differences in the work task and in its physical setting which stemmed from the production processes. High levels of job interest coincided with more pleasant working conditions, opportunities to develop individual routines and rhythms of work, the exercise of discretion, freedom of movement and a sense of being an essential part of a team into which the operator could see his work fitting. On the other hand, differences between the Works in attitudes towards supervision reflected differences in the role of supervisors which in turn were shaped by differences in the administrative system. The greater the element of monitoring and organizing that the supervisor had to do, the more likelihood there was of criticism from the operators. The more the supervisor's role was concentrated upon trouble shooting and giving advice the more favourable were attitudes likely to be. This finding would appear to support the view that mechanical control over the work task is preferred to a personal or administrative system of control transmitted through the traditional authority structure.

References

1. Blauner, R. (1964) *Alienation and Freedom.* University of Chicago Press, Chicago.
2. Woodward, J. (1965) *Industrial Organization: Theory and Practice.* Oxford University Press, London.
3. Blauner, R. Op. cit. (See Ref. (1) above.)
4. Willener, A. (1964) Payment Systems in the French Steel and Iron Mining Industry, in Zollschan, G. K. and Hirsch, W. (eds.), *Explorations in Social Change.* Routledge & Kegan Paul, London.
5. Goldthorpe, J. H. *et al.* (1968) *The Affluent Worker: Industrial Attitudes and Behaviour.* Cambridge University Press, Cambridge.
6. For a development of this view point see:
   Goldthorpe, J. H. *et al.* Op. cit. (See Ref. (5) above.)
7. Goldthorpe, J. H. *et al.* Op. cit. (See Ref. (5) above.)
8. Blauner, R. Op. cit. (See Ref. (1) above.)
   Turner, A. N. and Lawrence, P. R. (1965) *Industrial Jobs and the Worker.* Harvard University Press, Boston.
   Brown, A. (1966) Artefacts, Automation and Human Ability, in Lawrence, J. R. (ed.), *Operational Research and the Social Sciences.* Tavistock Publications, London.
9. Sayles, L. R. (1958) *Behaviour of Industrial Work Groups.* John Wiley & Sons, New York.
10. Blau, P. M. and Scott, W. R. (1963) *Formal Organizations.* Routledge & Kegan Paul, London.
11. Gouldner, A. W. (1965) Organizational Analysis, in Merton, Broom and Cottrell, *Sociology Today*, Vol. II. Harper & Row, London.

JOAN WOODWARD

11 Technology, Management Control and Organizational Behaviour

It may be recalled that in the final paragraph of *Industrial Organization: Theory and Practice* (1) the point was made that patient and detailed exploration of what really happens inside industrial firms was a prerequisite to the development of an organization theory comprehensive enough to provide managers with a reliable basis for their decisions and actions. The Imperial College Industrial Sociology Unit has spent the last five years in research of the patient and detailed kind recommended. The question arises, therefore, of whether the progress made towards the understanding of industrial organization has been worth the effort expended.

The theoretical ideas relating to the development of organization theory arising from this research were presented in the first part of this book. All that remains to be done in conclusion, therefore, is to relate to this conceptual framework the case study material presented in Part II and to consider the significance of the research for the practising manager. The initial reaction of a manager to the case study material could very well be that it is the uniqueness of organizations that makes their study both fascinating and frustrating. The chances that the firms described resemble his own are small and he may therefore dismiss the book as having little relevance for him personally. It might increase his interest in getting some research started within his organization for during the last five years the amount of interaction between social scientists and industrial managers has increased considerably. More managers are now accepting that they can benefit from the work of social scientists, or more specifically from the application of social science research, within their own organizations.

Such a reaction would be a disappointment to the research group responsible for this book, for although the value of social science applications is not disputed, there are not enough social scientists available to service each firm on an individual basis and it is therefore important to make progress on a wider front. The development of the social sciences as academic disciplines generating a body of knowledge and methodology that can be communicated and used is essential to any rapid or widespread increase in the sophistication with which industrial managers and management consultants deal with the problems of organizational structure and behaviour they encounter. It is hoped, therefore, that industrial readers of the book will be able to link its two parts and recognize that comparative analysis—the study of variation between organizations—can have a practical significance provided that the causes of variation can be identified and clearly presented. Given such an explanatory framework, a manager ought to be able to compare his own firm with the firms described and understand how and why it is different. Such a comparison would enable him both to understand the current situation within his firm and to predict the likely effects of any major changes in technology or in the system of managerial control he might contemplate in the future.

Within this framework of comparative analysis one of the objectives at the outset of this research programme was to find an explanation of the fact that batch production firms differed more from each other in respect of their patterns of organizational structure and behaviour than did the firms in the other technical categories identified in the South Essex studies. The firms chosen for the original tracer studies, therefore, seemed on preliminary enquiry to be concerned with batch production. But as Part II of this book confirms, the term batch production covers a very wide range of technical situations. Of the firms described only two, Division X and Hollington, fitted into the batch production stereotype. The manufacturing systems at both Madingley and Electra Ltd. had more in common with unit than with batch production methods. Research had started on the Seagrass site before Wedderburn joined the research group, but two of the three Works (Works B and Works C) on which her study was based were regarded by management as batch production processes. Technically they were similar to 'Four' Works. But all these organizations had more in common with continuous flow processes than with batch production engineering.

The term batch production as applied to Mass-Bespoke was related to the fact that the products were programmed through the organization in batches and there was a high degree of standardization of products. These wide technical differences illustrated one of the hazards of this type of research; the classification of both technology and control systems depends upon a fairly detailed examination of the manufacturing processes. It is therefore difficult to build up a satisfactory research framework in advance. Although at the outset it was hoped to eliminate technology as an explanatory variable by controlling it, it was found impossible to do so. Thus it is impossible to say categorically that the variations in organizational structure and behaviour observed in the firms studied cannot be explained in terms of technology alone.

Even so, there was enough variation between firms that were technically similar, between Electra Ltd. and Madingley for example, and between 'Four' Works and Works C on the Seagrass site to suggest that not only the nature of the task but also the way in which it is controlled is a determinant of organizational behaviour. This was illustrated in Chapter 8 where a change in the control system was resulting in other kinds of change. Examples of all the categories of control identified in Chapter 3 were provided by the research. Madingley had a personal control system; it was at one extreme of the personal-mechanical scale. Works A was at the other, its control system being of the mechanical kind. Mass-Bespoke provided an example of multi-system or fragmented control. The way in which supervision working within a fragmented control system are forced to rank their goals in a diminishing order of nuisance value was epitomized in the remark made in Mass-Bespoke: 'You get one kick for quality and two kicks for production'. Lesser goals were at times sacrificed for the attainment of more critical ones and in any one field there was little incentive to do better than the target set. In 'Four' Works on the other hand, the system of control was single and integrated, and in contrast to their counterparts at Mass-Bespoke, the problems for the managers and supervisors working in this firm was to learn to live with calm and to reconcile their real life situation with their stereotype of a manager's job. If the computerization programme in Division X is put into operation successfully, learning to live with calm might also become a problem there. As Chapter 8 indicates, however, at the time Division X was studied, this seemed a remote possibility. Living with calm did not appear to create problems in the kind of long-established process industry represented by Works A on the Seagrass site; it was the accepted way of life.

Linking what has been said about control variables and technical variables in the firms studied, their significance for organizational behaviour seems to be related to the fact that together they determine the degree of uncertainty with which an organization has to contend. The switch in emphasis to uncertainty as a determining factor does not remove the problem of measurement from comparative analysis. As indicated in Chapter 2, uncertainty is no easier to measure than technical or control variables. In these particular studies, however, the number of firms covered was small and the fieldwork in each firm went on for a long enough time to enable both the research worker concerned, and the other members of the research group with whom he was interacting, to become familiar with its production and control systems. It was therefore not too difficult even without sophisticated measurement techniques to compare on a reasonably objective basis the degree of uncertainty with which the different firms had to contend. The order ranking from low to high degrees of uncertainty is given in Fig. 5.

	Name of Firm	*Described in:*
Low uncertainty	1. Seagrass Works A	Chapter 10
	2. Seagrass Works B	Chapter 10
	3. 'Four' Works	Chapter 5
	4. Seagrass Works C	Chapter 10
	5. Mass-Bespoke	Chapter 6
	6. Division X	Chapter 8
	7. Hollington	Chapter 4
	8. Madingley	Chapter 7
High uncertainty	9. Electra Ltd.	Chapter 9

Fig. 5.

The relationship between technical and control variables in determining the degree of uncertainty appears to be a complex one. Technology is itself dependent on a number of factors; the nature of the product, the range of products, the market served and the techniques and hardware available to process the appropriate raw materials and components, all of which can be sources of uncertainty.

As these case studies have shown, the amount of uncertainty in an organizational task is a major determinant of the way that the task can be controlled. A high degree of precision and explicitness in the objective-setting process is associated with mechanical and unitary control procedures. Referring back to Fig. 4 in Chapter 3, unit production is linked with personal single-system control, batch production with fragmented control and continuous flow production with single-system mechanical control.

But the case studies also show that the control system can reduce or increase the amount of uncertainty in the technology. It can be a source of the uncertainty with which the organization has to contend. Had this not been the case the rank order in Fig. 5 might have been different. There would certainly have been some clustering of firms. For example, there was about the same degree of uncertainty in the technology of 'Four' Works as of Seagrass Works C and Mass-Bespoke. The integrated and impersonal control system in 'Four' Works has contained some of the uncertainty, however, and in Mass-Bespoke as in Hollington the control procedures through which the task was planned and monitored exaggerated the degree of uncertainty. Computerization in Division X might reduce the uncertainty while the technology remains the same. It is not absolutely certain that the technology would remain the same, however, for the new control system might lead to changes in the technology, in particular in the variety in the product range.

Madingley and Electra Ltd. were also very much alike from a technological point of view. But it will be recalled that a control system had been developed in Madingley that attempted to contain some of the uncertainty in the technology. In Electra Ltd. the planning and control processes were described as 'all a bit vague, but this is inevitable'.

The ability of a control system to contain the uncertainty inherent in a technology may be a measure of its appropriateness. The reason why the uncertainty was increased in Mass-Bespoke was that a technology of a standardized production kind was linked with a batch production control system, and a unit production ethos. In Hollington, a batch production task was controlled by the mechanisms and procedures appropriate to unit production. The reason for this was that Hollington was tied to the control system of a wider organization where the technology was predominantly unit production. It is possible also to envisage circumstances where a control system has to be geared to the technology of a completely independent organization.

Concurrently with the case studies reported in this book, a study was made by one of the research team of a supervisory training scheme in a motor manufacturing firm. This involved an investigation of the first line supervisors' role. Although the technology was of the large batch production kind with standardized products, the first line supervisor was a trouble shooter operating in the kind of fragmented control system more commonly associated with small batch production. The reason was not that management was unsophisticated in its approach to managerial control, but that the system had to be geared to the high degree of uncertainty introduced through the firm's dependence on a number of suppliers' components who were operating on a small batch production basis.

But the design of control systems that reduce uncertainty arising from technology is the concern of the production engineer rather than the social scientist. The social scientist is more interested in the way that technology and control systems and the uncertainty they generate influence patterns of structure and behaviour inside organizations. As far as structure is concerned the case studies suggest that it is the degree of uncertainty with which an organization has to contend that determines the amount of overlap between the system that designs and programmes the production task and the system concerned with its execution. If the firms listed in Fig. 5 were placed on Fig. 3 the sequence would be identical. High uncertainty as in Electra Ltd. is linked with total overlap and low uncertainty as in Seagrass Works A with total separation.

The behavioural consequences of this difference in structure were discussed in Chapter 3. The case studies suggest, for example, that in Seagrass Works A the successful achievement of the production task depended less on the exercise of control through personal and hierarchical authority than it did in Electra Ltd. In terms of the three categories of management activity listed by Klein in Chapter 5, the case studies showed how, in the conditions of high uncertainty operating in Electra Ltd. and Madingley, the energies and skills of management concentrated on setting up adequate systems of work organization and control for each order or set of equipment manufactured. Where there is a medium degree of uncertainty as in Mass-Bespoke, emphasis shifts to monitoring the system, planning workflow, coordinating materials and services needed, keeping quality and costs within reasonable bounds and operating generally as a trouble shooter. In low uncertainty organizations like 'Four' Works or the Works on the Seagrass site, management activity is primarily directed towards the improvement of the system and planning ahead for major system changes without interfering with the ongoing operations.

The differences in the demands put on managers and supervisors in different technical and control situations can lead to a credibility gap between management tasks and management training. There is little point in training supervisors to be 'motivators' of men if the successful completion of the organizational task does not require them to be this or if the reward and punishment system in which they operate is geared to a trouble-shooting role. Training of the kind implied was badly needed in Mass-Bespoke, for, as Chapter 6 has shown, supervision had a large part to play in the control of both the quantity and quality of the work produced. But this was certainly not the case in all the firms studied. An added interest in the study of Division X was that during the period of the fieldwork a considerable amount of energy was being expended on a management training programme. This programme was almost entirely directed towards increasing the effectiveness of managers in the exercise of hierarchical and personal authority; the significance of management still being seen as the apex of a pyramid of personal control and responsible for both system design and system operation. Away from the training centre, however, middle management involved in the computer application were becoming aware that if it was successful this concept of management would soon be remote from the reality of their day-to-day jobs. They could see that if the computer application was successful they would be making a much smaller contribution to the ongoing production task and their discretion area could be reduced. The changes in their role were creating anxiety and their involvement in an inappropriate training programme was increasing the stress in the situation.

This illustrates the fragmentation and inconsistency that can arise when two groups of specialists simultaneously attempt to introduce changes into an organization that are in conflict with each other. In Division X there was no contact other than social between the people responsible for the computerization and the Personnel Department. It would certainly not have entered the heads of either group that it might be necessary to plan future developments in their individual specialist fields in collaboration with each other. Moreover, the specialist training of the people concerned had not given them any common reference points or a common language.

The divergence of the paths pursued by the different groups of specialists operating in Division X links with what was said in Chapter 3 about unitary and fragmented control systems. As Table III shows, fragmented control systems are associated with medium uncertainty batch production, and unitary control systems with low uncertainty continuous flow and with unit production. The growth of functional specialization in management has obviously contributed to fragmentation. It is into the development of specialist techniques that most of management's intellectual effort is generally put; people have spent their entire industrial lives making detailed contributions to the perfection of technical process or control procedures, or looking for solutions to piecemeal problems. The question arises, however, of whether this concentration on specialization has been the result of misdirection in management education or whether it results from the fact that fragmented control is inevitable in batch production.

Among the firms described in this book only the three at the top of the low uncertainty scale had unitary control systems. One of these, Works A, was a continuous flow production firm and Works B was very like Works A in terms of the degree of uncertainty in its technology. Only in 'Four' Works was unitary control associated with batch production, but even here batch production was linked with a chemical process, and although there seemed to be a central mind operating in the organization, the technology with which it had to deal was not characterized by high uncertainty.

None of the firms studied were of the high uncertainty unitary control system type. The reason for this seems to have been that simple unit production, where individual orders although they may overlap, go through the system sequentially, was not represented. In this kind of production the sources of uncertainty are the type of market, the uniqueness of the products and the inability to predict the organization's future. The nature of the task does, however, enable management to know what the state of the production system is at any moment of time and to comprehend the organization as a total system of resources. Once the production system has to contend with a number of different products or components that have to be dealt with simultaneously within a limited set of production facilities uncertainty of a different kind has to be contended with. If the rather special conditions of high uncertainty in unit production are left out of account, these case studies demonstrated that the greater the degree of uncertainty the more difficult it is to integrate and unify control procedures, and to centralize the decision-making processes.

Kynaston Reeves and Turner, who are continuing the study of the relationship between technology, control and organizational behaviour, identify the inability to comprehend the production system in its entirety as the defining characteristic of batch production. In conditions of high uncertainty it is impractical or uneconomic to collect enough information to know exactly what is happening at any given moment in time. The result is that people working at different points in the system have access to only limited amounts of information and therefore form different conceptions of what the total system is like. Among these different and limited conceptions are those of the different functional specialists. The implications of this for behaviour in organizations are now being studied in depth. The fact that in several of the firms described in this book, managers appeared to be living in a fantasy world as far as time control or delivery dates were concerned may be significant in this connection.

As products become increasingly standardized, uncertainty decreases and information becomes cheaper to obtain. Various administrative and mechanical monitoring processes can be used to collect enough information to allow the state of the production system to be known. The computerization in Division X fits into this framework and its chances of success therefore depend on the amount and sources of uncertainty in the technology.

To sum up, what was said in the Introduction must be stressed again. The publication of this book does not mark the completion of a discrete stage in the work of the research group, nor is it claimed that there have been any startling breakthroughs in the way of new middle range theories. It is felt, however, that more insights into the relationship between technology and organizational structure have resulted from the study and categorization of control processes, as has the realization that not only the nature of the task but the way that it is planned and controlled is an important determinant of organizational behaviour.

The way that the research was developing at the end of the period covered—the focusing on the degree of uncertainty rather than on technical variables as the defining characteristic of the organizational task—will, it is hoped, enable the same conceptual framework and methodology to be used in the study of non-manufacturing organization.

Finally it is believed that the work done by the research group has demonstrated that if the patience lasts, detailed exploration of what really happens inside industrial firms can lead to the development of organization theory, provided that the cases studied can be linked within a viable comparative framework.

Reference
  1. Woodward, J. (1965) *Industrial Organization: Theory and Practice.* Oxford University Press, London.

R

Appendixes

I (Chapter 8) Development of an Organizational Objective

Organizational processes	Cycle I
SEARCH	1956–59
	The research into getting involved in the use of computers
Feasibility	Ascertaining possible alternative courses of computer application and a report recommending the specific kind, place, method and time of application.
Acceptance	Acceptance of report by Main Board.
CONSOLIDATION	1960–62
	The development of computer programmes in Companies
Interest group formation	Formation of three broad specialized functional groups—the Computer Unit, the Division and the Companies.
Sub-goal formation	Computer Unit's concern with *technical* problems involved in application; Division's interest in establishing a coordinated divisional structure; and Companies' commitment to previous autonomous manufacturing conditions.
CONFLICT/CHANGE	1963–65
	Conflict and pressures for change due to the abortive attempt to base computer programmes on existing manual production control systems

Conflict	Company resistance to Divisional integration and computer application.
Change	Decision by Division to limit application to Companies 1 and 2.

Organizational processes	Cycle 2

SEARCH	1964–65
	The attempt by the Computer Unit to find the basic logic of manufacture; attempt by Division to ascertain environment conducive to integrated data processing
Feasibility	The ascertaining of whether an integrated control system was possible within the Division; 'workable' proposals by the Computer Unit and Division to this end.
Acceptance	The attempt by Division to involve all Company managements in an active role in the computer application by setting up working parties and arranging for special management courses.

CONSOLIDATION	1965
	The cautious compiling of new information for revised programmes
Interest group formation	The formation of Company teams to assist in the application; formation of interest groups on the issue of who *should* assume responsibility for the application.
Sub-goal formation	The attempts by Division to coordinate subgoals; subgoal formation on the whole issue of control; who is to have it, what kind will it be, and how will it be used?

CHANGE/CONFLICT	1965
	The realization by Computer Unit that present equipment is becoming overloaded and built-in time delays are hampering objective
Change	The commitment by Main and Divisional Boards to the purchase of new generation machinery in 1968.

Conflict	The criticism by Company and Divisional personnel about new plans when only partial success has been shown to date.

Organizational processes	*Cycle* 3
SEARCH	1965
	The research into the problems of attaining integrated data processing and the advisability of obtaining a 'real-time' computer
Feasibility	The ascertaining of the 'need' and finances for such a project and a report specifying the scope, use, advantages, and schedule of proposed introduction of the new computer.
Acceptance	The attempt by Division to involve senior Company personnel in 'Divisional' projects, and initiation of a series of lectures, Company visits, and computer courses to gain Company commitment.
CONSOLIDATION	1965–?
	Senior and middle management computer courses and rewriting of programmes with the idea of transfer to new machinery

II *Outline History of the Research*

It may be of interest to the reader concerned with the organization of
research activities in the industrial sociology field if something is added
to this book about the way this research project developed, how the
research team operated and the events that led to the publication of this
book in its present form. Is it possible to use the task analysis approach
to examine the research organization itself and see whether the concepts
and ideas developed by the research team in studying other organizations
can provide plausible explanations of what happened?

When the project started in 1962, the fact that a five-year research
grant had been provided by the Department of Scientific and Industrial
Research meant that the team was going to have the advantage of being
able to operate on a longer-term basis and with greater resources of both
finance and fieldwork facilities than is normally the case in industrial
sociology research in this country. In general the research framework
within an academic institution is such that the problems of the longer-
term financing of research and the provision of adequate career opportunities for research personnel make it difficult to embark on projects
that are neither of short duration nor narrow in scope.

As research resources were likely to be available in fairly plentiful
supply, it would have been possible to follow up the South Essex research
by selecting one or more of the theoretical assumptions that emerged
from it and attempting to verify the theory by using quantitative
techniques of the survey kind. Such a course of action had considerable
appeal, not least because the new Unit was operating in an environment
where there is probably the greatest concentration of academic scientists
and engineers in the country, to whom measurement is important and
who regard only scientifically reproducible fact as respectable. In such
an environment, the building up of their self image as scientists was
important for the members of the research team.

But for a number of reasons this course was rejected. One reason was
the constraints referred to above of undertaking industrial sociology

research in an academic setting and the difficulties that can arise in reconciling personal with group goals. In projects of the survey kind, it is not easy to provide the individual members of a research team with adequate opportunities to develop their own ideas or to improve their career prospects by using their research as a basis for a higher degree or by publishing. Other considerations were equally if not more important however. In particular there was a reluctance to take up a fixed theoretical position on the basis of the South Essex research results. Organization theory is still at the stage where the generation of ideas and concepts has to take precedence over theory verification and for this purpose qualitative data, provided it can be systematically analysed on a comparative basis, is as appropriate as quantitative data.

It was realized, of course, that the choice of the less explicit research objective would lead to difficulties in exercising close control over the research and the three original members of the research team set off on their tracer studies with no mandate other than to develop ideas about management control and about the way that control systems are linked with technology and organizational behaviour. They were given the minimum of direction, the list of questions given in Chapter 3 being the only documentation. This list provided the main basis of discussion at the early research meetings.

The lack of explicitness was perceived by at least one member of the team, probably with some justification, as mismanagement of the research. It had been hoped, however, that within the comparative task analysis framework and with the background of the South Essex research as a common starting point, the carrying out of the tracer studies in parallel with regular discussions through which experience and observation would be shared, would result in the emergence of a conceptual framework consisting of sets of categories with their associated properties and relationships through which it would be possible to link together the three facets of organization in which the group was interested. This framework would then be available for use by new people joining the group and as a basis for further studies. The time target set for the construction of this framework was within two years, the intention being to present it as the conclusion of a book that would also contain a detailed account of each of the three tracer studies.

This target was not reached. As has been suggested, the main problem at this time was the lack of explicitness in the objective set. This led to doubts about its feasibility and a reluctance to accept both the objective itself and the method for achieving it. The tracer study method has a number of theoretical advantages—these have been commented on briefly in Chapter 3—but it is not an easy method for a research worker to use. The practical difficulties vary according to the experience of the people involved. An experienced research worker with sociological insight who has built up his own framework for the analysis of data is likely to find a tracer study tedious, time consuming and repetitive. He may also feel that his data is being forced into a framework that he cannot accept. The collection of detailed information about the mechanics and procedures of control can be perceived as a more appropriate research technique for the production engineer than for the social scientist.

The most difficult problem for the inexperienced research worker, particularly when his background training had not included much social science methodology, is the amount of data generated by such a study. It was found in practice that the research worker can get so bogged down by the detail of his study that he has difficulty not only in conceptualizing but also in getting down on paper a coherent account of what has happened. The detail also made the sharing of knowledge and experience difficult.

Thus, although the individual case studies produced some interesting data which was subsequently useful in the generation of theoretical ideas, it soon became apparent that no common product would emerge from the tracer studies. Indeed, there was a period in which the problems loomed so large that the only good thing that could be said about what had happened was that the research workers had got out into the field with the minimum of delay. Thus if any new ideas ever did emerge, they would at least be based on empirical reality.

The first cycle of the research project ended with the efforts to write up the data collected. In one case, progress was made up to the point at which a first draft was complete. From this a paper was subsequently prepared for publication.* At this point, however, the research worker responsible left the group to take up other work outside the Imperial College.

The difficulties experienced by the other two research workers both in writing up their material and also in drawing comparisons between the two firms which were at least superficially similar from a technical point of view, led to the beginning of the second cycle of the research and the emergence of a new objective. The research workers put forward the view that no conceptual framework linking technology, management control and organization was likely to emerge unless better techniques for measuring technical variables and for comparing firms on a task analysis basis could be developed. The result was that the work described in Chapter 2 was begun. Contact was maintained with the firms already studied for they were among those in which the measures developed were tested. It is interesting to note that what happened to the research programme was very similar to what happened to the development programme in Electra Ltd.† There, too, a failure to meet a product

* See footnote to Chapter 5, page 85.
† See Chapter 9.

objective led not to systematic attempts to solve the problems but to changes in the objective itself.

As Chapter 2 has made clear, many difficulties arose in the course of the efforts made to measure technical variables. But as the objective was a more explicit one the reaction to the difficulties was to put more effort into solving the problems than into trying to change the objective.

During this phase of the research more people began to become involved, bringing in wider background knowledge and experience. Between July 1965 and August 1966, three more sociologists joined the group, and a number of engineering graduates taking industrial sociology at post-graduate level participated for short periods. A third cycle of objective-setting and realization began with a new search process. This third phase of the research overlapped with the second, the reason being that the new members of the group were unable to accept the existing objective of finding a way to measure technical variables. This was partly because they did not see it as a workable or operational objective. Moreover, they felt that the measurement of technical variables was not only too narrow a task but also inappropriate for a group of sociologists. It is interesting to note that by this time the relationship between the group and the wider organization of Imperial College within which it operated had undoubtedly changed considerably. It now seemed more important to the research team to project a socio-logist image than to project a scientist image, and there was a reaction against what was seen as an over-emphasis on measurement and all that it implied. The divergence of views created anxiety as far as the direc-tion of the research was concerned. One complicating factor was that ambivalence could be detected in the attitude of the newer members of the team. Their reaction against measurement did not mean that they were content to accept completely the fact that sociology must rely on intuition, judgement and other 'non-scientific' processes. This dilemma was only resolved well after the research described in this book had been completed by the publication of Glaser and Strauss's *The Discovery of Grounded Theory: Strategies for Qualitative Research* (1). This book, by being specific about the way that non-qualitative data can be systemati-cally and rigorously handled, helped the research workers to legitimize their approach within the Imperial College environment.

The outcome of this third search process was a return to an objective very much like the one with which the research had started in 1962. The interesting question was, could the same sequence of events be prevented from occurring again?

One indication that there was a better chance of realizing the objective was the fact that the larger number of people involved and the wider range of background knowledge available was resulting in an inter-change of information between the research workers much more productive of ideas than the earlier search process.

Another difference was that the methodology was modified. The tracer study approach was not completely abandoned as a means of collecting data—indeed it proved increasingly valuable as a method of training graduate students—but less data was accumulated, more short cuts were taken and other techniques were included with it. More use was made of survey techniques covering various levels of staff in the firms being studied. In some firms attitude studies were undertaken, usually at the request of the firms themselves. The general effect was that more emphasis was put on interviewing and less on longer-term observation; the interviewing varying in its degree of prescription and formality according to the circumstances of the particular case. This more flexible methodology resulted in more of the work being done in pairs or in small groups, and this helped to prevent the feelings of isolation experienced by the research workers in the early stages. These modifications in method did not mean that the basic conceptual approach had changed; the later studies continued to focus on organizations as wholes, and as systems for getting work done and the questioning centred around the actual as much as the perceived character of the work of the people interviewed.

Gradually the theoretical framework outlined in Chapter 3, linking technology, managerial control and organizational behaviour, sought for at the outset, began to emerge, individual members of the group identifying with and working on different facets of this framework. This was a satisfactory outcome, for it demonstrated that in a research project of this kind, individuals can pursue their own interests and at the same time participate in a wider activity, the result of which may be more than the sum total of their individual contributions. The two approaches came closer together, their mutual dependency being recognized.

The next restatement of the research objective came in the spring of 1967, when a decision was taken to publish this book in its present form. It had become clear that the original publication objective was not going to be realized. In any case there was now too much case study material available for it to be presented in detail in a single publication. It was decided, therefore, to commit to paper the theoretical framework that had emerged so far, together with enough descriptive material from the case studies to illustrate various facets of it. It cannot be over-emphasized that this decision did not mean the researchers felt that their framework was now complete and comprehensive or that it provided plausible explanations of all the incidents that they had observed. But it was an appropriate time to take stock. The period covered by the original research grant was coming to an end. Some assessment had to be made of how the money had been spent and a decision taken about whether to continue the research programme.

Moreover, although the theoretical framework was still in the process of formulation, it was now possible to present it in a form in which it could be used by other research workers studying similar problems. This was demonstrated in the study described in Chapter 10. When Wedderburn joined the Industrial Sociology Unit, she and her team were already working on the Seagrass site. The framework in which the Imperial College group was working was already sufficiently comprehensible for her to see that the Seagrass site offered a good opportunity to test out some of its propositions. It was also useful in helping to provide explanations of some of the differences that had been observed between the Works on the site. The Seagrass research workers were able, therefore, to use the ideas and concepts that had by then been generated by the group and to feed back into the ongoing research concepts and ideas of their own.

Once the decision to publish had been taken, the details of the publication plan were worked out and made explicit. Intermediate time targets were identified in respect of both individual papers and the total publication, leading to the final completion of the manuscript in April 1968. It was recognized, of course, that there might be an element of unrealism in these plans, but like those prepared by the Works Order Control Section of Madingley,* they would, it was hoped, help to inject order into an uncertain future, and from a supervision or editing point of view make the activity easier to control

The more limited and direct approach to the case study material seemed to be helpful to the research workers who had earlier been unable to complete the writing up of the original case study material. It facilitated the systemization of the data and made it more manageable

Individual authors differed of course in their ability to meet their personal time targets and in the amount of work they had to do between the first and final drafts. It is even more difficult to set quality than time standards in an activity of this kind, but an interesting concensus developed of what was acceptable and what was required to be rewritten

The most serious miscalculation in the plan was in the amount of work that would be necessary to turn first drafts into a manuscript ready for the printer. This was underestimated with the result that the delivery date had to be put back for nine months. Moreover, to ensure that the new target would be met, tighter control had to be exercised during this final stage.

This was now easier as there were sanctions that could be applied. Pary 1 being complete, the publication of the book no longer depended on the contribution of any one individual and had any of the case study papers not been ready by the end of the time specified, publication could have gone ahead without it. The authors were sufficiently committed to

* See Chapter 7.

the publication of the book and sufficiently anxious to be associated with it to make this a real penalty. People reacted differently to the pressure; this was partly because some had more serious problems and heavier workloads than others, and partly because they varied in the extent to which they were prepared to accept control. As the deadline approached there were mutterings from some of 'what a way to write a book'. These were very reminiscent of the mutterings about 'what a way to send a computer out' that had been heard in Electra Ltd.* at the time the final pressure was being applied.

This account of the way the research project developed shows how the sequence of events and the pressures and problems to which the research workers were exposed and their reactions to them were much the same as those observed in the firms studied where there had been a large development content in the task, or where product or organizational objectives were not precisely defined. It is probably true to say that had they not been sensitized to these pressures and problems by their research experience, the failure of the research team to achieve its own objective would have been a more serious one.

Reference

1. Glaser, Barney G. and Strauss, Anselm L. (1968) *The Discovery of Grounded Theory: Strategies for Qualitative Research.* Weidenfeld & Nicolson, London.

* See Chapter 9.

Name Index

Subject Index

Adjustment mechanisms, defined, 48; *see also* Control mechanism(s)

Administrative structure, technology and, 14, 15–16; and constraints, 14, 15; production task and, 14

Administrative system, defined, 5; technology and, 6

Attitude(s), to pay, 6; towards quality after takeover, 67–8; computer application and differences in, 169–70; of workers and technological constraints, 203*ff*; work situation as an explanation of differences in, 203–4; differences in technology and, 203, 203n; towards company as an employer, 207–8; towards senior management, 208; towards supervision, 208–9, 215; towards work task, 209, 215–16; to pay and fringe benefits, 6, 209–10, 215; in relation to behaviour and technology, 210–11, 215–20, 230–3; prior orientation to work situations and, 211*ff*

Batch production, *see* Production systems

Batch production firms, search for explanation of differences in patterns of organizational structure and behaviour amongst, 235*f*; *see also* Production systems

Behaviour, *see* Organizational behaviour

Bonus system(s), *see* Control mechanism(s)

Change, technical, x; and the individual, 5; salient characteristics of technology and organizational, 16; instance of control and organizational, 150, 153, 155, 170; resistance to, 154; preparation for environmental, 144

Communications, information in control cycle, xi; systematic feedback information as part of total control, 117; as dysfunctional, 135; action consequences of inadequate, 137*ff*; non-specific to specific communication in order control, 142; need for uniform information systems in computerization programme, 158; inappropriate, 152; *see also* Organizational behaviour

Competition, impact on organization structure and behaviour of different types of, 85–6

Computerization, research study of, 146*ff*; and managerial control, 146; feasibility project, 147–8; proposals for, 148; programming problems and, 148, 159*f*; extension of, 148–9; interaction between structural changes and, 150–75 *passim*; search for organizational objectives for, 150*ff*; of accounts, 150–1; of stock control, 151; of production control, 151–75 *passim*; logic of production processes and, 152, 154, 157, 159, 165; for batch production plants, 151; organizational conflict and, 154*ff*; technical problems of, 148, 153–4, 161–2; perceived limitations of, 155; appreciation courses for, 159; task, division of, 159; organizational behaviour and,